Words Are Magic

WORDS ARE MAGIC

Story Guides for Human Beans and Other Perishables

BY John Thomas Tuft

FOREWORD BY
Allen H. Fisher, Jr.

RESOURCE *Publications* · Eugene, Oregon

WORDS ARE MAGIC
Story Guides for Human Beans and Other Perishables

Copyright © 2023 John Thomas Tuft. All rights reserved. Except for brief quotations in critical publications or reviews, no part of this book may be reproduced in any manner without prior written permission from the publisher. Write: Permissions, Wipf and Stock Publishers, 199 W. 8th Ave., Suite 3, Eugene, OR 97401.

Resource Publications
An Imprint of Wipf and Stock Publishers
199 W. 8th Ave., Suite 3
Eugene, OR 97401

www.wipfandstock.com

PAPERBACK ISBN: 978-1-6667-7911-0
HARDCOVER ISBN: 978-1-6667-7912-7
EBOOK ISBN: 978-1-6667-7913-4

06/19/23

To Ginny and Margie with all my love and gratitude

And Lillie, for finding me all over again.

CONTENTS

FOREWORD by Allen H. Fisher, Jr. | xi
PREFACE | xiii

GINNY | 3
GRIOT | 5
JACK GOO AND ME | 7
METANOIA | 9
CONTRONYM *CHANAN* | 12
THE KINGDOM OF GOD IS LIKE AN ABORTION | 14
TOUCHDOWN JESUS | 16
THOUGHTS AND PRAYERS | 19
THIRSTY PEOPLE | 21
WHERE DRAGONS SLEEP | 23
KNIGHTS OF FANTASIA | 26
CAROLINA CHLOE | 28
SEA OF LONELY | 30
SATAN | 32
SHUT UP AND DANCE | 35
THE BESPOKE CHAIR | 37
DESTINY'S CHILD | 39
STREETS OF PHILADELPHIA | 41
PLANT A STICKER | 43
JOHNNY SMOKE | 46
CORAM DEO | 49
THE BLACK MILE | 51

PADRE PEDRO | 53
PARE MY SOUL | 55
JOE SANTA | 58
RAY AND BRUNO'S RESURRECTION | 60
RUN AWAY TO MARS | 63
CRUCIFY ME | 66
THE CHERRY TREE | 69
JESUS WOODSTOCK | 72
JESUS THE FRIENDLY GHOST | 75
THE KITTEN AMENDMENT | 77
THE HOUSE YOU LIVE IN | 80
THE RAG MAN | 82
I WILL BE THE WIND | 84
THE CONTEST | 87
THE LAST OUT | 90
MILEPOST 62 | 93
THE BROTHERS CARAMEL-SLAW | 96
THE MIDDLE OF NOWHERE | 99
COTTONHEART | 101
BRACHIATE OR BREAK | 103
BOOG: SEMPER FI | 106
OPHELIA | 108
AT FIRST LIGHT | 110
AT THIS TABLE | 112
IF'N I'M FORGOTTEN | 114
IF I BE WRONG | 116
HURDY GURDY MAN | 118
iPHONE JESUS | 120
JUST AS I AM | 122
JACKPOT | 124
BEAUTIFUL WAR | 126
THE SECRET TO LIFE | 128
BILLY'S TRAIN | 130
BE THE SONG | 133

BREATHE WHILE DROWNING | 135
BROTHER JOE BOB CARL'S GAS AND GOSPEL | 137
THE PRISONER | 139
THE UNICORN STORY | 142
THE GREEN DOT | 145
THE GOD CULT | 147
THE HOLY DARK | 149
THE HONORABLE | 152
THE SECRET | 155
TAKE ME TO CHURCH | 157
LIVING MEMORY | 159
START FROM ZERO | 162
THIS GLORIOUS SADNESS | 165
THE PONY MAN | 168
ARE YOU READY? | 171
THE WEARY WORLD | 173
THAT WASN'T ME | 175
LITTLE LION MAN | 178
ONE DAY LESS | 181
NEENEE'S TEA | 183
MY BIG, FAT BODY | 185
LAMENTATIONS | 187
LAST CHANCE | 189
THANKSGIVING FOR MONKEYS | 191
THANKSGIVING MAGNIFICAT | 193
A RED WAGON THANKSGIVING | 196
A CHRISTMAS RESURRECTION | 199
A BILL AND BOB CHRISTMAS | 202
DON'T READ THIS STORY | 205
THE LAST CANDLE | 207
POOPSIE | 210
IT'S A WONDERFUL LIFE | 213
PASS THE LIGHT | 215

FOREWORD

Forty years ago, more than two generations now, I met John Thomas Tuft at a support retreat for people new to the practice of ordained ministry. Our connections took root in a deep sharing of personal reflection and family histories. Since our first encounters in a retreat center near the Appalachian trail in eastern Pennsylvania, our friendship has migrated with us throughout many states. While far too much time and experience has shaped our own narratives across decades as we transitioned into roles from children and siblings to parents, grandparents, and now a great-grandparent, our rapport persists and for that I am grateful. Colleagues and friends of such long-standing are too rare in a disposable, transient age.

In the modern binary world of zeroes and ones where the tribalism and tyranny of either/or speaking and thinking serve to incapacitate our humanity, Tuft invites us to notice the hues and subtleties of life as we know it. In telling these episodes so well, he entices us into the details of the human drama all the while exposing us to the presence of God often overlooked.

In engaging his characters and their adventures large and small, we can glimpse demanding questions, ambiguity, and even doubt as necessary ingredients for the feast that is life. Tracing their steps and missteps can free us from our own and those of people we love. We may learn that there is more to life than words themselves can say.

I invite you to spend time with the stories before you. In them you may find far more than you dare imagine. While Tuft is a gifted writer and superb storyteller, be prepared to see yourself in these pages. Glimpses of your own delights, sorrows, disappointments, ruminations, ecstasies, and losses may sneak up on you. His warm affection for others shines through his regard and fondness for the characters in these stories. Sharing facets of their scars, triumphs, injuries, metamorphoses, relationships, frustration, and dilemmas, his pastoral compassion tempers the telling of deeper truths at play in, through, around, and behind the lives of ordinary people whether they realize it or not.

Taken together, these gems express the patient nature, attentive listening, soulful reflection, and deep compassion of an author who has passionately leaned into life. Some may find flashes of brilliance and insight, while others who can hear and see with the ear and eye of the heart will perceive an abiding faithfulness that echoes through eternity in the realm of the divine.

Who knows? Perhaps your own life is more worthy of reflection, friendship, passion, and grace than you first thought. You may find yourself a friend. Listen! Prepare to be surprised; there is more here than meets the eye. Enjoy the adventure.

Allen H. Fisher, Jr., May 2023

PREFACE

SOMETIMES IT CAN BE hard to tell where my pain ends, and my life begins. Equally, it can be hard to tell where my joy begins and the light of grace shines, blinding me through the shadows and erasing the delineations of darkness and form. Forgive me for waxing poetical but I struggle to define for you the origins of this book. Quite simply, I decided in 2019 to write at least one story each week and post it on social media. I did so because it was all that I had to offer, and it was the best that I had to offer. These stories are my offerings.

I readily admit that they are offered from a broken vessel. I wrote the one about Ginny as I was sitting in an independent facility where she and I both resided. She was ninety at the time, suffering from dementia that robbed her of short-term memory. By short term I mean not even an hour. She did not remember to come down for meals, so I began going up to her apartment and bringing her down, sitting with her, singing with her, and becoming enriched and healed in part by the relationship. I had come to that place out of assisted living, a kind of nursing home situation for those waiting to die, quite frankly. Ginny was going to be on her way to such a facility in due time. Her stories of her early life growing up in a family of twelve children in South Carolina, told every meal, every day until I knew them by heart, became the ambience of mealtime.

I was there with nothing. And I wanted to say thank you for everything. Like surviving over thirty years of opioid drugs for the incessant pain. Surviving two major car accidents: one into the side of a brick house as my car sped down an ice-covered mountain road, the other spinning into a utility pole and totaling my car. Surviving countless trips to the emergency room, fifteen surgeries, a dozen years or more in physical therapy only to have to start over each time. Surviving having lived fifteen years with a morphine pump in my body and having a numbing drug added after the second accident that led to total memory loss for those years. Surviving severe depression to the point of actively contemplating suicide.

My children placed me into assisted living, a desolate landscape of despair. I want to say thank you to them. Thank you to the staff and administrators. Thank you to the friends who still live there. I should be dead now, but I am not, and for that I am grateful. As I walked out after one year, a young CNA came running up to me and threw her arms around my neck. "Mr. Tuft, nobody ever leaves here like this. Don't forget us." I have not forgotten. At the independent living facility, I began to write poems on the plain paper placemats. I still have friends there, as well. Among the stroke victims, the infirm, the depressed, the fearful feeling lost and forgotten. To them, a heartfelt thank you.

And now to you as you begin to read the stories, a deep gratitude. I write because I have to, I cannot not write. Stories are in my blood. Words are magic and writers are wizards.

JTT

STORY GUIDES

GINNY

I SAT DOWN TO lunch with my friend, Ginny. Ginny is 90 years old, and she has progressive dementia. In other words, she has no short-term memory. None. I have known her for a year because we live together in the same facility, an independent living building with cramped apartments and a common dining area. At the time, it was my first stop after living in assisted living for one year. A year spent waiting to die. And then not. It turned into a time of recovery, and I moved up in the world, to independent living with the elderly who have been forced to give up their own homes because their health is failing due to strokes, diabetes, early dementia. Mostly due to frailty. It is quite often the last stop before going into assisted living and into dying. Like I said, though, I was moving up. I was stepping back into life.

Ginny looked at me with her clear eyes. "Do you ever get a song stuck in your head?" It's a question she asks me nearly every day. "Sure, Ginny." I break into Tim McGraw's 'Neon Church', "Well, I need Jesus, or I need whiskey, whatever works best to get me through . . . " She laughs and in her South Carolina low country accent says, "I cain't get Amazing Grace out of my head today." Around us in the large dining room are wheelchairs, motorized carts, walkers, canes, and those souls who depend on them now for any chance at all. "So, sing it!" I encourage her. "No," she demurs, "no, people will think I'm touched."

"Well, I don't care." So, I launch in, full throated, "Amazing grace, how sweet the sound . . . " Ginny joins in, reluctantly at first. Then stronger, " . . . I once was lost but now I'm found, 'twas blind but now I see." Bystanders and wait staff stop to listen, some shaking their heads at this outburst. We sing three verses. The people around us are now strangely quiet.

Ginny smiles, rests her hand on my arm as we turn back to our salads. "Thank you. You're such a good friend, waiting to eat with me at lunch today." I cover her hand with mine. "No, Ginny, being with you makes me a better man. Maybe I'm just touched." She looks at me with a question writ large in her eyes. Even though I know what is coming, it is still jarring. "What's your name? I feel like I've met you before." I swallow hard and give her hand a reassuring squeeze. "That's okay. I'm John. I come to get you each meal . . . " I stop. This isn't what she needs. She does not, she cannot remember who I am or why she knows me.

"Well, it's right nice to meet you. People call me Ginny. I love to sing. Do you ever get a song stuck in your head?" I look at the tabletop for a moment, then back to her clear eyes. "I do, Ginny. I do. What song is in you today?"

Maybe I'm just touched . . .

GRIOT

THE LITTLE TOWN LIES fifty miles north of Pittsburgh, with the dubious distinction of lying approximately halfway between Youngstown, Ohio and Grove City, Pennsylvania—neither of which is known for being particularly forward thinking. Before you come at me, both my son and daughter in law are graduates of Grove City College, but this story takes place in New Wilmington, PA, home to one of their rivals: Westminster College. New Wilmington, population 2204, and the surrounding pastoral Lawrence County is home to a large population of the Old Order Amish. The 16-, 17-, and 18-year-old version of Jack, as I was known then, worked summers there, laboring to set up in preparation, serve during and deconstruct for the feeding, sheltering and cleaning up after the attendees of the New Wilmington Missions Conference. It was 12-14 hour days of hard labor from constructing a dining hall, lugging hundreds of mattresses, thousands of tables and chairs, to digging endless postholes, dishwashing for 3600 settings each day (I still have nightmares about the pots and pans), to cleaning the fieldhouse bathrooms for 500 high school boys loosed upon the earth like a pestilence.

It was all done under the supervision and bright, but irascible, eye of Doc Wayne Christy, a wiry New Testament professor and tennis and volleyball afficionado. It's hard to tell which meant more to him, sports or scriptures, and saints preserve you if you missed setting up a spike in the nightly volleyball matches in his yard against the dreaded college kids. With all due respect to those nonwinners, we didn't dare lose. The work hardened our young muscles, the sun tanned my skin and bleached my blonde hair, and I point that out for no better reason then that there were 700 high school girls there, also, for the conference. Amen. Come along if you will, and I'll show you the tree on the campus of Westminster College that I sat under each evening of the conference with the lovely Miss Linda Michaels but couldn't muster the courage for a kiss until the last minute of the last evening . . . Jack's a shy guy at heart, but you already know that.

Slippery Rock Creek runs through the area, past the old grinding stones of McConnell's Mill, through the gorges and forests seeking rivers and runs. Some say there are intimate mysteries and shaded shadows of ancient tales that rise with the evening mists along its tree lined banks. Drive the back roads, through the hills and pastureland, past the neat frame houses under giant trees, sturdy barns standing like sentinels in the evening dews and damps, steering around the ever-present horses and buggies of the Plain People, until you are lost on a dirt lane, that leads to a hidden path, that leads to an old cave. It is home of the primed depths where stories begin—form and rise; some unbidden, some needing a gentle midwife. Some kicking and screaming, newborns breathing oxygen for the first time.

The guardian of that sacred grotto, that repository of our stories, all our poems and songs, is the griot (gree-oh). Earth's only true royalty, much in demand at weddings and funerals, family reunions and cultural gatherings, books and prayers, the griot began their existence in West Africa, but now their spirits freely roam the land. Collecting and inspiring storytellers of all stripes. I met one during my second summer in New Wilmington.

Summer mornings in New Wilmington would find four teenage boys pushing a 1949 Chevy flatbed truck down Market Street past The Tavern on the Square restaurant, Doc at the wheel ready to pop the clutch. The first chore after breakfast was to humor the cranky starter and get it going with manpower. Get it up to speed, legs churning arms burning, into gear, and grab the slatted sides and swing up onto the back of the truck because you didn't dare stop, and ride on down the street to campus, hair flowing in the breeze, sun on our faces, fearless and unbowed. We pulled up to the back of the fieldhouse on a small incline, loaded folding chairs onto the back; 100 on, 1100 to go. Leave the slats off the rear, it is easier to unload them. Climb on top of the chairs. She won't start. Doc drifts it down the slope, pops the clutch, and I go flying.

The pavement is rushing at my face. In a blink, I'm face to face with the rear tire. Chairs tumble around me. Everyone screams. Everything stops. Except Doc. Unaware of the calamity, he drives on. Having hooked my one foot into a side slat before we started is all that saves me. I'm swinging wildly, pavement an inch from my face, the tire grabbing at my shirt. All ends well. Later, I'm stacking chairs in the belly of the outdoor auditorium stage, alone, when he steps out of the shadows. "Jack," the griot says, quietly. "I have your stories. Come for them when you are ready." Then he is gone. I step back into glare of sunlight beating off the waters of Brittain Lake, knowing that someday I will be back. I will be back to reclaim those stories.

Words are magic, and writers are wizards.

JACK GOO AND ME

THIS IS FOR MIKE, east of Tulsa. . .

When I was a child my older brothers called me Jack Goo. We don't need to go into what that's all about. I remember those years as being a mixture of dread over what people would think of me and joy at the sheer pleasure of playing. Long summer days of playing ball, any kind of game involving a ball, and before that, endless games of make believe.

Susan, Dan and I were the "little kids" of the family, so we were inherently tight, closely guarded each other's backs, confronted neighborhood bullies (okay, Susan did most of the fighting) and explored the mythical woods of Minnehaha with canteens of KoolAid and make-believe weapons. We flew imaginary planes like SKY KING, raised proud stallions like FURY, fought the bad guys like ROY ROGERS, and on and on ad infinitum.

All the while my oldest brother tinkered away on a god forsaken jalopy that was silently praying for a merciful death under the old cherry trees at the back of an expansive lot next to a dilapidated wooden garage held together by graying whitewash. Because that's what older brothers do.

Why, you ask, was my childhood filled with dread? Two words: Evangelical Calvinist. No, not me. My father. The minister. Reverend obedience to me is obedience to God is obedience to Sacred Scripture is obedience to me and round and round we go. And you kids better do nothing to embarrass me, NOTHING, in front of the church members. No pressure. And, to top it all off, women are inferior to men.

I kind of think dread sums it up, don't you?

Recently an Uber driver said to me, "You're not getting out of this car until I get your autograph. You are a walking, talking miracle!" I obliged. And silently thumbed my nose at John Calvin, the Rev. in front of my name notwithstanding.

We buried Susan goin' on ten years now. I'm not a very good brother to Dan, but I promise to do better. Honestly. And if you want my humble opinion, women are better than men, but maybe that's just me. And oh, I write fiction now. . .and poetry. Maybe someday a song or two. Who knows! Predestination or prestidigitation be damned.

Yesterday I rode around in my oldest brother's new pick up listening to his music and talking with him about the miracle that is our lives. And I got to meet some people who are very important to him. It left me filled with wonder.

Because that's what big brothers do.

I'm Jack Goo.

Words are magic and writers are wizards.

METANOIA

I WAS ON MY way to apologize to a dead woman. Driving up Ohio River Boulevard toward the Divine Providence Nursing Center in Beaver Falls, PA, converted from the very hospital where I had been born, I reviewed what had transpired the week before. Andrea, age 62, would have been my son's kindergarten teacher were it not for the cancer ravaging her organs. Her only child, 32-year-old Sonny, had discovered her crawling up the street at 3 am, bleeding, screaming, crying that he wanted her dead. I showed up at her admission, noting her disheveled appearance, snarling demeanor at her son and staff, and promptly decided he'd made the right decision. Now I needed to apologize. The assessment determined that he'd been overmedicating her, leaving her disoriented, crazed, and above all filled with fear.

The woman who greeted me on this visit was calm, collected, smiling. "Preacher, how good of you to come. Here have some of this candy my friend brought me." (Okay, I might have a reputation for a sweet tooth.) I pulled up a chair and as we talked, she told me, "I don't know what to do with Sonny. Henry and I gave him everything we could. His education, his first apartment, welcomed his wife even though she's a bit strange." She fussed with the pink silk ribbon holding her hair off her face. "All I have for him is my money. Isn't that sad, Preacher?" She brightened. "But they say I can go home now and have a private nurse. I miss my house. Henry and I built it. I do miss him so." She grew quiet. Fidgeted with the threads of the blanket. "Preacher, do you know what I want more than anything?" Big breath, a trembling sigh. "That just one time, before I die, that Sonny would look at me and say, 'I love you. Mother, I love you'. That's all I want." Silent tears coursed down her cheeks.

Weeks later I stood at the front door of a large house, signs of neglect showing in the flower gardens that ringed it. I was bringing her communion. For the last time. My knock was answered by the sound of running paws and a loud thump that made the door shudder. A tall, large woman in a nurse's outfit opened the door and glowered. "Who might you be?" After ascertaining my credentials, she let me in. A large, panting Doberman pinned me to the spot with a fierce glare. "Mrs. Beeges!" The nurse's stern voice penetrated the dog's protective instinct. "Stay!" Both the dog and I trembled. Mrs. Beeges finally turned and loped down the hallway. Andrea's room was filled with flowers. Everywhere. Of all kinds. "Preacher! You came. Make some room. Isn't this glorious?"

As I prepared the meal fit for the royalty of the meek, and uttered the ancient words that touch the ultimate, a summer storm broke. Thunder crashed and rain pelted the windows. I made a move to close them. "No, let them be, Preacher. Listen to that rain." So together we watched the leaves of the bushes dance in timeless rhythm. "Sonny barely speaks to me. He comes in . . . Mrs. Beeges growls at him . . . and stands down there at the foot of my bed for a minute or so and then leaves." Lightning split the sky and the winds picked up intensity. "I miss working in the garden, Preacher. Did I tell you what my Henry did? He asked me once about getting a car. So, you know what I said?" She gasped in pain. Then she laughed. "I said, just as long as it's a convertible. A red one!" She took my hand and squeezed. "I rode around town with the top down. It was glorious! Preacher, they better have red convertibles in heaven or else I'm coming back." She grew quiet as the storm raged unabated. "All I have for my Sonny is this money. What does that say about me, Preacher?"

Later that week there was a knock on my office door. Sonny burst in without further warning. "Who the hell do you think you are?" he demanded loudly. He thrust his finger in my face. "I'm warning you, you slimy bastard, stay away from my mother. I'm putting her back in the hospital right now. And so help me, if you go anywhere near her . . . You will NOT do her funeral. You're scum, Mister. Stay away." With that he stormed out.

Some days later I found myself outside a room on the top floor of Sewickley Valley Hospital. I entered the room. Andrea lay on the bed, gasping for breath, her mouth gaping open in her agony, showing gray and purple. I pulled a chair close to the bed and took her hand after swabbing her dry lips with glycerin. I didn't know if she was aware or not. I read the 23rd Psalm as best I could. As I murmured the Lord's Prayer, a ghastly moan came from her, the cry of a pleading heart, doing her best to have her lamentations heard. As I started for the door she cried out, "Sonny?!" I felt rooted to the floor. "Sonny?" The ground threatened to open and swallow me. Finally, I went back to her side. Ever so gently I knelt on the bed and put my mouth close to her ear. "Yes . . . " I paused, " . . . Mother. Mother, I'm here," I whispered as I stroked her brittle hair. Then I took her ever so gently in my arms. "I love you.

Mother, I love you." Her body trembled and tears washed her cheeks. "Oh, Sonny. Oh, my Sonny. Mommy loves you too."

I sat in my car for the longest time, drained, too spent to cry although I was filled with tears. I stared through the windshield, watching the rain seeking new direction as it caressed the glass. Wondering. Isn't this glorious.

Words are magic, and writers are wizards.

CONTRONYM *CHANAN*

THE ELEVATOR DOORS SLID open. I drew in a deep breath and stepped out into the hallway of the Experimental Cancer Treatment Unit of a major hospital tied to a major research university system. This story is not about me so suffice it to say it is not my most favorite place on earth to visit. The corridors are long, and the acrid smell of disinfectant and harsh chemicals passing through bodies and excreted again—wash, rinse, repeat—are not the comforting embrace needed in this place.

At the time, various groups of perishables referred to me as Reverend or Preacher Boy, take your pick, and I was tasked with interpreting the unimaginable to trembling souls thirsting for concrete expressions of faith in what is not seen, heard, tasted, or touched. And I weep as I write these words because I know what is coming yet have no explanation for it other than contronym *Chanan*. A word that means one thing and its opposite all in the same configuration of letters. And the word for today is the ancient Hebrew word for grace; the verb to be gracious. The holy mystery that is always, always staring us right in the face. Because it is always, always up to us . . . to make it real. If there is any trace of grace in stained glass, robes, and fragrant rituals then, for my money, there is certainly grace abounding in the piss, shit, and vomit stinking of chemotherapy. The grace that is life. The grace that is death.

Trisha has a particularly virulent brain cancer. At age 33, she is married and the mother of two. She is bright, articulate, vivacious, and a downright joy to be around. Yet many is the night, before this, that she called me around 10pm in tears. It is always the same thing: the state of her marriage to Jack. He disappears most evenings, claiming he needs to wander and think. She is left alone and wondering. "Why does he do this?" she cries. "Am I not enough? How do I explain to the kids?" Jack pastors a vibrant congregation of perishables on the other side of the county. I am a friend to them both. Which is why I am here, pushing open the door to her room.

Trisha's head is partially shaved. A port for medication into her brain is sewn in place into one side of her skull. Another patch is shaved on the back of her head from the surgery to place a shunt from her skull into her abdomen. I sit on the side of the bed. "John, I want to talk to you," she says, using my favorite title. "I want to go home . . . " before she can finish, a seizure strikes, twisting her mouth cruelly and making one arm flap uselessly. We wait for it to pass. "I'm telling the doctors to stop all treatment." We speak to each other with our eyes, for we both realize what she is saying. Not asking. Telling all those who care for her that she needs to extend this grace to herself. Not out of some resignation to fate or folly. Not out of fear or embarrassment of being a burden. Rather as a benediction on a life well lived.

My heart breaks as I nod that I understand. I'm losing my friend. A treasured light in my life. And she needs a goodbye. We all need goodbyes. Now, she needs mine. So, I smile. She squeezes my hand in appreciation. "I found a new wife for Jack," she adds, with her own crooked smile. "Tell me goodbye by agreeing to officiate at their wedding." And she laughs as only she could at the absurdity of grace. "She knows how to love him and to be a mother to my kids." I am speechless. "Does she know this?" I finally manage. She nods and a single tear escapes, tracing its way down her cheek. And we sit there together as the shadows of the day lengthen around us. The contronym of Chanan. She is leaving life. She is leaving life growing here where she has been.

About a month later I drove out to their home. The house is full of family and friends. Evidence of the grace of her life. "She's waiting for you," someone tells me. I go into her room. Her neck is arched, jaw dropping open. The end is near. I sit on the bed beside her. Reach out and stroke her hair. No words. There are no words. My heart is screaming to her not to leave, but I can only whisper, "Thank you." She manages to raise her head, open her eyes, and smile at me. Then she is gone . . . and I catch the scent of roses outside her window drifting in a lazy dance with the breeze.

Words are magic and writers are wizards.

THE KINGDOM OF GOD IS LIKE AN ABORTION

The kingdom of God is like. . . a farmer who goes out to sow his seeds and Mother Nature takes over and the forces of the marketplace do their thing and somehow food ends up in your mouth.

The Kingdom of God is like. . .a four-year-old girl who picks her way across a floor littered with Barbie dresses and accessories and body parts to look into her father's pain drawn face and ask the question that plumbs the mystery of all mysteries, "If you were a red marker, where would you be hiding?" And upon finding said red marker, proceeds to draw a hand puppet twixt thumb and index finger and animates it to proclaim boldly to said father, "Pain, get out!"

The kingdom of God is like. . .a preacher who gets up into the pulpit on a fine Sunday morning, looks out over her flock, shuffles her notes, murmurs her ritual invocation, faces the expectant perishables, and can only choke out a whispered, "I got nothin."

The kingdom of God is like. . .a 16-year-old girl, sitting in a quiet room with only the suggestion of faltering breeze in the air, nervously twisting a bottle of antibiotics in her hands, saying plaintively, "I cried all night, but my parents ignored me. Finally, Momma came up and said, 'What are you going to say when you get to heaven and that baby asks you, why'd you kill me?'" And the man listening can only hold her hand while helplessly hoping his harlequin prayers hover nearby.

The kingdom of God is like. . .two men who go up to the temple to pray. One makes much ado about how 'right he is with God, how righteous he is in making others live godly lives, how proud God must be of his Herculean effort to make others into his own image.' While the other man says, "I don't have any seeds left. I don't know where red markers hide. I could only hold her hand while the other hand wiped her tears. I got nothin."

The kingdom of God is like. . .looking in the mirror each and every day. . .and asking, Who am I going to be. . .today? Knowing full well that the only real options are grace and humility. Today and always. That's all. Everything else is not worth having, for what does it profit us to gain the whole world. . .

God is a choice. Live like that.

Words are magic and writers are wizards.

TOUCHDOWN JESUS

ONCE UPON A TIME, in the mythical, fading coal country of southwest Pennsylvania there was a place called Tipple Town. It's a small place with people with big hearts. There's an old drug store, an abandoned Five and Dime, Taylor's Groceries, and a gas station. Where they pump your gas, check the oil, and clean the windshield. Going to the doctor means going to Uniontown. Anything more than that means a trek to Pittsburgh. The Baptist Church anchors one end of Main Street. The Real Baptists are further off in hill country. The Presbyterians anchor the other end, the Methodists proudly own the middle, Episcopalians are on a shady side street, and all the good Catholics belong to the four county Southwest PA Parish. Every fall, come hell or highwater, everyone turns out for high school football. Everyone. In 1969, that means coal miners, mill workers, deck hands from tow operators on the Monongahela River, yard crews from the railroad. And their families. Having a boy on the football team is a point of particular pride.

One of the local pastors had a son named Jack. At 16 years of age, he is Chip Hilton handsome, six feet tall and 180 pounds of star quarterback, destined for a scholarship at Pitt. One day his mother came to him and said, "Jack, there is a family down the street who need someone to babysit their boy, Joey. He's 12 and he has leukemia." Jack protested, "But Mom, summer camp starts next week. I've got to get my reps in with the guys in the weight room." But his mother persisted. Then insisted. As mothers in Tipple Town are wont to do. So it came to pass that in the summer of 1969, with too many of the good sons of Southwest Pennsylvania fingering their draft cards as Vietnam played in the background, Jack, with much fear and trepidation, began to spend a couple of hours in the evenings with Joey.

The treatments had left Joey bald. As a cue ball. As no 12-year-old, no matter where they live, should be. In fact, that's what he insisted Jack call him, Cue Ball. And Jack obliged, as boys are wont to do. (Look it up, it's an old word.) "So, what do you want to do?" Jack asked with practiced nonchalance. Quarterbacks are like that. Joey shrugged. "Wanna play checkers?" He looked small, pale, always wrapped in a colorful afghan crocheted by his mother. As mothers baffled by their children facing their mortality are wont to do. When they aren't walking as far away from the house as they can so their boy won't hear them screaming through the tears.

So, the big strong quarterback with a future mapped out for him, sat with the pale, weak Cue Ball with numbered days, and they played checkers. And talked. About nothing and about everything. Sports, fishing, hunting, cars and the promised land of driving, food, gross things they enjoyed doing to freak out their moms, the inscrutabilities of dads. And girls. Lots of talking about girls. And the promised land. As boys are wont to do. Summer football camp started but the good coach of the regional high school let Jack leave camp in the evenings for a couple of hours to spend with Joey, the Cue Ball.

Football season started. The Tipple Town boys were a good team. In contention for the playoffs for the state single A championship. The whole town was abuzz. Jack was a hero. But Cue Ball had to go up to Children's Hospital in Pittsburgh. So the Sunday before the last game, the one where everything is on the line, Jack used his newly minted driver's license to follow the Mon and see his friend. In a cold, too brightly lit hospital room, too far from Tipple Town, the two sat and played checkers. And made a secret pact. As two friends are wont to do.

It's the night of the big game. For all the marbles. The team from Freedom, PA, a railyard town north of Pittsburgh, where tows of coal glide by in silence on the Ohio River, is an equally good team. Jack is in his element. Every so often he glances at the sidelines. Where a small figure huddles against the cold in his wheelchair, wrapped in a colorful afghan. The game is close, the lead seesaws back and forth. Fourth and goal, ten seconds on the clock, Tipple Town team driving to score. The crowd is going wild. Jack rolls out, heading for the end zone for the winning score. Joey the Cue Ball leans forward, cheering with all his failing might.

Suddenly Jack veers to the sideline. The other team crashes toward him. Jack stops. Puts the ball in his friend's arms. Picks him up out of the chair. Stumbles toward the goal line. Trips on the colorful afghan. Falls to the ground. The ball comes loose . . . The next day there is a picture on the front page of the Tipple Town Tribune. There in the foreground is Jack, on the ground, covering his friend, Cue Ball, in the end zone. In the background is a huge defensive lineman from Freedom who goes by the nickname, Congo. He is kneeling, arms stretched out. In one hand is the football. That he's extending toward Jack and Cue Ball's hands. In the background is the stunned into silence crowd. Above the picture is the headline: TOUCHDOWN JESUS

So, on a clear autumn night, if you're in Tipple Town, and it's the last home game of the season, make your way to the high school football field. Just come prepared. Because at the end of the game, as the Hunter's moon shines brightly, casting moon shadows through the beams of the old coal tipple at the north end zone, the crowd stands in silence, makes their way to the field and when they walk away it is covered. Covered with cue balls. As the good folks of Tipple Town are wont to do.

Words are magic, and writers are wizards.

THOUGHTS AND PRAYERS

It was a midnight call. Coming from three time zones away. To a nondescript home in the nondescript town of East McKeesport, the Nazareth of Western Pennsylvania. It was a minister-to-minister call, a strange breed of communication, if there ever was one. "I have a message for you. You are John, right?" Umm . . . yeah. "Okay, I looked you up in the Presbyterian Church Professional Directory. Because I never heard of you." Umm . . . okay. "I don't quite know how to tell you this. I feel a bit silly." Umm . . . that seems to come with the job. "Well, I had a dream. And in the dream someone told me that I was to find you. And I was supposed to pray for you. And you will be healed of your affliction." Umm . . . someone. Someone like who?

A long, long pause. "I don't know. I'm not sure. Maybe an angel." Maybe an angel. Maybe an angel?! Riiigghhtt!! And this angel did what? Gave you a fortune cookie with my name inside? "I know how you feel. I've been putting off this call for a week." Check out the window. No burning bushes. Although East McKeesport does have some lovely Christmas lights along Broadway, Punta Gorda Avenue, Park Street and on into North Versailles' Taylor Plan. Not too unlike where you are, maybe. "Listen, Reverend, I've been praying about this ever since. Do you think I want to sound like . . . like an(and here he uses a word you might think Reverends don't use, but I'm here to tell you, you would be wrong.)"

And it came to pass that the reverend set his course toward the East. He went before his congregation and told them about the dream. "I must travel there. Pray with him. And he will be healed." And they were astonished. Then they admonished. "We've never done anything like this before. Are you unhappy? We give you four weeks of vacation. And two weeks of study leave. Let us pray for the afflictions of this other reverend. It will be enough." So the first reverend was down cast and forsaken. And he sought refuge and spiritual comfort in the local neon church, " . . . with a jukebox choir, full of honky-tonk angels with their wings on fire, straight pouring out that Johnnie Walker healing . . . "

A woman came out of the crowd and quietly took a seat nearby. She had a reputation. She said to the reverend, "You look troubled. Pray tell, what can I do?" He told her the story of the dream. So she went and got her mother so she could hear the story. And the mother said, "I've saved Tupperware money. You can have it." And the bartender said, "Tonight's tips are especially good. Take and use them, all of them." And a boy came in selling hoagies for a band trip and he saw the crowd and wondered. He ripped up his order sheet and gave all the money to the reverend who'd had the dream.

Thus it was that in the fullness of time, the reverend from the west set off on a great journey seeking the reverend in the town in the East, bearing his gifts of great thoughts, and great prayers. And the unmatched kindness of strangers. Who knew the value of dreams. And the invaluable treasure of hope.

And, thus it was, in the fullness of time, and it came to pass, that at one point, on the last leg of his journey our hero boarded an airplane bound for Pittsburgh. It was designated USAir427. On a warm evening, with no warning, a stone's throw from the runway, it dropped out of the sky. And littered the wooded hillsides of Hopewell Township. Bearing east/southeast.

The reverend from the East was summoned to the crash site. To aid the first responders. To walk the slippery with blood ground. To witness the flames and the horror. To weep with the hopeless. To bear with the broken. To bind up their wounds. To be emptied. To ask what cannot be answered. To be healed in a crucible.

Prayer is down and dirty. It has grime under its fingernails. Breath of stale beer. Bloodshot eyes and needs a shower. Tats and brats. Go big or go home. Steelers for the win, fourth and goal, last ten seconds on the clock fervor. Homeless woman on the curb feeding a kitten humility. Toddler on the potty chair, first time, first try expectations. Prayer believes all things. Hopes all things. Endures all things.

Or is that love? Is there a difference?

Words are magic, and writers are wizards.

THIRSTY PEOPLE

When Mama Sadie put on her black and white polka dot dress everyone knew things were taking a turn toward the serious. Mama Sadie only wore the dress for Sunday going to meeting, funerals, and dealing with high falutin' folks like the mayor or chief of police or the all too rare occasion of going to the Woolworth's lunch counter for pie and coffee to celebrate another successful drive for the library or the March of Dimes. She drove around town in a pink 1963 Buick Skylark with a black top, horn-rimmed glasses perched on the end of her nose, hands positioned at 10 and 2 on the steering wheel, and her piety firmly tucked like the good Methodist that she was, into the shiny black handbag with the gold clasp on the seat next to her. And every evening when she locked the doors and turned out the lights, she paused before her framed photograph of the 35th President of the United States to whisper, "Gone too soon," before retiring for the night.

"The greatest gift we can give is dignity," Mama Sadie would say. "That's what my Arnold used to tell me when he went out the door each morning, four of the a and m, to go do his milk route. They're not customers, he'd say, they're thirsty people." She stopped to sigh. "I cleaned houses for the folks who ran the mills and if there's one thing I learned, it is this. People are designed for love. Period. Nothing, and I do mean nothing, can fill that hole. And if you know that you are loved, you treat others with dignity. Just like if you never are loved, then other folks are just something to use or push out of the way. Period. 'Nuf said." Arnold passed away when Sadie was barely fifty, and her life became more of a struggle, albeit a dignified one. She simply would not allow herself to deal with it in any other way. Even then, however, the next ten years aged her twenty.

So, when Henry Chalmers, III, came courting, Mama Sadie did not quite understand. "I'm no spring chicken, Henry. My hair's gone gray, everything sags, and I ain't got much more than the clothes on my back." Henry drew himself up straight and proclaimed, "I want to give you everything that you have ever desired." "All I want is for you to take me as I am," was Sadie's dignified reply. "That's all I want from anyone or for anyone." But she let Henry talk her into putting on the black and white polka dot dress and take her somewhere fancy, the new Applebee's on Route 28. "I want to buy you a new car, new furniture, and bring you presents. I like to spoil my women," said the eager suitor. Mama Sadie took all this in, pondering it in her heart. Then she asked, in a voice so quiet that Henry had to lean over the table to hear, "What do you get out of this, Henry?" Henry sat back, a big smile on his face, "Well, I get to go around town with Mama Sadie on my arm. People will see us coming and think, why those folks got everything!"

Mama Sadie picked up the extra rolls and wrapped them in a napkin and carefully placed it into the shiny black handbag with the gold clasp. As she let Henry help her with her coat, she said, "They're not customers, Henry. They are thirsty people." Henry scratched his head at this and as they were getting into the car, the police chief pulled up alongside, calling to her, "Mama Sadie, we need your help." He motioned for her to get in and they sped off. Henry followed, curious. He caught up to them outside the moldy trailer on the outskirts of town. Kyle Kendrickson, disheveled and drunk, was being pushed into the back seat of the police car. An ambulance prepared to cart away Kathy, a small woman with bruises and cuts and haunted eyes. The four Kendrickson kids, ages 3 to 13, sat on the couch, looking defiantly desperate and hollowed out. Mama Sadie opened her handbag and split the fancy Applebee's rolls between them.

She turned to Henry. "You want to give me everything? Love these children. Then I will have everything, as will you." Then she sat down among the kids, in her black and white polka dot dress, and put her arms around them. Henry backed away, not prepared for this kind of extravagance. She looked to the police chief. "Homer?" He nodded. "I sent a deputy to get your car, Mama Sadie." And so it came to pass, that the evening that began with urgent desires for love and attention, ended with Mama Sadie driving her 1963 pink and black Buick Skylark back to her little house, horn-rimmed glasses firmly resting on the end of her nose, hands at 10 and 2 and her black handbag resting next to her, held by the fragile hands of a 13 year old, while the other three squabbled in the back seat.

After they were in bed, Mama Sadie locked the doors, turned out the lights and paused in front of the picture of the 35th President, and beside it the picture of her Arnold. And with a sad smile, she whispers, "Gone too soon." 'Nuf said.

Words are magic and writers are wizards.

WHERE DRAGONS SLEEP

Jessie slid into the back seat of the Uber car, fastened the seat belt, her eyes fixed on the screen of her phone the entire time. She felt the car move forward and cast a quick glance at the back of the driver's head. White hair curled out from beneath a Pittsburgh Pirates cap. Thick lenses in the black frame glasses with a flip up pair of dark shades gave him the appearance of a bookie's accountant, complete with a brown suede vest over a flannel shirt. "Gd'evening, ma'am," he said in an accent she couldn't quite place as she caught a glimpse of his eyes in the rearview mirror. They were a startling emerald, tired but not unkind. Jessie grunted a noncommittal sound and returned to staring at the phone's screen. "I'll be taking you to see where your dragons be sleepin'." He held up a large paper cup. "And I'll be having chocolate coffee, yes indeed. You're welcome to sippin' if you please."

Jessie looked up, alarmed. "What? Dragons? No, I'm going to home... I mean, to my house. Just take me there." The driver pointed to the screen of the phone in a holder on the dashboard. "Your home is in the middle of the Westinghouse Memorial Bridge? Nothing there but down, miss." Jessie, clearly annoyed, was short with him. "I like to walk some. Just take me there. Now." The driver nodded. "I think it be best if I take you to see where your dragons be sleepin'." A long pull on the chocolate coffee. "Sure you don't want some?" Jessie ignored this offer. "I'm going to report you to Uber," she threatened, stabbing a finger on the screen. The driver shrugged. "Uber doesn't know how to take you to where your dragons sleep, ma'am." "This is kidnapping!" Jessie yelled. "Is there someone willing to pay a ton of treasure for you?" came the calm reply. Jessie shrunk back in the seat. "No." A nod of the cap, "Then why would I kidnap you? I don't want to hurt you. Your sleeping dragons already do enough hurtin'."

Jessie dropped the phone in her lap and leaned back. "What is it with you and dragons?" The driver flipped down the shades over his eyes. "Your Freddie liked dragons, right? He was what, 3 or 4 years old?" Jessie bolted upright. "How do you know about Freddie?" There was panic and pain in her voice. "I'm the dragon keeper. I know where dragons sleep," was all the man said. Jessie slowly crumbled and then is wracked with hard sobs. "I was so mad at him. He did something like a little boy will do and I screamed at him. So loudly that I terrified my own little boy." The driver waited in silence. "He ran up to his room, grabbed his dragon lamp and ran out the door. I heard the brakes of the car out in the street and then ..." She can't go on any further. The dragon keeper handed her back some tissues. Through her tears, Jessie managed, "But now he's gone, and I don't know where. I'm afraid. I'm so afraid."

"Ma'am, the thing about dragons bein', well, dragons live where people are afraid to go. It started when there were bottomless pools of water, deep in the dark forest. And mountains that reached into the clouds, too high to ever climb. Or caves, dank and steamy that no one had the courage to enter. So, they put their dragons there." The driver paused as he turned off the highway and onto an old service road. "Then we say dragons collect treasures. Hard piles of gold and diamonds. Only dragons can sleep on the jagged edges of their treasure." He stopped the car in front of some foreboding, deserted-looking greenhouses. He switched off the car and turned to look at Jessie.

"Missy, if you ask me, we develop a whole mythology about our guilts and fears and why we need them to be real, and why we hide them away like treasures. We get comfortable with the uncomfortable. We keep our pain and our dark secrets and other dark memories, our trauma, or hurting someone—we put them all in dark places, like they are a dragon's treasure. Guarded by fire-breathing beasts with hard scales. In the deep pools, dark forests, impossible mountains, or dank caves of our own hearts. Ya followin' me ma'am?" He got out and opened her door and invited Jessie to follow him. "I'm not sure," said Jessie in a nervous voice. "Where are we?"

"Where dragons sleep," came the dragon keeper's reply. They walked through the gathering gloom of the night, past scary looking empty buildings with scars and empty eyes. Jessie stayed close to the driver, unsure of what lay ahead. At last, they reached an old, abandoned greenhouse. Lots of broken glass littered the ground and what looked like dragons' tails poked through the walls and roof, twitching in the night breezes. "They used to grow heritage roses here, but they abandoned it decades ago," said the driver. He put his hand on Jessie's shoulder and guided her through the doorway. Inside it was dark and dank, the sound of dripping water echoing in the emptiness. The man reached over and flipped on the lights.

The room filled with a fiery glow. That revealed a riot of colors and delights. The old rose plantings had continued growing all those years.

Along the walls and right up through the roof, busting out glass panes. Reaching for the heavens. Jessie covered her mouth in wonder, turning in circles to take it all in. "Sometimes," said the dragon keeper, "if we don't turn our pains and guilts and worries into dark treasures where dragons sleep," he flipped the shades up and looked into her eyes with a smile, "they become beautiful in the most wild of ways."

Words are magic and writers are wizards.

KNIGHTS OF FANTASIA

RANDY IS THE FIRST to arrive for the meeting of the Knights of Fantasia. He struts down Jefferson Boulevard dressed in his Harry Potter at Hogwarts best: a long black cape that sweeps the ground behind his heels, trimmed in gold and burgundy paisley around the entire edge of the dramatic garment. Randy knows that he draws looks as he passes by, and secretly gloats that these strangers know nothing of his extraordinary powers. He sweeps into the diner with an urgent flaring of the cape, making it swirl out around him as he turns to face the room. "Is my table ready?" he asks with his best Dumbledore voice. "Do not pity the dead. Pity the living, and above all, those who live without love." Then he adds, to his puzzled audience, "Do not fear. Snape will set me free." He does a slow turn, sees the eyerolls and shaking of heads and gathers the cloak tight around his slender frame. They don't know it, he assures himself, but they are in the presence of greatness. Real and imagined, as all greatness truly is, after all.

Next to arrive is Kimberly. Kimberly is the custodian for the local parish down the street. Her family is glad that she found employment of some sort with her "being on the spectrum and all," as they speak of her struggle to find her place. As each generation seems to successively compete for their own diagnostic ticks, and fret over how to define their traumas as uniquely life-shaping, Kimberly's approach is "tell me what you want done and I'll do it." For her, the Knights of Fantasia means that she belongs somewhere. She has her people. She enters the diner in her jeans and peasant blouse, rubber gloves jammed into the back pocket. She pulls out a bottle of spray from somewhere, mists the table-top and chairs, then proceeds to wipe them down. Cleanliness is next to godliness, after all.

Guy makes his entrance, dressed in an old lime green leisure suit, white shirt, and bolo string tie. He has to keep hitching up the pants over his beer belly. Guy likes to carry a big, fat wallet in his back pocket, jammed full of pictures and paper money. In the other back pocket is the greasy comb that he frequently takes out to run through his thinning dark hair. Guy is proud of the fact that he has successfully resisted the beard craze. He wants to look good on camera. For the ladies. His mission in life. As a Knight of Fantasia, his self-assigned role is to cruise the online live porn sites, like PornHub. When he finds someone to save, he joins her live feed and texts encouragement. Even Bible verses, especially the ones in red ink, from Jesus' own mouth. Guy just recently realized that there's much more to porn though. All types for all tastes and pleasures. It's a big world and Guy wants his place in it to not go unnoticed. At the very least, he's going to need a bigger wallet. Maybe the other Knights can give him advice. That's what friends are for, after all.

Marianne comes in as quietly as she can manage. In a time gone by, Marianne was an "indigent admit" to the Blue Ridge Psychiatric Facility. She has become institutionalized. At different times, the staff has considered discharging her out into the world. But they don't know if the world is ready for Marianne. She wants the safety and surety of the big facility, no group home for her. Nobody is quite sure even what her admitting diagnosis was any longer. Finally, a program was devised where she gets a daily pass outside, but she can return to the Blue Ridge every evening for a safe place to sleep and get food in her belly. Marianne tells them she has to stay so that she can finish the epic poem she's writing on the walls of her room. The Knights of Fantasia are her touchpoint with outside reality. "The oceans are filled with the tears of God," begins her poem, begun with her own blood in her cutting phase. "Avoiding the fresh water of the lakes of our fears and the rivers of our sorrows . . . " The Knights are her encouragement, after all.

Daniel the Puppet King is the last to arrive, the Silver Knight of Fantasia. "I am the Paraclete of this Paradise," he proclaims, striding into the diner in his furry outfit, complete with a swishing tail and pawprint mittens, and taking his seat at the head of the table. The other Knights take their places. Daniel leaves the mask of Daniel Striped Tiger in place over his face as he goes around the table giving each Knight a chance to talk. Randy, Kimberly, Guy, and Marianne all give updates on their trying their best to be Knights of Fantasia. After each one finishes, Daniel the Puppet King goes to them, takes a tube of bright red lipstick from his pocket, cups their chins in his hand, and "I give you the seal of the Holy Kiss," he solemnly intones as he draws a red X on their foreheads. He knows that they all need this kind of love. Who among us does not . . . After all.

Words are magic and writers are wizards.

CAROLINA CHLOE

CAROLINA CHLOE ALWAYS LEFT a bowl of cream on the back step, tossed a piece of cornbread out the window before serving it to her family, and kept the front door painted a 'Haint Blue with a touch of periwinkle to keep the spirits of the dead out of her home. She sang Auld Lang Syne for Samhain and funerals, as well as New Years, was famous all through the mountains for her clogging, and sang her way through annual planting and harvesting seasons in the original Cherokee version of the Earth Blessing. She stomped through the hills, famous for the dogwood rod she carried, used in divinations of course, and when a cauldron sat in a prominent place in her front yard, you could rest assured she was open for business. Such are the ways of an Appalachian Granny Witch.

"Tis for healin'," Chloe always admonished those who dared question the ramifications of being a Granny Witch. "These hills and hollers are alive, you know. My people come here generations ago. Many generations. Mountains are more than just big rocks, you know. They're alive. You can take your fancy phones and computers and all you want, but they ain't got no spirit to 'em. And if there's no spirit to a thing, it's just a thing." She fixes her one clear eye on a visitor: "If there ain't no spirit, there ain't no music. That's what you gotta understand." She stares out the window for a spell. "You can go into Ashvull' all you want, but the closer to a city you get, the fainter grows the music. I'm just tellin' ya."

Carolina Chloe was known far and wide in these here parts for her aforementioned corn bread and her big heart. In fact, it's nigh on impossible to be tuned into the ebbs and flows of the rhythms of the very ground under your feet, the melodies of water and trees, the ever-rehearsed scales of birds and beasts, and not end up with a big heart. An Appalachian Granny Witch is nothing if not tuned in. And she didn't ask to be tuned into the spirits of the deceased of neighbors and the different clans that filled the hollers, and their ancestors' spirits. It was just part of the deal. No good Granny Witch turned her back on anyone in need. Anyone.

Carolina Chloe had a daughter name of Summer Rose whom she loved more than her own life. "My man died up in Ashvull' nigh on five years ago. Summer Rose is only family I got nowadays. We don't have much, but we're happy. No, all the healin' in the world couldn't help my Charles. He was a good man. Summer Rose favors him a bit. She's eight now. All she wanted for Christmas this past year was a baby doll. So, I got Johnny Sayers to take me to the store in Ashvull'!" Carolina Chloe cackles with glee at the memory. "I've been saving up my herbs and potion money because a girl needs to have at least one special friend in her life when she's young. That's what a doll is, you know." Carolina Chloe nods sagely and stops for a moment. "Whisper her secrets to her, share the good times, comfort in the bad. I'm just tellin' ya. They can be healing."

She sighs, then gathers herself. "Anyway, I was sayin', Johnny takes me into the city and we're cuttin' up laughing at all the so serious folks walking around with them little things in their ears, staring at their phones like they's expecting magic all the time!" She laughs till tears trickle down. "You couldn't give them the evil eye, says Johnny, cuz they never look up!" More laughter till Carolina Chloe is coughing. Then she grows quiet. "I made a special dress for Summer Rose's doll. Yes I did. I had a piece of my great grandmama's wedding dress. Almost blue as the sky. With gold trim and pearl buttons." She gets up and goes to the kitchen. Sets a bowl of cream on the back step before returning with steaming coffee. "It's a beautiful dress. Summer Rose 'bout had a conniption when she saw it. Dressed her new doll up all pretty. Took her down the mountain to show her friends. Puts her to bed real careful. Has her sittin' at the table every meal."

Carolina Chloe bows her head for a moment. "Bout kills me. Seein' Summer Rose so happy, what with her Daddy and all." Then lifts her head, mountain strong. "But I was up all night over at the Barkley's place. She was pregnant. I couldn't stop the labor, you know. Sometimes there's nothin' a body can do." She sips at her coffee then stares out the window. "Child was stillborn. They're agrievin' somethin' fierce. They want to bury her proper and all. With a viewing and everything." Carolina Chloe struggles to keep her lower lip from trembling. "I've gotta ask Summer Rose for that dress back. From her doll. For the baby. So it will settle her spirit." She stands, the weight almost more than she can bare. Reaches out and touches me on the cheek.

"But what's a mother to do? Tis for healin'. I'm just tellin' ya."

Words are magic, and writers are wizards.

SEA OF LONELY

THERE WERE SO MANY times he just wanted to give up. It wasn't supposed to be like this. All the countless hours spent traveling from city to city. All the upturned faces hanging on his every word. Saints and sinners, they're all the same. Pass the grace and cash the check. He pours himself a strong one, gulps it down, pours another. Pulls out his wallet. Thumbs past the pictures of his wife and children, perfect strangers. Pulls out a card, punches in the number on the bedside phone. "She'll stay the night for a thousand, buddy." He demurs. Everybody has their standards, after all. The knock at the door startles him. He pulls off the cleric's collar, tosses it onto the dresser where the cash is neatly folded on the far corner. When he opens the door, he is taken aback. It is a man, maybe in his thirties, plaid shirt, jeans, muddy boots. Dark skin. Who looks him in the eye, reveals a sad smile, and says, "Show me your scars."

And it was day. And it was night. And it was good.

Her fingers tremble as she struggles to fit the key into the lock. Her heart is beyond broken. It is crushed. She finally gets the door open and throws the key at the dresser. It slides across and falls to the floor. She sits on the side of the bed, head in her hands. Will the tears ever end? How could he do such a thing? They were to be married. Two weeks before the wedding, he sat her down. Looked her in the eye. And said, "I never really loved you. No, please don't touch me. No, no, it's not you. It's me." She is utterly alone. Her brain feels like it is on fire. Her soul gasps for air. There is a knock at the door. "No, no please go away!" she screams. The knocking continues. She avoids looking in the mirror as she stumbles to the door, opens it. It is a man, maybe in his thirties, she's never been sure. He's in a plaid shirt, jeans, muddy boots. Dark skin. Who looks her in the eye, reveals a sad smile, and says, "Show me your scars."

And it was day. And it was night. And it was good.

The hallways stink of disinfectant that never quite covers the smell of urine. The young boy clutches his father's hand as he dodges the wheelchairs filled with wispy-haired gnomes who make feeble gestures as they reach to touch him. He is on his way to see his mother. For the last time. Except he doesn't know that. What child should? Ever? They had been trying to enter the Promised Land. The people in the uniforms took his mother in one direction, him in another. The cages are cold, the cement floors hard. Some children are taken away. He is frightened. Did his mama forget about him? Now his father stops outside of a door in an endless hallway of doors. Takes a deep breath, kisses his rosary and pushes on the door. His mother is there, ever so still. Forlorn. Weak. The boy sees a doctor beside his mother's bed. A man, maybe in his thirties, he's never forgotten that face. A white coat covers a plaid shirt, jeans, muddy boots. Dark skin. Who kneels down, looks the boy in the eye, reveals a sad smile, and says, *"Muestrame tus cicatrices."*

And it was day. And it was night. And it was good.

A teenager sits in the middle of worship, people all around. Yet utterly alone. They all stand, they all sing. They all mutter words. They all bow their heads and hope against hope to make a connection. The heavy cross hangs above all of them, its shadow falls on the wooden table in the front with the intricate carving. Does it matter? What about any of this matters, they all wonder. The flickering light reveals the scars on his wrist, illuminating the fear in her heart. Body of a man, the soul of a woman. The desires of a human being. The loneliness of a human being. There is a rustling at the disturbance of a late arrival. The teen feels someone sit next to him. She looks up. It is someone in their thirties, maybe. In a plaid shirt, jeans, muddy boots. Dark skin. Who looks them all in the eye, reveals a sad smile, and says, "Show me your scars. Please, all of you. Show me your scars."

And it was day. And it was night. And it was good.

Words are magic, and writers are wizards.

SATAN

Old Leo makes his way up the church steps, slowly, but with practiced, patient purpose. He is known around the small town as the "bee man" because of the hives he carefully nurtures out back of Johnson's Orchards, but in all of his eighty-three years this is the first time he has ever questioned the ways of Mother nature and the providence of the good Lord. Both at the same time, and with equal vehemence. He opens the door and steps inside the cool sanctuary with the vaulted ceiling and polished pews for the perishables.

He makes his way down the aisle, his faded coveralls held up with a tarnished buckle on one side and a piece of rope on the other. He doffs the unfashionable brown fedora, revealing the mane of white hair that perfectly matches the thick beard that still harbors a few crumbs of toast from breakfast earlier that morning, along with scalding coffee—black only, now mind you. Ever since Mabel passed, life has only been kept palatable with routines, the simpler the better. That is the only way to keep away the feeling that he is always sleeping on the edge of a frown, as the Good Book says. Or was it some country singer? He can't remember. Hard to tell the difference some days.

Reverend Joanne pauses mid penance prayer as Old Leo passes his usual pew in the front and comes and stands right before the pulpit, and asks in a soft voice, "Have you seen Satan?" Mrs. Gafferty, three pews back, leans forward. "What did he say?" Her friend, Esther whispers loudly, so no one can miss it, "He said, he wants to speak to Satan?" Mrs. Gafferty, being a bit of a Presbyterian, asks, "Satan who? Satan wouldn't be caught dead in here!" Fred Barnett, one of the eternal ushers, hurries forward. "Old Leo ain't been the same since Mabel passed. Why's he looking for Satan in here?" Penance is forgotten as Reverend Joanne tried to restore some semblance of somber worship.

She quietly insists, "Leo, why don't you take a seat, and we'll see what we can do." Old Leo waves her off and lifts his face to the ceiling. "Jesus Christ, doesn't anybody listen? My Mabel is buried right out yonder there." He doesn't have to look out the window to picture the cold granite headstone with daffodils planted around it, in a small sea of granite headstones covering souls of fading memories. "All I'm asking is, where is Satan? I'm always telling him to get behind me, but I turned around and he wasn't there." Reverend Joanne abandons her prayers to try and make this a teaching moment, because . . . well . . . seminary and all that.

"Leo, a lot of times we all feel stressed and anxious to the point we want someone to blame. But blaming Satan for our own shortcomings isn't the answer." It's a gentle remonstrative, a clear conflict of interest, not to mention language, because nobody wants ministers telling them they are wrong. About anything. Especially about Jesus's crazy uncle, Satan. "Sit down, you old fool," Esther chimes up, in a clearly remonstrative tone, without interest beyond getting on with worship. Mrs. Gafferty pipes up with, "He's going to come after you with his flaming sword." And clucks for good measure. Fred Barnett is quick to correct. "That's Gabriel, look it up, Gafferty!" Because this is a friendly, high school cafeteria kind of church. I'm sorry, I meant to say, an everything in its place, decently and in order congregation of perishables.

A discussion ensues in a total disruption of the worship service about angels and demons and other Dan Brown level theological niceties and mysteries. And possibilities. What's a good discussion of heaven and hell and punishment and reward without considering the possible outcomes . . . for one another's neighbors? What else is a good imagination for, wonders Reverend Joanne, surveying her flock and quietly slipping her sermon notes off to the side. This is not seminary and all that. Old Leo takes this all in, and in stride. This is not his first encounter with the human race. Mabel used to gently chide him over his obsession over and his fascination with the bees. Not remonstrating at all, now mind you. Honey is a joint effort, a community working together that fascinated Old Leo.

He lowers his gaze as the hubbub continues and makes his way back to the doors. As he steps out, he replaces the worn fedora with a sigh. At least a honeybee can only sting once. Losing Mabel is always going to hurt. He hears a loud greeting from down the street, beside the blue mailbox on the corner. "Satan? Is that you?" At the sound of his voice, the golden retriever gives a happy bark and bounds toward Old Leo. The greeting between the two old friends is as warm as a prodigal being found can be. "C'mon, Satan. Get behind me. Let's go home."

And they did.

Words are magic and writers are wizards.

SHUT UP AND DANCE

The train departs Lynchburg at 12:14 in the dead of night. He slowly climbs the stairs and enters the car, seeking his seat among the soul-weary travelers. He sags into the seat with the ache of a thousand sleepless nights and the tiredness felt in his bones of wondering if everything in his life has really added up to this. A midnight train to Philadelphia, another leg in the journey from "now I lay me down to sleep" to "how in the hell did I sell my soul so cheap?" His eyes begin to close then snap wide open again with nothing to see but the strangers huddled over their filtered talismans or the shadows slipping past beyond the windows. But it's better than the scenes that play out on the back of his eyelids every time they sag low with his sighs.

If life is defined by what we value the most, the lines on his face matching the scars on his heart speak of treasures befitting royal beggars. As the Virginia countryside slips by in the moonlight, he takes a travel magazine from the seat pocket and begins to leaf through the glossy pages filled with colors and smiles, temptations and treats, beaches and hotels. He knows that chasing a dream becomes mostly about the chase because the dream never quite lives up to the anticipation. And when you are not there for a loved one, it does not matter why, all that is remembered is that you were not there.

His daughter married six months ago. He missed it. Just like he missed so many of the important events in her life. He snaps his eyes open to stop the unreeling of the things he has missed. Too many pictures of pain. The man reaches into the pocket of his jacket and pulls out a pocket-knife that includes a small pair of scissors. He carefully selects a page and begins to snip away, slowly, methodically. When he finishes one page, he moves on to the next, his tongue jutting a bit out of the side of his mouth as he concentrates. When the train reaches Washington, DC there is a layover while the engines are switched.

The traveler looks out at the people at the other windows of other trains. Can he handle one more dream? He climbs down to the platform and scurries from one trash receptacle to the next, taking out plastic straws and discarded popsicle sticks. At the "All aboard," he gets back in, cradling his treasures in one arm as he asks the conductor for some tape. For the rest of the journey, he is absorbed in the anticipation and the labor. Before he knows it, he is climbing the long stairs in the 30th Street Station in Philadelphia. He searches among the rows of old wooden benches beneath the neoclassical arches, offering being empty, except for the one gift he has to offer.

She is waiting at the counter in the center of the vast room, talking to a police officer who handles a large black dog. He approaches them, waiting until the dog decides he offers no threat. He speaks her name, holding out his gift in one hand. "I brought you this," he smiles. She turns, sees him, sees the gift he brings. "Oh Daddy, how could you? Can't you get anything right?" and she grabs the travel magazine that he offers and throws it on the shiny countertop. Then she spins around and walks away.

She is in such a disgusted hurry that she never sees the magazine slide across the counter, teeter on the edge and drop to the floor. And the police dog who sniffs at it, then touches it with a paw. Or the little girl who runs over to rescue the gift and picks it up with great excitement. Which turns to wondrous delight when she opens it, and a bouquet of hope and dreams emerges. Daffodils, daisies, tulips and even an iris pop up from the pages. She shrieks with delight and turns to share it with the traveler, but he is gone, onto the next train.

And it came to pass, that after a boys' night out, as grown men are wont to do, and Jesus being nowhere to be seen, his BFFs decided to sail across the lake in the dark. It was an impetuous decision but making impetuous decisions had hooked them up with this guy in the first place. They get out onto the lake and a storm blows up, a big one. They are afraid of the storm, and of the realization that when they get home their wives may knock some sense into them . . . When out of nowhere, they see the Big Guy, walking toward them in the storm. Peter says, "Hey, I want to try that." Jesus says, "Go for it. Watch me to see how it's done." Peter jumps out and makes it a few steps before reality sets in and he starts to sink. "Now what do I do?" he screams at Jesus. Who looks at him, sinking lower and lower, shrugs, and says those words that echo through to this day: "Shut up and dance!"

Words are magic and writers are wizards.

THE BESPOKE CHAIR

The children found it in Old Man Peterson's weathered barn, as is wont to happen when kids set out on adventures. They climbed over bales of moldy straw and poked around in the ancient furniture seemingly discarded at random; a bureau with no knobs and a cracked mirror, a glider with no runners, a kitchen table that had lost its balance, an overstuffed chair now home to a clan of mice, and various pots and pans and dishes piled on, over and around a strange wooden rocking chair with the carving of a hippopotamus in the back. Cici insisted that the boys help her move all of the old dishes so that she could get a better look at this discovery. When she could finally see it she squealed in delight and dragged it over the straw to the front door. Old Man Peterson heard the commotion and limped out to the barn. When he saw Cici standing there with a look of amazement, he stopped in his tracks and seemed to have trouble uttering the words, "That's Miriam's bespoke chair."

"What's that?" asked Cici. "Why's it be broke?" asked one of the boys, because—well . . . boys, you know. Old Man Peterson came closer. "It's her bespoke chair. I made it for her to rock her babies, sitting in the front room, looking out at the mountains. Had to be just so. Comfortable for her and with a hippopotamus carved into it." He reached out and ran one calloused hand over the dark finish. "I cut down the tree, selected the parts for her chair, shaped and fashioned it just the way she'd like it. Her bespoke chair." He let out a heavy sigh. "What's the hippopotamus for?" Cici was intrigued by all of this bespoke business. "Why a hippopotamus?"

OMP gave a sad smile. "It's the sign of maternal strength. Courage and calmness until someone comes after their babies, then all hell breaks loose." Cici studied the chair for a long moment. "But it's out here in your old barn. Did she not like it? Did she even ask you to make it?" Cici, as usual, had questions. Lots of them. The man's face grew quite solemn, and he fidgeted a bit. "Not exactly," he finally muttered. "It's the wrong kind of chair." "Whataya mean?" asked one of the boys. "Doesn't she know how to sit?" asked the other boy. That elicited a small smile from OMP. "She wanted a captain's chair. Her bespoke chair is the chair of a captain. So, she left to make her own chair."

Three curious faces stared up at him. "Captain? Like in the army?" asked one of the boys, because . . . well, boys. "No, a ship," exclaimed Cici. "She wanted to be captain of a ship, didn't she?" OMP nodded. "She had her dreams, her goals, her hopes. She had her heart set on it and so she left. I got angry and threw all her things, including my bespoke chair for her into that old barn. Her life was with the sea, not me."

Cici thought for a moment. "You weren't happy for her?" OMP shrugged. "I suppose. I know she's happy. Captain of a big ol' hospital ship, going places all over the world to help people get better. She went on without me." One of the boys tugged on OMP's overalls. "Why didn't you go with her? She could have sat in her hippopotamus chair on the ship!" It made perfect sense to him because . . . .well, you know, boys.

The other boy started to argue with the first one. "You can't be a captain on a ship in a rocking chair. Besides she didn't want it, so she can't ever have it, bespoke or not." As I've said, boys . . . you know. Cici stayed quiet for the longest time as OMP wiped the sweat from his bald head. "She didn't want to be what I wanted her to be," he said, "and I didn't want to look at it any more or think about her anymore." Cici piped up with, "I could use a hippopotamus." Something in her voice made OMP ask, "And why is that?" She didn't say anything at first, using an index finger to trace the round, solid shape of the hippopotamus in the dark wood. Finally, "I'm eight and a half years old. I'm in my third foster home now because my mom's in jail. Who knows, a hippopotamus bespoke chair might keep me safe."

OMP knelt there in the dirt of the barnyard and looked into Cici's eyes. What he saw in her eyes spoke to what was missing in his heart. And that is how the bespoke chair, created for one person who did not want it because she needed something different, became the bespoke chair for someone who needed it very much for purposes of her own. Because . . . little girls have needs, just like the rest of us . . . and sometimes it's all a hippopotamus chair can do to help . . . humans, you know . . .

Words are magic and writers are wizards.

DESTINY'S CHILD

THE OFFICER PULLS THE cruiser over to the curb. He's parked in front of a modest brick home, in a modest subdivision, of a modest suburb, of a modest city, in a most immodest country. He hates this part of the job. A car pulls in behind him. A small woman, perhaps 80 years of age, struggles out of the car, knocks on his window. "Well, c'mon and git, if you're comin'." He reluctantly climbs out, adjusts his Sam Browne, and escorts her up the sidewalk to the modest porch. He reaches for the doorbell. "Wait a secon'!" She carefully removes the snuff from behind her lower lip, unceremoniously dumps it in the flower bed beside her. "It'll be good for 'em." The officer watches, bemused. "You ready?" She nods and he rings the bell.

The door is opened by a woman in her 40s, who looks so tired it makes the officer gulp. She takes in his oh so neatly pressed uniform, with all the accoutrements of force hanging on the wide black belt. Fear widens her pupils. "Ma'am, can we come in?" She pushes on the door. "Did you find him?" "Is your husband home, as well?" The older woman elbows him aside, "Let us in, Honey. It ain't good news." The officer knows it's pointless to resist. "No, my husband's out preaching a revival. Did you find my boy?" The officer takes a deep breath as the older woman perches on the modest couch, feet dangling. "Yer man ain't here?" she demands to know, making a tsk-ing sound.

The officer breaks the news as gently as he can. "Your boy's at the Medical Center. The nurse called about a 16-year-old male, severely beaten, they're not sure . . . ," he hesitates. "We're looking for who might have done it. But we need more information." The mother twists at a tissue in her hands, says softly, "Maybe he'd be better off dead." The older woman clucks, "You don't mean that now." The mother's anguish is all too real. "You don't know what it's like. We had a perfect little boy, all happy and wild . . . ," her voice catches. "And then one day. One day he tells you . . . " The officer swallows hard. "Ma'am, he needs you now. Can his father come home?" She shakes her head. "When he ran away from that place that's supposed to fix him, well, his father washed his hands of him." The older woman pipes up. "He ain't got rabies! He needs his momma and his daddy. Lord Almighty!"

"But it's not right. It's not natural, him being that way." The mother is defiant, or maybe defeated. The woman on the couch rubs at her lower lip. "What's unnatral' about wantin' love, Honey?" The officer tries another tack. "Is there someone we could call for you?" "Oh heavens, no," she worries. "We don't want people to know. They've been praying for him all these years. Fat lot that's done." The older woman hops down off the couch. "I need my snuff." The officer steps in. "Destiny, settle down." The mother worries aloud. "Maybe I should call his father . . . just in case."

"You know, don't ya?" Destiny steps toward her. "If that boy of yours dies, what's goin' ta happen? I'll tell ya what's goin' to happen!" She draws herself up to all 4'10" of herself. "Jesus himself is goin' to meet him at them Pearly Gates. That's right, I tell ya." She's spittin' fire now. "This is pitiful, as my Momma used to say. Damn pitiful. Jesus is goin' to say, 'Boy, cum here.' And Jesus' goin' to spread his arms wide and say, 'Boy, let me hang on yer neck!' And he ain't talkin' about no fool gold cross. Hell no. Where I come from, hangin' on your neck means let me give you a forever hug. A forever hug, I tell ya'!"

The officer realizes he's done all he can do and shows himself out. He pauses on the porch as the voices still reach him. "You don't know," protests the mother. "You don't know what it's like. You want the best for your child. But then he turns out to be . . . one of those!" The officer recognizes the deadly quiet that follows. A storm is abrewin'. "Child, let me tell you sumthin'." He goes down the first step. "Why in God's name do you think I'm here?" He takes the second step. "I don't know you from a turkey squat." He reaches the sidewalk. "Fer crackin' ice on a tin fiddle, that fine policeman is my boy. MY BOY. He's 'one of those' thank ya very much!"

The officer climbs into his cruiser. Glances in his rearview mirror. Spots the colorful yarn of the Eye of God, dangling from his mother's mirror. Keys open the radio mike. Clears the static. "Destiny's Child. Destiny's child here. Back in service. Over." And drives away along the very modest street.

Words are magic, and writers are wizards.

STREETS OF PHILADELPHIA

Once upon a time, on a lovely Saturday autumn morning, I stepped out of my hotel in Center City, Philadelphia, turned left and headed for Rittenhouse Square. "Mister, hey Mister!" I looked around for the source of this small, shrill voice. "Mister. Down here. Hey, Mister. Whatcha doin'? Where ya goin'?" I looked down. There among the ever more common collection of homeless humans sat a waifish girl of about 9, lanky brown hair below her shoulders, wearing the simple, broadcloth smock of the Plain People. "Mama says I ain't to be talking to strangers, but you ain't no stranger, are you Mister!?" Before I could answer she rushed on, "Name's Sarah. Pleased to meet ya." She extended her hand and when I gingerly took it, she grabbed on, and hopped up to stand beside me. "I'm just tryin' to do believen, that's all."

"What . . . well, um . . . ," I searched for my grown-up words. "You wanna help?" she asked. "Every Saturday Momma and me come into the city to the market over yonder," she indicated the quaint square a block away, where vendors in stalls hawked produce, canned and baked goods, and arts and crafts. "Help you sell?" I asked. "No, goofus. Mama's got Sally and Robert and Hannah and Drexel to help her." She looked up at me, saying slowly, carefully as if to a child, "Do-you-want-to-help-me," then a sweep of her arm, "give them fudge?" From somewhere she produced a shoebox lined with wax paper and overflowing with squares of heaven. "You give the homeless people fudge?" She sighed at my question, tilted her head to one side, and rolled her eyes. "Fallen angels. Didn't your Mama teach you right?"

"Sarah . . . right?" She nodded so I pushed on, ever more aware of the agitation of some of those sitting on the plastic bags nearby. "Sarah, does your mother know you're here?" She shrugged. "She says I'm always in her heart. Didn't your Mama teach you that?" She took a bite of fudge. "I'm just trying to do believen, that's all." A gentleman in a ragged jacket, sores on his grimy hands, approached and made an elegant bow. "Sarah, may I have another?" She giggled. "Sure, Mr. Reepicheep. Then I'll go get you some coffee." She handed me the box of sweet treasure and fearlessly skipped toward the ever-present Dunkin' Donuts shop on the corner.

I felt a tug on my sleeve and turned around. "She's one of us," said a small woman dressed in an old housecoat and wrapped in a much too large pea coat. She tucked some loose strands of frizzy hair underneath a watch cap. "Calls me the White Witch." She smiled before continuing, "My husband was Navy, 22 years. We lost everything in ought 8. He was a proud man, but that was too much for him." She turned away to hide her trembling lip. A large man in stained fatigues stepped forward and belched in my face. "She calls us fallen angels. Huh!" he snorted. "You be nice to my new friend, Aslan" Sarah called as she returned, balancing two trays of steaming cups of coffee. "Here, pass these out," the half pint commanded the shaggy figure.

I watched as her disciples tended to each other, sipping the hot coffee and nibbling the lifeblood of fudge. Sarah planted herself in front of me again. "Mama says it ain't polite to stare but there's no excuse for not noticing. Mama says we're all just angels trying to find our way home." She stared at me with eyes that saw right through me. "I think Mama might like you." She pointed a finger at me, "Mind you, I said might!" She put her small, cool hand in mine. "You'll tell her won't you?" I was confused. "Tell her? Tell her what? Your mother?" She nodded with such a solemnness that I felt a holy breeze pass between us. Without another word she handed me the box of fudge, turned, and disappeared back around the corner, with all of Narnia following behind.

I found myself in front of a small booth in Rittenhouse Square. Families from the surrounding neighborhoods were enjoying the sunshine. The woman behind the table looked at me with a curious expression. "Where did you get that?" I looked down dumbly at the shoebox of fudge. "Sarah gave it to.." Before I could finish, she gasped, and dropped the tin of candy buckeyes she held, scattering them all to kingdom come. "What did you say?" Her eyes looked wild, afraid. I held up the box. "Sarah said her Mama . . . " The woman yelped in pain, loss, wonder. "I'm Sarah's Mama. My Sarah's been gone a year now. Her little heart gave out. She used to come with me . . . " She couldn't finish and turned away.

I sat on a bench the rest of the afternoon. Sipping coffee. Nibbling on fudge. Wondering if all any of us are doing is tryin' to do believin.

Words are magic, and writers are wizards.

PLANT A STICKER

The hallway feels like it is a mile long. My steps are halting, almost baby-like as the pain tears at my fraying spirit. Protestant chaplain for The Medical Center Beaver in Beaver County Pennsylvania in the inauspicious year of 1992, and I'm starting my morning rounds the way I always begin them: a stop at the surgical suite and then on to the Intensive Care Unit. The ground the hospital is built upon would not support the ten stories that were planned so they instead built it low and wide . . . and long. Three floors of long, long hallways. Sometimes it feels like the seasons could change in the slow time march traversing the trail from the timeclock at the rear employee entrance to the snack bar up near the main doors. Trudge past the doors to the Emergency Department, knowing that at some point in the coming hours the beeper on my hip will summon me to tragedy . . . or carnage.

And fear. Most of all is the fear that arrives barely announced. Ambulances arriving from all over three counties or the dreaded whomp-whomp of an Air Life Flight chopper on the pad. The evening before I attended a traumatic stress incident debriefing. Nurses, nurses' aides, respiratory therapists, techs, any and all who were part of the all-hands code earlier that morning. The doctors? Perhaps a first-year resident had dared to come to this circle of human need. A young woman, 8 months pregnant, life-flighted in after running off the road, crashing and impaling on the gear shift stick on the floor. Frantic efforts to restore her pulse without success. Blood drenched scrubs all that held human spirit intact as attention turned to the baby. The keen frustration and awful sense of loss as all heroic effort was to no avail. "Damn, lost them both," became the lone epitaph in the all too still room. Then, on to the next case. The next prayer. The next genuflection of grief and goodness.

I set my sights on the snack bar and settle in behind the counter for, well, me being me, a couple of warm chocolate chip cookies with my coffee. "Chaplain, you look tired," says Sally, a volunteer with a soft smile and a husband battling his third go round with cancer. "It's these hallways," I respond with my tired joke. "Thank you for stopping to see Bob. He enjoyed talking to you. If I could only get him to church . . . " her voice trails off as she busies herself with refilling the half full cups gathered round this outpost of restoration. I tug the 5x7 yellow cards from my jacket and sigh. My ICU patients and charges. The top one is Hank's. The top three are Hank's, he's been in there that long. They are covered with the date of each visit and the notes I scribble about our visits, our chats. And stickers. Of all kinds and colors.

Hank cannot speak but he can certainly communicate. He's in his late sixties, no family, seriously ill, on and off a ventilator. My first visit he looked at me like I'd stepped off a spaceship. Vigorously motioned to me to put away the pathetic pamphlet of prayers and lamentations offered up and pull over a chair for the privilege of his presence. He grabs his pad and pencil, writes, "Got any scotch?" I can't help but laugh and we're off and running. "Do you think the nurses would mind?" I ask. He shrugs and his pencil moves, "It was their idea." We spend a few minutes in this vein before I stand to go. He waves me close. Reaches under his covers and pulls out a page of stickers, the precursors to emojis. Big, brightly colored stickers of pandas and pies, cartoons and candy, flowers and horses and everything in between. He wants me to bend over and when I do, he plants a sticker on my forehead.

As soon as I leave his room, I pull it off and stick it on the card. It becomes our daily routine. I stop in and take a seat. I learn about his life as a teacher of Latin and literature. Note by slowly scrawled note, I learn about Hank's life, its ups and downs, loves lost and lingered, dreams pursued, and dreams lost. I bring in a chess set and although I never once heard his voice, there is no mistaking the sheer joy he has in beating my pants off. Every morning, he's my first stop in ICU and he's always so glad to see me. The nurses tell me he gets anxious if I'm running late, so I make sure to get there. I'm there when the tube is down his throat and I'm there when he can barely keep his eyes open. But always, every time, he motions for me to bend low so he can plant a sticker on my forehead, touch my cheek, and make my moment better.

I finish my coffee, collect the cards, and head off to see Hank. The hallway is no shorter as I make my way to the ICU. I round the corner and slide open the glass door. Hank's bed is empty. My heart sinks. Nobody called me. The chess game we were playing waits forlornly on the bedstand. I feel someone at my side. A nurse gives me a sad smile and hands me something. "He wanted you to have these." She turns to go. "Your visits meant so much to him." I look down. I'm holding his packet of stickers.

I spent the rest of the day seeing my patients, maybe for the first time. And for each of them, I leave them with a touch on the cheek, and I plant a bright sticker on their forehead. The nurses just nod and go on to the next case.

Words are magic, and writers are wizards.

JOHNNY SMOKE

They called him Johnny Smoke because when he was the star tailback for the East Allegheny Wildcats in the year of our lord 19 and 69, the coach said when Johnny ran, all you saw was smoke. That was the year that the shiny new high school opened, east out the Lincoln Highway to the Kmart plaza, hang a right on to Route 48, and in half a mile there it rose on an old slag heap and coke cinders pile, like a sphinx of hopes and aspirations for the generations of descendants of steelworkers, WABCO workers in Wilmerding and Wall, East McKeesport, North Versailles, and, lest we forget, Crestas Terrace. The era of getting a job after school at Kings Family Restaurant or killing time at the Burger King. Students from the St. Roberts Catholic school got their first inescapable taste of the real-world mixing with heathen protestants and the lines of race being papered over with forced busing. And if a young man did not get into Penn State or Pitt, a union job in the mills or a job pushing a broom at Continental Can in West Mifflin, he could take full advantage of an all-expense paid trip on Uncle Sam's dime to the garden spot of Vietnam.

It was the year before the ultra-modern Three Rivers Stadium would open, after the ushers' union declined the request for female ushers to wear miniskirts, and the following spring on opening day, fellow students would fall to their deaths while trying to jump from one pedestrian ramp to another. But by then, Johnny Smoke was an infantryman, slogging through rice paddies while taking orders from some fuzz faced Marines second lieutenant and taking fire from an elusive enemy. With a soundtrack of constant helicopter rotors slashing thick humidity, Jimi Hendrix, Creedence Clearwater Revival, incoming fire from AK-47s and screaming rockets, or the ominous silence of B-52s high overhead dropping "lazy dogs" along Ho Chi Minh Trail, the awful "whoosh" of napalm igniting and sucking oxygen, Johnny Smoke knew he was not there to win anything but his and his buddies' survival.

Johnny put in his 13 months hell tour, twice narrowly avoiding the disaster of pits full of pungi sticks smeared with feces, two lungsful of Agent Orange, somehow avoiding the plague of heroin, and went stateside for thirty days. He tried to talk to his old teachers at East Allegheny, but really, white kids and black kids shouting and swinging in the indoor courtyard outside the cafeteria, algebra and English lit be damned, was as disorienting for him as making his way through jungle in pitch darkness and absolute silence. Johnny Smoke went to the Marines and asked to go in country once again. Because he still had buddies there. You don't abandon buddies or dishonor their blood. Ever. The ranks were swollen with dumb draftees, kids in chamo and 8 weeks of basic at Paris Island. Somebody had to look out for them.

So, Johnny Smoke went back. It is exhausting trying to keep teenagers focused on anything, but in Vietnam focus meant living or dying. Johnny took his responsibilities seriously. He became a combination of Hell's tour guide and tough SOB den mother. By some stroke of military genius, he got a kid from back home, Lenny from Wall, in his platoon. He used threats, bullying, reason, charm, whatever it took to keep Lenny alive. They would sit and argue over which family back home has the cutest girls: the Knezevichs, Manns, or Kellars? Would you rather go to a Pirates or Steelers game? What time of night was best to drag race and with which carburetor? Did anything exciting ever happen in Wilmerding? Whose French fries were best, Kings or Eat N Park? Both Johnny Smoke and Lenny from Wall made it safely back to North Versailles and life went on. Lenny remained in the military and retired a full colonel.

Fifty years pass. Johnny Smoke is in a nursing home. Time, wear and tear, and the luck of the draw take their toll. Johnny suffers from dementia. In his mind, it is always time to reup for service in Vietnam. He wakes up every morning, frantic that he's going to miss the plane. Searches desperately for his uniform and weapon. "My boys need me," he cries. "I got to get them all home." He is beside himself and nothing can console him about letting down his buddies. One day a shadow fills the doorway. Johnny Smoke looks up. There before him, in full uniform and regalia of a colonel, stands Lenny. Johnny salutes him. "Marine, come with me!" Lenny commands. He gets Johnny Smoke in the car and drives to East Allegheny Junior/Senior High School. Marches him across the parking lot and into Joseph Churchman Stadium. Out onto the field to the fifty-yard line.

There on the slag heap and coke cinder pile of history, Lenny from Wall slowly salutes Johnny Smoke. Then he hands him a fancy written proclamation, signed by the President of the United States. "From a grateful nation: For your service, bravery, and sacrifice. You have done your duty. Well done." Lenny takes an arm to guide Johnny Smoke home, murmuring so only the two of them hear it: "You don't abandon your buddies. Or dishonor their blood. Ever."

Words are magic and writers are wizards.

CORAM DEO

He wasn't supposed to die. As she sat in the car in the parking lot of Grace's Convenience Store and Grill and Ice Cream Shoppe, that's the thought that kept running through her mind. Over and over and over. He wasn't supposed to die. But he did. He died. Far from home, all alone, abandoned and forgotten. And now she would never have the chance to tell him that she was sorry. Now her waiting and denials and fears would never be released, never assuaged, she would never heal. She could never look into his eyes and say the needed words, never hear what she longed so badly to hear. And the pain and sorrow of it all felt like it was crushing her.

Her best friend always told her she had the heart of a child, a little girl's view of things. She felt the pain of others too keenly, she cried at arguments, got angry at people being mean to others, and trusted beyond reason. All that made her very shy, and all that that combination had gotten her in her school days was that everyone thought she was stupid. "Silly Sarah, silly, stupid Sarah," was still the singsong taunt in her head whenever she felt someone thought she didn't understand something. Or when facing something she wasn't sure about; sure she could handle, sure she would be accepted, sure that her ideas would be good enough, sure that she even looked good enough. Silly stupid Sarah.

Except for him. "Let your imagination get ahead of you, but never let it get away from you." That was the first thing her literature teacher, Mr. Ichigo Ichthus, had told the class and she knew right then she had found her spot. He let the class call him Mister II (Eye Eye) because Ichigo Ichthus is a mouthful and teenagers want nothing if not shortcuts. "Good writers are soul reapers and soul illuminators," he always said at the beginning of a new unit of authors. "Some even call them wizards who spin words as magic." Mr. Eye Eye had paid careful attention to her, encouraging, and challenging her at the same time. He set the bar high and expected her to give nothing less than her best effort to try to reach it.

The thought of that time ten years ago brought a bit of light to Sarah's eyes as she sat now in her car, wounded by the news. She had applied for the school paper, full of hope and eagerness. But Mr. Ichthus had said no, she wasn't ready. In her head she heard silly stupid Sarah. So she went to the principal and told him that Mr. Eye Eye had been inappropriate with her. Ichigo Ichthus was summarily fired and could not be hired anywhere else. For all these years she kept the truth as her precious secret. The last she heard of Ichigo Ichthus was that he was somewhere out west working in a nursing home as a patient aide, changing diapers and feeding mushed up food to those many considered barely above homeless derelicts.

The knock on her window startled her. A young man peered in at her. Her heart pounded. Could it be? She was certain she had never seen him before but somehow he looked all too familiar. Sarah hesitated. Unsure. Uncertain. He motioned for her to roll down the window. "I have something for you," he shouted. Sarah rolled the window down. "What? Who are you?" He motioned to her to get out. She drew back, afraid of this stranger who somehow seemed to know her. And she was stunned to the core when he said, "Silly stupid Sarah, come here."

That did it. Sarah threw open the door and jumped out. "What the . . . ? Who the hell are you to call me that?" To her surprise the man smiled. "Come and see," he said, and held out a business card. Sarah slowly reached out and accepted the card, her hand shaking with both rage and fear. She held the card under the streetlight. The only thing on it was a simple drawing of an eye and a fish. "Good writers are soul reapers . . . " the young man's voice drifted off into the mists. "Who are you?" Sarah whispered.

"I'm Junior," he said. Sarah fell to her knees, tears streaming down her face. "Mister Eye Eye?" The man took her hand and pulled her back to her feet. "My father sent me. He's not here anymore." Sarah gasped out her pain. "I never told him . . . I'm so sorry. I'm so sorry." Junior wiped the tears first from his own face and then hers. "He knows, Sarah. He knows." Sarah pulled her hand away. "I was horrible to him. I can't forgive myself." Junior said, "Look at me." Sarah looked. "My father wanted you to know that he's sorry." Sarah buried her face in her hands. "He's sorry? No, no, he did nothing wrong. No, no, no."

Junior took her hand again. "He just wanted you to know, Sarah. He's sorry for all the pain you've been in. He never regretted being your teacher." He took a step back and turned to leave. "It is done with, Sarah. It is finished. Live like that."

Words are magic, and writers are wizards.

THE BLACK MILE

Scotty grew up in an All-American town, with an All-American family, attended an All-American church, and played All-American sports at an All-American high school. In 1969, at the age of 18 he was given a number in the draft lottery, drew a high number and ended up in boot camp at the ripe old age of 18 and a half. Inducted into the Army and indoctrinated into the eternal shibboleth of "following orders," he was shipped to Vietnam to explore the last of his teen years as the point man in a squad of 'night creepers.' While other nineteen-year-olds were exploring the vagaries of college life or listening to Guess Who sing "American Woman" on their way to a shift as grunt labor in a steel mill, Scotty was walking the black mile. He led a file of grunts through the pitch black of a midnight patrol through rice paddies, around a sleeping village and into the jungle to try and ambush a supply route.

The black mile is the deep darkness, so black you cannot see your hand in front of your face, but you keep going. Being absolutely quiet and invisible. Through a landscape that is invisible, and if the darkness suddenly grows quiet, all the night noises abruptly cease, you know that there is mortal danger at hand. Step by careful step he treads, because those creeping behind him depend on Scotty for their lives. Scotty has some kind of sixth sense about finding his way along the black mile, feeling the texture of the darkness in a way even he does not understand. But one of the irrefutable rules of war is that no one involved on the ground, wielding the weapons, stalking close encounters with death itself, is invincible. In truth, there are no superheroes. It is human beings hunting each other for as many reasons as there are lies in a day.

The blackness is ripped apart by the painful glare of magnesium flares. Guns and mortars open up on the night creepers. There are curses, grunts, cries of panicked fear. Explosions, noise, pandemonium, and pain. Terror mixed with plaintive cries for mothers. Scotty keeps his head and directs them in defense. It is all they can do to keep the attackers at bay. They fight until dawn. In the pale light, casualties become real. When the choppers finally arrive, Scotty drags himself over a skid, plops in the doorway, numb. Just before it dusts off, a corpsman runs over and hands him a package. It looks like any other package of meat, maybe two pounds, with a splinter of bone that sticks his palm, drawing blood. Like any other package except for the dog tags wrapped around it, identifying it as The Kid, 18-year-old Clarence, from Syracuse. Scotty cradles it close, promising to get The Kid home, so he can drink the Devil's tears with his fellow fallen soldiers.

After forever and a day, Scotty rotates home and takes a job in one of the coal mines that feed the steel mills along the mighty Ohio River. The mine goes down and down, mile after mile, extracting fuel for fortunes and the unfortunate alike. Scotty keeps his head down, does the dirty work, tries to ignore the dreams and screams that haunt his nights. The darkness is almost comforting in its familiarity. Then one day, there is a cave in, a collapse in the mine and Scotty and his squad of miners are trapped down below, a black mile from the surface.

Scotty helps the men take stock of their situation. No food, no water, no more batteries for their lamps. But there is one path, he thinks, for their escape. They must first go deeper into the blackness, away from the shortest route which is blocked, find the ventilation shaft for the planned expansion of the mine, and climb through the darkness. Knowing that he must become a chimera of folly and fortitude, Scotty promises to lead the men out of there, or die trying. And so, they set out through the eerie quiet and pressing darkness. Admitting that strange sixth sense into his mind once again, Scotty leads them in night creeping, trying desperately to ignore the screaming inside his head that only he can hear.

Continually calling out to them and cajoling each one by name, Scotty penetrates the black mile. Inch by inch, he leads them out of the blackness and toward the light. When they finally emerge, Scotty finds a seat away from the others and as the sun rises over the wooded hills, someone hands him a packet of food to help him revive. But it is too much. He is back in the jungle, seated in the doorway of the chopper, wondering why he did not bring everyone through the black mile. It breaks him. He just wants to drink the Devil's tears with his comrades.

Twenty years later, the mills are gone, and Vietnam is one country. Scotty lives under a bridge, while far away other soldiers still creep through the night thinking no one has ever done this before. Alone in the darkness, Scotty traces the old scar on his hand. Eventually, he quietly pleads, the black mile has to lead him home . . .

Words are magic and writers are wizards.

PADRE PEDRO

Padre Pedro was standing in the kitchen of the seaside cottage when he first heard the strange noise. He came to the small homey abode every year, enjoying the view from the cliffside perch, thirty feet or so above the restless waters. He'd take his cup of tea out onto the front deck, relax into the old wicker rocker, and just soak in the sea air. Which is where he headed now, wandering slowly through the pungent cloud of garlic and chiles, red of course, used in his homemade Mexican *carne con chile rojo* or the ones for his *guajillo chile* sauce that he loved with his scrambled eggs in the morning, Before he stepped out the front door he looked at the wooden plank nailed over the door with the words burned into it: *La ola se rompe a mi alrededor, pero la ola no me entierra.*

As he eased into the rocker, lost in the sound of the pounding surf below, he heard it again. A weak but urgent mewing carried on the wind. He sipped at the tea as he watched the gulls wheeling and dealing above the waves. There it was again. His knees complained as the old priest hauled himself to his feet and went to the edge, leaned on the railing. The lines on his face deepened as he tried to listen hard. Lines of weariness, lines of fading hope, lines of too hard memories. Forty years of parish work can do that to you. People need so much. People want so much. People are never satisfied. And God, what about God? God needs so much. God wants so much. God is never satisfied. Padre Pedro never could figure what was the end game. Drop over while elevating the host some day during Mass? Maybe the waves could tell him. So, every year he made his way back to this refuge. To listen.

His fingers slipped into his pocket like they had a mind of their own, it was so much a part of his being. They closed around the pearls of pleading, worn to perfection by his fingers over the years. It was a gift from his mother upon his ordination, her own rosary beads. They'd been with him through thick and thin. At his dear mother's funeral when he stood there feeling so lost and alone. Years later when his closest friend told him he was leaving the priesthood. The Holy Rosary was his guide, his companion for his shuffle o'er this mortal coil. The sound came again, jolting him from his reverie. He eased his way off the deck to make his way over to the top of the stairs, leading down to the beach. The crying sounded desperate.

Padre Pedro put on his glasses and peered down. There, in the tide pool. Among the rocks. A kitten, trapped as the waves lapped closer and closer, higher, and higher. He grunted. His knees would not be happy about making the climb down, let alone the climb back up. But a creature was in need. He set the mug of tea on the stoop and made his way down. As he approached, the kitten's cries grew louder as water splashed over the top of the rocks. The kitten was pure white, except for a patch of black fur around one eye. "Ah," said Padre Pedro, "*mi pequeño pirata!*" He reached down to rescue the poor creature, but its leg was stuck fast in the rocks.

Padre Pedro wiped at the spray that coated his glasses as he tried to free the kitten. "*Lo siento, no soy que querias, mi pequeño pirata!*" But Padre Pedro was exactly what the little pirate kitten wanted. And needed. It looked up with such trust in its eyes as the waves grew higher and higher, that the old priest was deeply moved. He painfully sank to his knees, then onto his back and reached his hand as far between the rocks as he could. Finally, he felt the soft fur of the kitten and supported it underneath with his palm. "*Estoy aqui, mi pequeño pirata. Estoy aqui.*"

A young couple strolling on the beach found them the next morning. Padre Pedro looked very much at peace, a beatific appearance to his now smooth face. And a kitten that looked like a pirate sitting on top of the highest rock. They were somewhat curious about the rosary beads around the little one's neck. The police determined that the old priest with the painful knees had been trapped by the incoming tide. They couldn't have known, however, that as the water lifted Padre Pedro's hand, it lifted the pirate kitten free. And to this day, no one has ever been able to explain the wooden plank resting in the old priest's other hand. Or how it had freed itself from the nails. Or who had burned the words into it: *La ola se rompe a mi alrededor pero la ola no me entierra.*

"The wave breaks around me, but the wave does not bury me."

Words are magic, and writers are wizards.

PARE MY SOUL

"In the end, it is just you." The old man, skin the color of a too ripe banana, eyes a bit bloodshot from the morning's libation, whatever that might be, cackled a bit at the end of each sentence he spoke. "You certainly got the right jacket on, buddy." Cackle. We were in the McDonald's in Roanoke, Virginia, across the street from the Berglund Center for the performing arts and coliseum. School buses unloaded students for some sort of field trip experience as I devoured a McGriddle and Coke, breakfast of champions. The man was referring to my Pittsburgh Steelers jacket, a certain conversation starter as I journey through life. I was on my way to a doctor's appointment, one of life's futile indignities for as the old man said, "In the end, it is just you."

In this day and age of coaches for all aspects of life: parenting coaches, writing coaches, marriage coaches, birth doulas, death doulas, faith coaches, clergy coaches, sex coaches, career coaches, healthy living coaches, healthy eating coaches (don't bother with me), decluttering coaches, memoir writing coaches, throw your life in the air and see what comes down coaching- seems perfectly suited to the "don't tell me what to do" tenor of current living. Coach me on it, but I'll figure it out. Cackle. As I was placing my order at McDonald's, the woman behind the cash register nodded appreciatively. "You got the best jacket. Good to see you." Be careful, we're everywhere! Cackle. As I finished my repast and stood to clear the table, the old man leaned in close. So close, I could feel the stubble from his shaved head scratching my cheek in a moment of peculiar intimacy. "You got to play an April Fool's on your lady there," he whispered, a gleam in his eyes, and yes, the cackle. A quick glance over his shoulder at my significant other. "Get in the car and tell her she forgot her pocketbook!" Cackle.

In the end, it is just you. On occasion, I get asked what do I think happens when we die. My honest answer is, "I really don't care. Does it matter? It is called death for a reason." Maybe not the Easter message that you might be looking for, right? I'm practicing paring my soul. Cackle. I took me and my Steelers jacket to the doctor's appointment. She turned out to be younger than my youngest daughter, doing her internal medicine rotation with the Virginia Tech medical school next door. And not impressed with my jacket or team preference. It got me to wondering. Human beings are this amazing sack of self-containing skin with all sorts of gooey biochemical processes going on inside, that even generates its own electricity, who somehow believe that life is about self-discovery. Maybe I need a soul paring coach. Is it all about finding what I want and going for it? You might have figured out by now that I go through life asking questions. My significant other tells me she can tell when I am in 'counselor listening mode.' I look at her and nod as she speaks, then respond with a question. Just how I roll . . .

I left the doctor's appointment relatively unscathed, two prescriptions already making my phone ping with notifications from the pharmacy back at home. The awful irony of these handy dandy technological devices moving information in the blink of an eye, while also feeding the spectacular rise in the aptly labeled "deaths of despair" as overdoses and suicides and gun violence reflect back to us, and everyone else, the emptiness and confusion in the mirror of our souls. Social media has exposed us in its harsh light; the good, the bad, and the ugly, in the most Southern sense of that word. Each group competes to scream the loudest: "Have you seen how they treat us?" While secretly terrified of the old man's words, "In the end, it is just us."

Lunch was in the bucolic town of Bedford, at The Train Station. Just what the name says. Inside is a mixture of men in caps with names on their work shirts eating while their pickups rest in the parking lot, librarian/quilting circle types, retirees, young families with babies, two female friends where one is monopolizing the conversation with loud stories, broad gestures, eyes wide— as I try to be too polite to eavesdrop as writers are wont to do, and the requisite old codger in baggy clothes seated alone at his favorite table, eyes a bit rheumy, fingers gnarled, heart pure. His soul is pared to the core. We present ourselves to be seated and the young woman comes out from the ticket cage with two menus. She has the appropriate mixture of forced smile and practiced indifference that shouts, "I'm in my late teens to early 20s, don't f**k with me." Her gait is made a bit odd by the one leg being made of black titanium, strapped to her upper thigh. But she is steady and true, leading the way to our meal.

The food is a surprise, a good surprise. As I'm eating I feel a tap on my shoulder. A waitress passing by leans in to say, "I see you're wearing the right jacket. Good to see." Indeed, I am, and it is. My SO rolls her eyes. "You and that jacket!" I look her in the eyes, nod, and say, "What can I say? We're everywhere." I tried to get her one for Christmas, but . . . .there's always next year. If I have a goal in the years that I have left, it is to keep learning how to pare my soul. Death is about grief. The trick is to know what it is that we grieve. And grieve . . . however long, however painful.

We get back to the car to go pick up the puppy from the groomer. "Hey, you forgot your pocketbook!" I exclaim. She rolls her eyes. "Just how old are you?" I smile, rub the faint brush burn on my cheek from the old man's head. Then I cackle. . .

Words are magic and writers are wizards.

JOE SANTA

It is tucked up against the foothills of the Blue Ridge Mountains in north central North Carolina. It is a small all-American town built at the confluence of two rivers, the Mayo, and the Dan. Hence its name, Mayodan, proudly occupying space in Ripley's Believe It Or Not, as the only town in the entire world holding that name. It is the proud purveyor of the annual hay bale (round and square) sculpture competition—my favorite is the hot rod tractor entrant—and the humble host of the Rockingham County Quilt Square Trail. Once you pass the shuttered textile mill on one side of town, the drive down Main Street is a welcoming array of azaleas and dogwoods, set around neatly kept homes.

Once you pass the park with its whitewashed gazebo, you enter a downtown that peters out about a block in any direction. The good folks of Mayodan have several churches to choose from if they are so inclined, ranging from Baptist to Methodist, Episcopalian to Moravian to independent and proud of it, from a newer looking brick building erected after a tornado knocked down the old structure, to a tiny box holding its own on a side street. You make the full circle past the Bridgestone airplane tire plant, post office and fire station on the edge of town, next to the two competing gas stations where one is always a penny a gallon cheaper depending upon whose turn it is, and you might think you've seen all there is to see, know all that there is to know about Mayodan.

And you would be wrong. Like far too many small towns in far too many places, the people of Mayodan sent their sons and daughters off to war. Wars of far more justification than you could shake a stick at, against enemies natural or unexplainable. So it was that Big Willie, the sexton of the church at the end of Main Street with the tallest steeple and the biggest bell, was called to serve. Big Willie was married to Daisy, and they had a boy, whom everyone called Little Willie. Big liked to sneak Little up into the belfry to help him clean the big bell and survey the town, all the way to the gas stations. One day before he left, Big, after again reminding his son that he shouldn't tell momma about their secret spot, took Little up and held him close. "Remember," he said, "that while I'm gone to listen to your momma, say your prayers, and watch for daddy to come home. Can you remember that?" "Yes," said Little, "I'll do you proud, Daddy. I'll listen to momma, say my prayers, and watch you home."

And he did. All through that summer. All through that fall. All through Thanksgiving and Christmas and beyond, Little Willie did what he'd promised his daddy. He heard adults worrying on street corners about the battles and losses. He saw times grow grimmer as people lined up for food, some for shelter. Medicine was rationed and nobody smiled very much. He tried to remain brave as he minded his momma and said his prayers to the ceiling. And every Sunday after church, he slipped away while momma talked to the ladies and went up to the belfry to watch Daddy home.

Thus it was, that Palm Sunday arrived, in the Year of Our Lord. Little Willie fidgeted and fussed, more than a little frightened as Momma sat silently, tears wetting her cheeks. She kept folding and unfolding the letter she received the day before. Mrs. Winters, who smelled funny, reached over, and patted him on the head. Somehow that made it worse. He watched in worried wonder as Momma held the letter to her lips and kissed the ink on the page. He listened with the ears and heart of a child as the story of some guy riding on a donkey meant people cheered like they were watching him home. Then everyone got to leave with a long, green leaf in their hands.

While Momma got to talking to the ladies, Little wondered if he should even bother. Things were just so sad. Finally, he made his choice, made his escape, and scampered up the ladder to the belfry. The big bell looked neglected, but he paid no nevermind. He stood on his tiptoes and stared hard out toward the gas stations. A breeze off the mountains stirred the palm frond in his hand as a truck pulled off the road out where NC Highway 704 meets Main. The far door opened, closed, and the truck pulled away. There. He saw someone. A weary figure, leaning on one crutch. Little Willie looked hard, scarcely daring to breathe. But it was no stranger.

Everyone down below heard his cry: "Joe Santa! Joe Santa! Joe Santa! Here he comes!" Daisy looked up in astonishment as Little flew down the ladder. "Momma! I watched him home. Joe Santa, Momma. Joe Santa! Here he comes." Out the door he ran, palm waving. Daisy followed, alarmed. The others came out, too, all the greenery waving in the sun. They stood in wonder in the street as Little Willie ran toward the lone figure, shouting for all he had: "Joe Santa! Joe Santa! Here he comes! Daddy! Daddy, I've watched you home. Joe Santa!"

And it was good . . .

Words are magic, and writers are wizards.

RAY AND BRUNO'S RESURRECTION

It is a nondescript barber shop in a nondescript strip mall on the corner of a busy intersection in a nondescript old mill town along the Ohio River. Wedged in between a paint store on one side and a vape shop on the other, sits Ray and Bruno's Olde Italy Barbers. Both Ray and Bruno hailed from the Salerno region of southern Italy. Their mothers were sisters from a family that went back generations. The cousins played together, exploring the grounds of the great cathedral on the hill, going down to the shore on adventures. Early on they discovered the joys of playing mumblety peg and spent hours with their friends in childish abandon. In the mid- 1960s both of their families decided to immigrate to the United States. Ray and Bruno were 6 and 8 at the time. Life in America soon settled into a routine. Both of their Papa's getting up to go work in the J&L mill on rotating shifts. Attending school and trying to master the weird intricacies of English. They soon learned that in America, around a city like Pittsburgh, there was always of community of Italians to remind them of where they came from. As it should be.

Neither Ray nor Bruno's father wanted them to follow them into the mills or mines. College was not an option, so after high school both of them decided to enroll in the Barber School of Pittsburgh. The hope and dream were to save enough one day to open a shop together. They passed through the school, found jobs, and saved toward their dream. Meanwhile, in the mill town things prospered and it spread up the hills and out along Brodhead Road. New housing developments sprang up and with them the soon to be ubiquitous strip mall/shopping center as the family car became the main mode of transportation. Ray and Bruno met the loves of their lives, married them, and moved into one of those new housing plans not too far up Brodhead Road from the space they had leased to open Ray and Bruno's Olde

Italy Barbers. One fine day in 1980 they had their grand opening. They even chipped out part of the parking lot in the rear so they could invite their friends and customers to a game of mumblety peg in the soft clay.

Ray and Bruno's soon became a destination for the men of the area. The mills were struggling, and guys needed somewhere to gather and share the news and share the pain. Ray and Bruno had three chairs in a two-man shop, various odds and ends of furniture along the walls for waiting, and half the surface of the mirrors became covered with newspaper clippings. Stories about the Pirates, the Steelers, the mills coming back, the dashed hopes for the mills coming back. Lots and lots of local high school sports stories, as well, decorated the various mirrors and pale green walls. Ray and Bruno took turns bringing in big pans of Italian cooking at its finest, homemade. To the uninitiated, it might have seemed a bit strange, walking into this community in a shop for the first time and being offered a meatball sub with Salerno's best marinara sauce while he waited for a straight razor shave and trim. Or to be immediately questioned about whether or not he carried a worthwhile pocketknife to try on the clay out back. If he dared . . . and if he wasn't wearing his best shoes, all the saints be praised. Loser bought the wine, as it should be.

The memories of good times can help us survive the sure to come bad times. Men being boys and boys trying to be men is one of nature's reliable cycles and calculations. Shouts of competition and cries of loss, learning to play and playing to win don't always agree. Life is for fully living never negates the obvious that life only moves in one direction, towards its end. Even our inventing of Palm Sunday, Good Friday and Easter cannot change any of that, but only underscores the fact that cradling life in our own hands like precious water in the desert and offering sips to those who thirst, serves to make every week holy. Such it was that both Ray and Bruno discovered as they aged that they shared a degenerative heart condition. Since they came from the same blood line, they matched up pretty closely in the transplant registry. Both had equally good lives, good families, good memories, equal need for the life-saving potential of receiving a new heart.

And it came to pass that a young man was killed in an automobile accident, a young man who registered to be an organ donor. His heart was healthy and matched the requirements for Ray to receive as his new heart. Or Bruno's, as well, for that matter. Only one could receive the heart. The doctors and nurses on the transplant committee were at an impasse. Precious minutes were ticking by. A decision was needed. Two phone calls went out. Two phone calls were answered . . . .

Ray opened the door to the Olde Italy Barbers and slipped inside. Bruno waited there, a fancy wooden box in his hands. The two face each other in silence, as two kindred souls can do. One would receive salvation wrapped up as more years of life, not without risk. The other faced certain death in short order. Ray shrugged and smiled. Bruno laughed and opened the box. Inside were two brand new knives. They each selected one and then, arms flung over each other's shoulders, they stepped through the back door, to play a game of mumblety peg. And accept their sure and certain resurrection. For what it's worth. As it should be.

Words are magic and writers are wizards.

RUN AWAY TO MARS

FIVE YOUNG BOYS SET off that summer afternoon. Hours later, only four came back. The five were the McKinley triplets—Kyle, Kenny, and Kearson, Little Johnny Rapson, and Moon Saint, aka Sammy Shune. How Moon Saint got his nickname is lost in the lure of that time and place, but the legend lives on. Some children are just put together differently, and Moon Saint was one different child, on that most folks agreed. Sometimes it is nature and nurture and other times there are more egregious reasons. Especially when you see a child building a wall around themselves, laboring mightily to create a prison for their own protection. All that was known for certain that day is that all the boys who returned, the triplets and Johnny, said the same thing about Moon Saint. "He ran away to Mars."

Meanwhile, on Mars, Moon Saint unpacked his brown paper grocery bag. He had his special suit that shielded him from all harmful rays and lack of oxygen. He carefully buttoned it tight and took out the special space food from the airtight plastic containers. While he ate one of the paste sandwiches with space jelly on it, he dug around in the bag and took out a box of sidewalk chalk. The light was growing dim on the rock walls surrounding him, but he had a mission to complete. As he thoughtfully chewed, he selected the yellow chalk and scrawled on the wall: "Here on Mars no child will be hurt or hated." Satisfied he sat back and tapped a piece of blue chalk on his cheek while thinking. After taking a swig of water, he picked another spot and wrote: "Here on Mars nobody laughs at you when you are sad." He hesitated, then added: "Here on Mars no one goes to bed hungry . . . or scared."

Down on earth, in the town of the five boys, the parents of the McKinley triplets and Johnny Rapson's mother put their heads together. Who would go tell Moon Saint's family that he had run away to Mars? They were known to be difficult, to put it politely. The dad drank heavily, and rumor had it that he hit Mrs. Shune. Mind you, no one asked them about it, but she always wore long sleeves and heavy makeup on her cheeks. But they showed up in church most weeks and helped with the fellowship dinners. She was real quiet-like, always, while Dad Shune was laughing and slapping the men on the shoulder, inviting them to go hunting on his mountain property. Neighborly to a degree, but no one really wanted to get involved. She seemed like a grim mouse to them, and now her boy was on Mars.

Moon Saint thought about getting some rest. Days are different on Mars, you understand. And the nights . . . the nights are colder, darker. He hoped there was enough oxygen to burn the candle he'd brought. Thankfully, it lit and he took up the pink chalk. Holding the flame in one hand he wrote on the walls: "Here on Mars no one is too slow, too ugly, too stupid to be here." The flame danced and shadows flitted across the rockface. Moon Saint thought he heard loud booming in the distance. Did Mars have storms? He couldn't remember. Before turning in for the night, he took the green chalk and wrote: "Here on Mars pain does not hurt so bad. Here on Mars bruises can be beautiful. Here on Mars no one is worthless." He hoped the candle would stay lit as he closed his eyes and tried to go to sleep. Outside the thunder came closer and the sound of rain hitting the creek grew insistent.

In the town, adults milled around in disarray while waiting for the authorities to tell them what to do, how everything would be alright. The chief of police interrogated the triplets and Johnny. But all they could get out of them was that Moon Saint ran away to Mars. Why would he do that? Maybe it was a better place to live. You cannot get to Mars, it's impossible. The boys all shrugged at that nonsense. You can get to Mars anytime you need to, they insisted. Everyone heard the storm brewing up in the hills and debated whether it was a good idea to set out in this kind of weather to find a misguided boy who thought he could run away to Mars. Make his worthless parents go find him if they really want to.

Here on Earth, a lot of time can be wasted trying to figure out who is in charge and who is worth saving. That is why it was not until the next morning, after it had stopped raining, that the people set out to look for Moon Saint. Just how far is it to Mars? It was early afternoon before anyone reached Parker's Creek. The runoff from the storm had it running fast and high. Seeing this, the boys got worried and told their parents about the caves they had found along the banks of the creek. The rocks were orangish red from the clay inside where the rushing water hollowed out spaces. Johnny reluctantly pointed out the old oak that marked the spot for the best one. A sheriff's deputy stripped down to his shorts and plunged into the water. After precious moments he re-emerged, holding high a flannel shirt and a Tupperware container holding the sacramental remnants of peanut butter and jelly.

Now as we all know, sacraments come with sacred writings. The wet deputy was in stunned silence as he climbed up the bank and sat down trying to collect his thoughts. "Did you find him?" everyone asked. Finally, he shook his head as he said, "That's all I found. Except on the roof there's writing." He choked as they all pressed close. "It says in orange chalk: To anyone who needs to live on Mars, Moon Saint loves you . . . "

Words are magic and writers are wizards.

CRUCIFY ME

Sherman could not sit still. He was nervous about even coming through the door into my counseling center office. His eyes never stopped darting around the room, his hands kept playing with the pack of cigarettes, and his feet bounced up and down. Finally, he asked if we could talk out in the courtyard instead, out in the open, where he paced as he started and stopped telling his story many times. Sherman had a history of abusing alcohol and was well on his way to losing complete control over it. He worked a dead-end job in a retail store, he was handsome, soft spoken, and gave the impression of a wandering soul with many a tale of woe.

Sherman had moved into the state just recently after some great disappointment in love, he told me. She was a beautiful, intelligent woman whom he adored. As a matter of fact, he was still in love with her. He had planned on being with her for the rest of their lives. A forever love. Somewhere along the line, however, her brother introduced her to cocaine. Over the ensuing months the drug had taken over her life. She insisted that she loved him, wanted him, wanted to be with him, needed him. But her actions said otherwise. The drug offered an immediate sense of well-being. The drug offered release and pleasure without asking anything in return.

Sherman said that he spent countless hours pleading with her to seek help. "Do it for me. Do it for our future. Do it for your kids. Do it for yourself. Just, please, do it!" Finally, she agreed to enter a treatment facility to detox and get help. Sherman told her that was an act of love and to ease her mind, he told her that he would stay with her two children. For three long months, she was in treatment. Sherman worked hard providing for all the needs and care for the children. At one point he even had to sell his much-prized stereo equipment to help pay for her treatment. But he did it, willingly. She was so much a part of him, no price was too high; whatever it took.

Finally, the day arrived when she was to be released from the treatment center. Sherman drove with great excitement and relief to the hospital to bring her home. Their new life awaited. Their new life together could, at long last, begin. She came out of the building, all smiles. Once in the car, she greeted him with an eager kiss. Then, as he pulled away from the parking lot, she opened her bag, rummaged around, and took out a small cellophane package of white powder. She turned to Sherman and asked if he wanted to join her in celebrating by getting high.

The young man's heart broke. Along with his spirit. A shudder passed through his body there in the courtyard as he recounted all of this to me. This final travesty, this mockery of his love, broke him. We sat in silence and stillness. Finally, he looked up and pointed to the cross hanging on the outside of the church building. "It would hurt less if she just crucified me." He made another appointment to talk some more, but I never heard from him again.

Another setting, this time a large medical center where I am a chaplain. A fifteen-year-old boy, Jerry, stands alone in a sterile hallway. His father lies in the intensive care unit, stricken by a massive heart attack. The same father that his boy had to go fetch home from bars ever since he was eight years old. Now, as the oldest, he must be the head of the family, as he has been since forever. Dad is a confusing mix of hearty laughs, loneliness, fear, weeping shame and anger. Jerry has been expected to be the one to take care of dad, the one who is punished no matter which child misbehaved. At 13, he was driving his drunk father home from the bars at 2am. Jerry feels alone, angry, uncertain, old, unable to let anyone see inside of him to his own fears.

Jerry dreamed of being a professional baseball player, but that is barely a memory now. He starred in Little League, and he used to eagerly scan the bleachers, searching for his father's face, imagining it filled with pride and joy, only to be disappointed. Every time. The coach encouraged him to keep playing, but Jerry has family to think of. There is no room for dreams. As we talk, his mother approaches, walking with hesitant steps, head bowed, fingers twisting nervously. She tells Jerry that the doctors have asked for a decision. His father is beyond help, being kept alive by machines. It is his decision, she tells him. It is up to this 15-year-old to decide whether to turn off the machines that are keeping his father alive.

Jerry tries to protest, but she is already heading for the exit, her drab winter coat wrapped tightly to shut out the freezing winds. Minutes tick by as Jerry stares down the hallway without seeing anything in its unrelenting brightness. Finally, he pushes through the doors to the ICU. He spends a long moment looking down at the form of his father. In the stillness of creation holding its breath, he brings his own fingertips to his lips, kisses them, and gently presses them to his father's tortured lips. To the waiting shadows, he whispers, "Yes. Turn them off. Let him go . . . "

At the end, when he turns to go, he stops, looks at me, and he asks, "Mister Chaplain, do you think it would hurt less if God crucified me?" On my action notes for the day, all I can manage is to scratch, *"Ecce homo. Quo Vadis?"*

Words are magic and writers are wizards.

THE CHERRY TREE

It stood as a sentinel at the far end of the large garden. It was planted by Susie and Jimmy when they first bought the lot. The day their Sears & Roebuck house kit was delivered, a pile of lumber, nails, hopes, and dreams, sliding off the truck right next to the hole dug out for the foundation, the young couple walked back to where Jimmy would plant his big garden. Next to that spot, together they planted a cherry tree. Eventually, they planted a few more, both sour red and sweet dark cherries. But it was the first one that always watched over everything. Watched over the land. Watched over the garden each year, from spring planting to fall harvest and all points in between. Watched over Susie and Jimmy as they weathered storms and gathered the fruit of their hardworking lives. Watched over them through lean times, fights, and failures, yet always found a way to show forth blossoms come each new spring. When the house was ready for them to move into, Jimmy took some extra lumber and built a most comfortable love-bench underneath that very tree. Here was home.

Jimmy worked in the blast furnaces of the mills down along the Youghiogheny River near McKeesport, then later to the Clairton works along the Monongahela. Their home just across the line from the small borough of East McKeesport into North Versailles Township was his refuge from his shifts in the bowels of hell. One year during the annual shut down of the furnace to reline it with treated brick, he built a garage between the house and garden for all his tools and the much beloved two-toned Studebaker Commander Starlight coupe. The Sears & Roebuck house was sturdy and comfortable, but he liked to tinker at making it better for his Susie. Come spring, though, there was only one place to find him. Out in the garden using the manpower of his own arms and legs to push the hand plow to turn the dirt. Then he would get his buddy Fred to truck in a load of fresh from the farm manure. The whole neighborhood knew when Jimmie was preparing his garden each year by that fragrance drifting on the wind.

Susie pitched in, working harder than most men, digging the dirt, hoeing around the plants, bringing homemade lemonade out from her kitchen to sit with Jimmy on the cherry tree loveseat and enjoy their life together. And when their daughter, Grace, was born Susie brought her out in the sunshine to sit on the bench while they did the work of encouraging the earth to yield its bounty. As the corn, squash, cukes, beans, carrots, and all, came in, Susie busied herself canning the vegetables and placing the jars in the fruit cellar they'd dug with the foundation. When the cherry trees matured and bore their fruit, Susie picked, pitted, and canned what didn't make it into pies and cobblers right off. Grace grew up and brought her beau to sit on the bench beneath the cherry tree to help him understand where she came from. Also, every Wednesday evening, Jimmy drove Susie down into East McKeesport, to the Presbyterian Church on Broadway for choir practice. One does not go through such a rich life without a nod to the divine aspects of community and fellowship.

When the new minister moved in across the back street with his seven scruffy kids, Susie brought them homemade vegetable soup and cherry crumble as a welcome. When the cherries ripened each spring, she would invite the three youngest, dressed in their '3 for $1 pack' of white tee shirts from the sparkling new Kmart store out the highway, to come help with the picking. Ladders were climbed, pails were filled and iced tea drunk on the special bench beneath the sentinel tree. Their white tees became permanently stained by the raucous pitting sessions around the old kitchen table. To them, Susie seemed ancient. And perhaps she was. Ancient enough to have endured seeing Grace married, then widowed by a terrible accident that left her struggling to get around on two canes. Ancient enough to see Jimmy retire, still driving that old Studebaker, slowly become hobbled by arthritis, and watching his garden grow smaller and smaller with each new aching joint. Ancient enough to wear her beautiful long hair, now gray, in a long braid wrapped around her head like a well-deserved crown.

Now Susie and Jimmy sat on the love-bench, marking the time and its passing by noting the branches over their heads becoming more gnarled and weatherworn each spring as it blossomed. The day came when Susie called the minster to tell him that Jimmy was in an ambulance, could he come pray with her. Time can be soothing yet unyielding. It was Jimmy's time to go. Susie needed a ride now to choir practice each week. The house began to feel empty even in its aching familiarity. Trips outside to sit on the loveseat became more halting even as they became more valuable. The tree seemed to bow before her, offering what it could. Time kept passing without thought to the future.

One last time, Susie came to sit beneath the cherry tree. She had not gotten this far in life by being afraid of decisions. The Sears & Roebuck house was too much for her. Her own health was in doubt. Grace might need special care. She ran her fingers over the old bench, imagining sitting here with Jimmy, the garden in full throated bloom. A petal from a cherry blossom floats down to kiss her cheek. This is the last time. The back of the lot with the garden is sold to a developer for townhomes. It's hard for her to imagine. What will become of the bench? The cherry tree? The old woman fretting about them both? Susie sighs. Yesterday, today, and tomorrow. Nothing stops them. But for now. For now . . .

Words are magic and writers are wizards.

JESUS WOODSTOCK

Jesus Woodstock was a farrier's assistant, son of a man who was a traveling knife sharpener, or cutlery, for 67 years. Joey Woodstock, dad of Jesus, was known for the paper lunch bag he wore on his head for a cap, with the edges rolled down, while he worked over the grinder, sharpening knives, scissors, gardening tools and whatnot. Jesus liked riding around in his father's old green truck, with the crudely painted on name and description of services rendered. But he discovered a love for horses when a girl he liked in the eighth grade had a sorrel pony in the old barn down at the bottom of their pasture. Soon he knew all about hoof picks, clinch cutters, hoof gauges, anvils, trimming knives, rasps, nippers—the whole kit and caboodle. By the time he was in his fourth year of apprenticeship, the blacksmith had named Jesus his assistant. Working on shoeing horses requires a lot of patience and muscle strength and Jesus Woodstock had a lot of both elements. Getting along with horse owners and trainers and veterinarians, aye, there's the rub. More agreement could be found in a conversation between universalist nontrinitarians and complementarians about the seven mountains of dominionism; i.e. Not a whole lot.

Jesus Woodstock loved his father as much as he loved himself and, in that spirit, he also wore a paper lunch bag rolled over at the edges as a cap when he worked. With the heavy leather apron of a farrier, his steel toed boots and muscular arms showing below the usually rolled up sleeves, Jesus Woodstock cut quite the figure of a young man. His work became so well known that people would request that he be the one to come shoe their horses and care for their hooves. "We need Jesus Woodstock," became the most heard request in the office of the blacksmith. So, it was not entirely unexpected that one day a call came in from The Greatest Clown Show On Earth, saying that they were coming to town and that they used a lot of horses in their act, could Jesus Woodstock work his magic on them? The Blacksmith was only too glad to dispatch the farrier's assistant. It would be for one day at a top rate.

Jesus Woodstock drove to the town where the Greatest Clown Show would perform and looked at all the horses, took care of their needs, then made use of his free ticket to watch the show. Clowns being an ersatz version of human foibles, fears, and failures, he found the show to be entertaining but unfulfilling and prepared to check the horses again as it drew to a close. But a strange and unexpected thing happened. A few members of the audience stayed and asked the clowns to keep going. So, they climbed on their horses and continued clowning. Soon word spread that the show was still going on and more and more people came to witness this unending show. The bigger audience fed the clowns need to perform and they just kept going. Hour after hour, then into a new day, then another. Newspapers took notice of the growing crowds, the buses parked in the parking lot, the never-ending entertainment from the clowns. They labeled it the Great Clown Revival and soon other shows started to wonder how they could measure up to this kind of competition.

Forgotten in all this were the horses. They were starting to come up lame. The head of the Greatest Clown Show sent for Jesus Woodstock. But he was nowhere to be found. Appeals were published, TikTok videos were made, social media discourse was launched asking for the whereabouts of Jesus Woodstock, the farrier's assistant. Why was he falling down on the job, failing at his duties, many wondered. The Clown Revival needed him. Finally, someone spotted him in a homeless encampment and the police were summoned. Fortunately, Jesus Woodstock did not have dark skin, so it was a safe bet to send the police for him. The officers caught up to him outside a ratty old laundromat. They recognized him by the brown lunch bag he wore as a cap. "What are you doing?" they demanded. "You are needed at the Circus."

Jesus Woodstock took an old woman by the arm and brought her in front of the police and gathering press. "This is Martha," he said. "She hangs around here because people coming out of the laundromat give her their extra change. Then she buys the ingredients for her special porridge. She makes it every day and brings it here to feed the birds all winter long in old Starbucks cups. She's getting older and a bit absent minded. I thought she might need some help." The police sergeant shook his head. "But the Clown Revival needs you." Jesus Woodstock took the arm of a sixteen-year-old boy and brought him into the circle. "This is Henry. I saw him hiding something in the dryer vents out back. Turns out it was a couple of automatic weapons. Henry is feeling desperate and thought shooting up his school would take away the pain." Jesus Woodstock shrugged. "I thought he might need some help."

"Grab your tools and come with us," the sergeant commanded. "We need to keep the Clown Revival going." Jesus Woodstock shook his head. "I can't. I sold them all so I could buy this laundromat. Why should I shoe the horses just to keep a circus going?" And he stayed where he was. If you happen to find the Jesus Woodstock Laundromat, just look for the guy with the brown lunch bag on his head. If you're not sure, check behind the building. I'm told that he keeps a sorrel pony in the back lot.

Words are magic and writers are wizards.

JESUS THE FRIENDLY GHOST

It came to pass that the Story Guide took them up to a high mountain, where they could look out over all the land. To the west, was the smoke from great and fierce fires. To the south, dark clouds brewed severe winds and a deluge that devastated the land. To the east, rose the groans of the people under the weight of a plague which was plaguing them. To the north, rose the cries of those seeking justice and freedom from fear because they looked different than those who ruled over them. And he told them a story saying: Sarah Jane woke up as the sun peeked over the hills, as she did every morning and when she walked out into the living room she discovered a gift had been left for her on the carpet. Wondering at this gift, she picked it up and took it to the nearest church, The Home of Jesus the Friendly Ghost.

"Welcome," said the good people of Jesus the Friendly Ghost. "What is this?" asked Sarah Jane, holding out her hands. "Should I be afraid?" "First," said the people, "do you know Jesus the Friendly Ghost? Because he knows who you are. We're all special because we know him. He is a kind of round, white happy-go-lucky boy who hovers nearby. His is an amazing backstory that just makes you feel all gooey inside, like a marshmallow. See, we keep roasting sticks on the wall to remind us of that feeling." Sara Jane asked, "Will he take my gift?"

"Not if you don't know him like we do," said the good people of Jesus the Friendly Ghost. "Ask him to make you special. Then live for king and country. In fact, give your gift to the king and he and Jesus the Friendly Ghost will be greatly pleased. Just bow your head and close your eyes and the Friendly Ghost who hovers nearby will listen to you, and you only. That's what makes us special. Don't you want to feel better about yourself? Don't you want all the best that life has to offer for your very own self? That is what Jesus the Friendly Ghost wants for you." And Sarah Jane returned home, still holding her gift.

Sarah Jane woke up as the sun peeked over the hills, as she did every morning and when she walked out into the living room she discovered a gift had been left for her on the carpet. Wondering at this gift, she picked it up and took it to the palace of the Mad King. "What is this?" asked Sarah Jane, holding out her hands. "Should I be afraid?" "Do you know who I am?" asked the Mad King. "I made this country great for people like you. Bringing me gifts shows how much you love me." Sarah Jane said, "The good people of Jesus the Friendly Ghost said to live for king and country. Will you take my gift?"

The Mad King looked blank for a moment. "You could give it to me on live television. I could gather all of my family and all my serfs and servile so that everyone could see me accept your gift like the one and true upholder of the kingdom that I am. The good people of Jesus the Friendly Ghost will love it. Absolutely love seeing their king receiving this gift, all the best people. We could do it across the street in front of that old building. That will make me look like a good king." And Sarah Jane returned home, still holding her gift.

Sarah Jane woke up as the sun peeked over the hills, as she did every morning and when she walked out into the living room she discovered a gift had been left for her on the carpet. Wondering at this gift, she picked it up and started out the door. At that moment her beloved returned from his long journey. "What is this?" asked Sarah Jane, holding out her hands. "Should I be afraid?" Her beloved stifled a sigh and mustered a smile. "No, Sarah Jane. You do not need to be afraid."

He gently took her by the shoulder and led her back inside. He saw the literature on the kitchen table from the Home of Jesus the Friendly Ghost, alongside the official stationary of the palace of the Mad King. Brushing them aside, he prepared a tub of warm water and soap. Then, ever so tenderly, he cleaned Sarah Jane's hands and arms and face and feet, putting her gift where it belonged. When he finished the story, someone in the crowd asked the Story Guide, "Well, what was her gift?" And he looked upon them and loved them, saying, "Her brain is broken with disease. Every morning she steps on her own excrement. Her gift is her feces. She has Alzheimer's and is like a child. Now go and do likewise."

And the self-righteous and self-haters, realizing that he had told this story against them, pushed forward to cast him from the cliff. But, as in all good cliffhangers, he passed on through, and left them to clean up the mess.

Words are magic and writers are wizards.

THE KITTEN AMENDMENT

NORTH STORER AVENUE IN Fayetteville, Arkansas, is a nondescript street on the edge of the University of Arkansas, home to the Razorback Hogs, some 20,000 students from all over the illustrious state gathered in the tenacious pursuit of knowledge . . . or something like that. At least that's what their parents want to believe. In the Winter/Spring semester of 1973 my trusty 1960 Ford Fairlane 500 was parked around the corner on Douglas Street, with its bald tires and perpetually empty gas tank and cranky starter justifying my investment of the grand total of $150. That spring the activity that demanded our attention each evening was to gather along the sides of Maple Street where it bordered the campus, watching traffic go past. Well, truth be told, we were watching for those souls daring to bare all and go 'streaking' through said traffic. Naked, except for shoes or sandals, running full speed through traffic, up and over cars, with the occasional full splat onto unforgiving pavement. I kid you not. I guess you had to be there . . .

I had a draft card in my wallet with its 1A designation and the news was filled with Nixon's Christmas bombing campaign of North Vietnam to force them to the peace table in Paris. I kid you not. In my two years at the illustrious institution, I had a grand total of two dates. One each with two different young ladies and that's all we need to say about that. I lived at 612 Storer Ave. in a large boarding house, where I washed dishes and cleaned bathrooms in exchange for a good portion of my room and board. And in a house full of college students, cleaning up the kitchen and the bathrooms was no mean feat. But enough about that. My major was premed/psychology, but I dropped the premed part after failing to slay the mighty dragon of organic chemistry. For a psychological statistics course we had to design a program for some reason, go to the basement of the psych building to punch the program into computer cards, then sign up for time to run it on the behemoth computer lurking in the corner. If the machine didn't gag on your cards, you passed the assignment. I kid you not. I guess you had to be there...

I was a thousand miles away from Pittsburgh, which may explain a lot about my choice of school. That was never more apparent than when an ice storm hit this very southern state. Complete chaos and gridlock ensued. Watching cotton hulls spread onto the slippery streets made this northern boy just shake his head in amazement. My first room in the boarding house was in the basement, a small windowless room where I discovered the previous occupant had left his stash of Playboy and Hustler and similar type magazines for me to discover. This type of literature had not been a part of the curriculum for Preacher's Kid 101. As such, I decided that it warranted further investigation and continued to purchase monthly updates... for research purposes, mind you. And that has nothing to do with the all-nighter I pulled before the Statistics final exam in which I sat down, stared at page one of a ten-page exam that required to build from the first problem. And promptly forgot the first formula that I needed to use on the first problem. Nothing. Nada. Blank slate land. I kid you not.

It was at the Univ. of Arkansas that, after my financial aid went through, the school refunded to me the money my father had paid for tuition. And I promptly purchased a stereo system for my now top floor room with two windows. It was a long trip home to face the music after he wrote that I should use the refunded money to pay toward the next semester. But he invoked the Kitten Amendment—I was his son, not a research project—and I spent the summer shoveling dirt, sand, and wet concrete so other people could have swimming pools in their backyards. In Pittsburgh, with its all of 6–8-week summers. Added to the $60 bucks for my car, I could return for the next semester, still scrubbing toilets and showers and endless dishes. I kid you not...

At the end of my second year in Fayetteville, amid rumors of old pickup driving Sam Walton up the road starting a new concept in cheap merchandising he called WalMart, and having decided to transfer back home to Pittsburgh, I got a six-week, good paying job being a counselor for incoming freshman to the U of A. Two batches a week of kids fresh from high school graduations turned loose on a big college campus. What could go wrong? I could tell them whatever I wanted. I would be back in Pittsburgh when they showed up to start classes in the fall. So, sure, the professors are all brilliant, classes are easy, no need to study, you'll find the love of your life, alcohol makes everything better, and parents are overrated. Actually, all I remember about them is twice a week sitting on the floor of the lounge while they had a dance, my friend and fellow counselor leading his band, and they always closed out with The Boxer, by

Paul Simon. And he always had a hip flask of scotch. And he inherited a stack of magazines when I left. I kid you not . . . maybe.

Oh, and that statistics exam? My professor invoked the Kitten Amendment and showed mercy. "John, I know that you know this stuff. You had a 98 average before the exam. I'm going to give you a score that still maintains your 'A.'" I kid you not. Sometimes, you really do have to be there to experience mercy . . . and to know when to invoke the Kitten Amendment.

Words are magic and writers are wizards.

THE HOUSE YOU LIVE IN

Morty gets up at 4am six days a week. It's not quite night and it's not quite morning. It is the time for nightmares and the time for very strong coffee. The others stirring at this hour are bread makers and donut dippers, sleepy cops and drivers of delivery trucks dropping off bundles of newspapers. By 4:30 he is shaved, dressed, fed the cat, and out the door. He climbs into his old panel truck, backs out of the driveway and heads across the bridge. He stops at the railroad crossing, looks both ways, then rattles across the iron rails and proceeds to the high slatted fence around Estelle's Salvation Recycling Yard, named for his now deceased wife. He stops at the gate, climbs out to unlock the big monster of a padlock, and pushes the gates open with a teeth-jarring screech. He pulls the old truck into the yard, swallows the last of his coffee and goes into the warehouse. There he counts out how many burlap sacks he needs for today's rounds, turns out the lights and sets out into the realm of broken dreams and unanswered prayers.

In the parlance of days gone by, Morty is a junk man, not just any junk, however. He gathers the detritus of the soul: the remains of the spirit. Emptying the slop bucket of plaintive unanswered prayers for it is filled with fear, as well as pleadings for sure ways around the laws of the universe and its daily grind. Or, collecting the soft rags of wishful murmurs rising like dust specks caught in a beam of sunlight, the beseeching of relief for pain, uncertainty, healing and light. They float out the windows and chimneys during the nights, slip beneath the crack in the door, to gather in tired heaps at the curb. There is the odd judicial robe or constitutional parchment, holy transcripts, or political speech, purporting to bear the weight of the world in their rows of ink or stains that might be marinara sauce, or might be blood. Whatever. It is now an abandoned, used up, worn out fashion, that readily drifts away. Junk, to be carted away and forgotten.

Back in the warehouse Morty carefully separates out all the dashed dreams and broken hearts. They can be repurposed into trinkets of jewelry or wall hangings. The unanswered prayers and lost hopes he sets aside while he searches through the cupboards and drawers until he finds what he needs. At his work bench, Morty selects bright layers of tissue paper that he folds and glues together, attaching string or yarn in just the right places. One special drawer is filled with votive candles and one each is attached to the tissue balloons, with an unfulfilled beseeching nestled into the wax, next to the wick. Morty takes his collection of mini hot air balloons to the banks of the river. There, with great care and reverence, Morty lights each candle, and as the breezes of the dawn play across the water, the little balloons float off, high and wide, ever rising, until they are indistinguishable from the last of the morning stars.

Then it is back home to the little house, lost in his loneliness, ready to sit and stare into the corners. Estelle loved their little house. He can feel her memory in every corner, picturing her puttering with her fine China, watering the plants that she loved to mother, talking to the cat the whole time. The Salvation Recycling Yard had been her brainchild. "Morty," Estelle would say, "we have been blessed. It's only right that we help with the impossible. It's like that song says: The house you live in will never fall down, if you pity the stranger who stands at your gate." And her being Estelle, she dove right into the impossible: unanswered prayers and lost dreams. Morty sighed and kicked at the cat, who knew enough by now to be on alert when Morty got back from his rounds. Estelle had a way of getting her way, but he always wondered if he had been enough for her.

A knock at the door interrupts Morty's reverie. He grunts his way back onto tired feet and opens the door. Before him is a child, no more than eight or nine. "I'm Jojo," says the child. "Estelle sent me to the house you live in." Morty is taken aback. "Estelle is gone. Forever." It is like a curse, this last word. Jojo is unfazed. "Whatever you say. But I'm here and it is because of Estelle." Now nonplussed, Morty remembers his manners and invites Jojo to step in. Jojo produces a small burlap sack and opens it. Slowly a mangled tissue paper hot air balloon emerges, still attached to a votive candle. "I found this in my tree. It is one of Estelle's unanswered prayers." Stunned, Morty can only stare at the small figure before him.

Jojo takes Morty by the hand and leads him back to his chair. "She asked for someone who would take care with you. She knew you would be lonely," Jojo says, gently pushing Morty into the chair and climbing into his lap, arms encircling Morty's neck. "I'm here to cry with you." It is a benediction.

Words are magic and writers are wizards.

THE RAG MAN

IT ALL STARTED WHEN Petey Peterson was sent to the principal's office. Seems he led a revolt in the elementary school cafeteria during first lunch period. And, well, if it wasn't nipped in the bud, the rest of the lunch periods might be full blown anarchy. Mr. Christopher, the principal, listened to the lunch ladies pour opprobrium on this unlikely 11-year-old reprobate. Petey, for his part, sat quietly with a faint smile playing across his lips. "We have rules! And there's a purpose for these rules. Children have to know that they have to take responsibility for their actions."

Mr. Christopher sighed, before interrupting, "What exactly did Mr. Peterson do?" Mrs. Kowalski drew in a big breath: "He tried to help Meghan Fields get a lunch. Her family is in arrears for $26 on her lunch account. Rules are rules, Mr. Christopher. If we let one child get away with it . . . " The principal matched the lunch lady's deep breath and raised her one, blowing it out through pursed lips. "What did he do exactly?" "He tried to give her his lunch. That's not the way this works, as you well know. Then, when we stopped him, he dropped his tray on the floor. Right in front of me!" One hand on her hip, she continued, "Then the other children stood up, marched over, and one by one, one hundred and fifteen of them, mind you, dropped their trays of food on the floor. Every last one of them!" The harried man turned to Petey, who was still calmly smiling. "What do you have to say for yourself, Petey?" Petey gave a shrug. "She was hungry. If she doesn't eat, none of us eat. The rag man said, Be Bold. And Be Brave."

Next up was Carla Whitehead, a third grader with a beautiful smile, and a soft voice. Carla disappeared during an active shooter drill. One minute she, along with everyone else, was scrambling to get hunkered down in the closets, being perfectly still under the desks, or cowering beneath the bleachers in the gym. The next moment she was gone. Nowhere to be found. Teachers and administrators were frantic. Distraught parents besieging the principal's office. Scary and solemn police officers turning the school upside down.

While the children gathered in the gym and held hands, the superintendent tried to calm the parents' fears. "She's only a child," exclaimed a mom. "How could you let this happen?" "If you can't keep even one little girl safe," shouted an angry father, "maybe we should just keep our kids home." As the police were radioing headquarters for more help, the front door opened. In walked Carla, smiling beautifully, as she spoke softly to the teenage boy all dressed in black, who held her by one hand. In his other he held a big backpack. Carla stopped in front of Mr. Christopher, who was beside himself. "What do you have to say for yourself, Carla?" She smiled and said in that soft voice, "He was scared. If he's scared, we're all scared. The rag man said, Be Bold. And Be Brave."

Things were getting back to normal when Miss Rush, a kindergarten teacher, showed up at the principal's door. "Mr. Christopher, you're going to want to see this." The intrepid principal grabbed a couple of aspirins and followed her out to the playground. All the school children were outside. But instead of laughter and shrieks and squabbles, the playground was silent. Completely and utterly silent. As if on an unspoken command the children separated themselves into two groups on opposite sides of the playground. With a minimum of noise, the two groups lined up facing each other, one group in the sun, the other group in the shade.

A fifth grader stepped out of line and, using a big, pointed stick, drew a line right down the middle between the two groups. Petey and Carla stepped away from the group in the sun and approached the line. When they reached the makeshift border they stopped. And lay down in the dirt. Petey put his arm protectively around Carla's shoulder, as though shielding the small child, holding her close, while swimming a river of desperation. If you simply glanced at the, one might mistake them for a pile of discarded rags. A first grader in the sun group spoke up, "They were seeking a home." A fourth grader from the shade group said, "If they don't have a home, none of us has a home."

And the Rag Man said, "Be Bold. And Be Brave."

Words are magic and writers are wizards.

I WILL BE THE WIND

AIMEE THE PROPHET DROVE around in a big Crown Victoria, an old police cruiser that still had the searchlight mounted outside the driver's window and the nudge bars on the front bumper. She was particularly fond of a McDonald's breakfast sandwich, the McGriddle with bacon, egg and cheese sandwiched between two syrup infused pancakes, as evidenced by the countless wrappers that littered the front seat. The back seat was stacked high with cheap paperback books, everything from Zane Grey to Agatha Christie to Eugenia Price to James Patterson's latest attempt to appear relevant. And every February and March, if you were lucky enough to be around when she opened the trunk, you would find it absolutely stuffed with Girl Scout cookies. Aimee the Prophet called them "food for the angels" and she spent her days looking for the angels who were "flagging in their efforts or thinking of falling." The work of a prophet is ill-defined at best.

What made Aimee a prophet was the old GI Joe walkie talkie mounted on the dashboard, a 1984 mobile field unit, tightly bound to the dashboard with an acre of gray duct tape. Every so often, on any given day, it would crackle to life with the callsign "This is Sunrise. Come in. Over and out." And Aimee the Prophet would take the mouthpiece and respond, "I will be the Wind. Go ahead, Sunrise. Over and out." She claimed that this is how she received her instructions on where next to patrol and find those who needed to know about Sunrise and the message from Sunrise particularly for them, and them alone. About remaining to be angels who don't give up hope or encouraging those getting close to taking The Fall. Such is the work of a prophet.

Needless to say, Aimee the Prophet had her detractors. Perhaps it was the car, maybe it was the way she looked. It's not every day that you see a 68-year-old five-foot and one-half inch figure getting out of an old Crown Vic, dressed head to toe in a crimson and burgundy organdy pantsuit, separated by a broad traffic-cone-orange sash, an oversized Smokey Bear hat on her head with overdyed jet-black hair stuffed up underneath the brim. On her feet she wore a pair of mottled green crocs over white tube socks. And to complete the ensemble, she had an official Star Wars plastic lightsaber thrust into the sash. Most people laughed at her, but Aimee the Prophet was undeterred. She answered only to Sunrise, the voice on the walkie talkie.

It was Valentine's Day when Aimee the Prophet got the fateful call. She had just paid at the drive thru for her two McGriddle sandwiches and soft drink breakfast when the GI Joe walkie talkie scratched to life. The McDonald's worker, 17-year-old Esther, said that she heard the call. "A voice said, 'this is Sunrise. Are you ready?' And the lady in the messy car and loud clothes said, 'I will be the wind. Over and out.' And I thought, that's weird. Use your cellphone, for Pete's sake! I missed the rest of it because the lady drove off, without her change, so my drawer didn't balance, which is so unfair!" The rest of the story is pieced together from eyewitness accounts and the report by the state police.

Guy Frommes at the gas station picked up the tale. "A car came in for gas. Guy was acting real suspicious like. In a hurry. I thought I heard a noise in the trunk but didn't think nothin' of it. He kept telling me to hurry up and all. Then when I was putting the hose back on the pump, I seen this little Valentine card come sliding out from under the trunk lid. You know, like those kind kids give out in school. So, I went to ask the guy what's up? But he peeled out and took off. I yelled to Earl to call the cops. But before he could, this old cop car comes busting past, with a little lady in a Smokey Bear hat shaking her fist and blinking the search light like a maniac! Never seen nothing like it!"

Corporal Roger Peters of the State Patrol picks up the story in his report. "I arrived on scene on the bridge over Peace River on route 68. It appears that the Crown Vic pushed the suspect's vehicle into the railing with the nudge bar, springing the trunk and freeing Freddie Banks, the 10-year-old victim. Suspect was discovered tied to the railing with a plastic lightsaber and some kind of orange sash. I tried to locate the driver of the Crown Vic but was unable to do so. I did locate a green croc shoe at the west side of the bridge, but I found no other evidence of what happened to the driver."

Freddie Banks completes the tale. "After the car wrecked, I jumped out. I saw the little lady in red going for the bad guy, but I wasn't scared. Next thing I know, he's all tied up and she's giving me this old hat." He touches the brim of the big Smokey Bear and continues, "Then she whispered in my ear and started walking. Next time I looked, she was gone." He shrugged. "Trooper Peters ripped that GI Joe thing off the dashboard and showed it to me. Some old toy, I guess. When he turned it over, I could see it didn't even have batteries in it." His eyes get a funny look in them. "But then it made a weird noise and a voice said, 'This is Sunrise. Is anybody there?'" Freddie smiled. "I knew what to do. I took the microphone and pushed the button and said, 'I will be the Wind. Over and out.'"

Words are magic and writers are wizards.

THE CONTEST

The Cathedral Church of Saint Peter and Saint Paul in the City and Diocese of Washington, commonly known as Washington National Cathedral, has hundreds of stained-glass windows, Gothic spires, and flying buttresses, along with a few other odds and ends that serve to make it look mighty important, even anciently so, one might say. Situated in Mount Saint Alban, off Wisconsin Avenue, in the Northwest quadrant of the District of Columbia it is the site of events of national importance such as funerals for presidents, and other such oddities. A lot less well known was the first attempt at a National Interdenominational Theological Preaching Invitational Contest, or NITPIC for short. Everything was all set: famous preachers from near and far invited, rules of conduct and concourse set, tickets sold to raise prize money (no television preachers permitted, thank you very much!) and only the most distinguished Bishops, Senior Pastors and Senators, Seminary Professors, District Superintendents, President of the Southern Baptists, other Holy Rulers, and of course, Executive Presbyters, served as judges . . . with the Dean of the Cathedral in charge, naturally.

The great weekend of the NITPIC arrived and attracted great crowds. All day, Saturday and Sunday great throngs heard great preachers. All sorts of great exposition, dispositions, prepositions, theological positions, syllogisms, and exegetical propositions were expounded. And some stories were told. Everyone likes good, handy illustrations, after all. Finally, the hour for announcing a winner of the $150,000 prize, along with publication of the winning sermon and picture of the winning preacher in USA Today, drew near. The judges were huddling when the Dean received a text message: 'One more. Rag man.' He climbed the circular stairs to the NITPIC pulpit high above the crowd and asked, "One more?" Then, hesitantly, face scrunched up, "Rag man?" Far in the back of the National Cathedral a figure pushed through the gathered people, an older woman who began limping down the center aisle. Her white hair escaped in all directions, her chin was stained brown with snuff juice, her mismatched clothes covered by an old Army surplus great coat, and on her feet a pair of gold-colored high-top Air Jordans with the big toes cut out because of her bunions. "Git outta my way, Sonny!" she belched at the acolyte who greeted her at the front.

She creaked up the stairs and settled in behind the pulpit. "Rag man said to tell y'all about my Daddy. My Daddy was a grocer. Fine store outside of Mobile. Known all over for his produce. Lots of fresh fruits and vegetables. He'd set them all out under them bright lights in the cases: apples, oranges, lemons, lettuce-4 kinds, mind ya'-beans from all over tarnation, and so forth." She paused, dug into a pocket of the great coat, took out a can of snuff and proceeded to tuck some back between her cheek and gum. "Where was I? Oh yeah, Daddy would say to me, 'Sibby, lookee here at all these perishables. All colors, all sizes, all different strains, and varieties.' Then Daddy would reach over and push the button for the sprayer. And all them perishables would look clean and shiny from the water on 'em. And he'd say, 'Sibby, them perishables ain't gonna last much longer, no matter how good they look. I can spray 'em, wash 'em, dunk 'em, sprinkle 'em. But if no one takes them home and eats them, what good are they? They'll sit here and rot, nevertheless. If nobody wants 'em . . . well, they're just compost. Or pig slop.'"

She stopped, sucked hard on her lip, leaned over the side of the pulpit, and spat a stream of tobacco juice onto the sacred ground far below. A moan of disgust went up from the gathered. Sibby looked out over the crowd and shrugged. "I ain't no preacher. Never said I was. The rag man asked me to tell you a damn story and now I done told it. It's just fruits and vegetables, but rag man, well he's funny that way about perishables." Another stream of juice splattered the marble floor. "Fat lot of good it did Daddy, though. When his store burned down, them sprayers didn't save him."

She turned and started down the steps. Halfway down she stopped, turned back. She was slightly out of breath when she spoke again. "Maybe . . . .maybe," and here she looked down at all the gathered princes and popes of the kingdom, "what you need up here is a sprayer button. Y'all could push it when you needed, and all them perishables out there would look shiny and clean. Useful like." She sucked hard on the stash in her cheek. "The rag man says, if by this time tomorrow, everyone of ya', if you ain't poor, or homeless, or hurtin' or broken . . . ." And Sibby shrugged, "or if you ain't on the way to befriendin' someone who is . . . " and she fixed her eyes on the gathered contestants and sighed. "Then all you're adoin' is makin' compost. Or, as Daddy would say, pig slop. And the world already done got enough of that." Another spit. "Amen, y'all."

The National Cathedral has never been the same since. And the first annual NITPIC was the last one.

Words are magic, and writers are wizards.

THE LAST OUT

The summer after my first year of seminary I was hired to be the chaplain of a state park camping ground. The first year of seminary is like any first year of graduate level training and education: a testing time, a weeding out of who can handle the subject matter, the demands of the workload where a 'C' is a question mark hovering over failure, the personalities of the professors and fellow students, along with the infernal internal struggle of what the hell am I doing here? A summer spent enjoying the easy-going atmosphere of Pymatuning Lake in northwest Pennsylvania seemed like just the ticket. My wife and I packed up the fire engine red 1969 Pontiac LeMans SE with the wide tires and powerful V8 engine, 0 to 60 in just . . . sorry, I need a moment . . . where was I?. . . with clothes, and two bikes on a bike rack clinging to the rear bumper and headed off into the summer, Presbyterian polity and the exegetics of the Book of Judges be damned.

One part of the time I eagerly anticipated was being a member of the park's softball team in the local church league. In the old trailer with the broken windows sitting in the middle of a field that we called home, I put on my bright yellow Pymatuning Carp tee shirt and green cap, jumped into Wonder Car, and headed off to play, my well-worn fielder's glove in the seat next to me. My fellow teammates were college aged laborers doing park maintenance for the summer who considered Seminary Guy with some skepticism. In a land of cornfields, ice cream socials and softball for the summer, the regulation ballfields were scattered around the countryside. My highlights included a most satisfying line drive over the centerfielder's head that rolled all the way to the lakeside, blocking the plate as the catcher with a runner trying to score, and playing a decent first base.

But this isn't a story of highlights. It's a story of Steve Blass syndrome. Steve Blass was a major league pitcher, a good one, for the Pittsburgh Pirates, who inexplicably lost his ability to get the ball over the plate. It just happened. Nothing helped to correct it. The Pymatuning Carp made it to the championship game for the summer. Our coach put me in left field. I inexplicably lost my ability to judge a fly ball. It simply evaporated. I could see the ball come off the bat, but I could not judge where it was going to land. Pretty soon every batter was trying to hit the ball to left field. Because Seminary Guy wasn't catching anything. Nothing. Nada. They flew over my head, dropped in front of me, skipped past me. Center fielder college kid started shading toward me, trying to help me out. Nothing helped. I finally begged the coach to take me out of the game. "Seminary Guy," he said, "I'm not going to do that. When you want to be in the game, you play until the last out. You played hard all summer. Now play through the last out."

Someone whom I care about, a lot, and respect, a lot, used to be a Special Education teacher who worked with the most difficult and impossible cases. Children with profound ailments, physical and intellectual disabilities grouped in classrooms in public schools. One of her students was a young boy of six. His mother was in active drug addiction during her pregnancy. After he was born, both his mother and grandmother tried to actively harm him, resulting in irreversible brain trauma. His life was hopelessly horrible. Undeterred, this teacher worked with him every day. Other teachers questioned putting in much effort or treating him beyond infantilizing him. She persisted in working toward the drawing out of a grunt of recognition or the grace of a smile. She read real books to him like Treasure Island and the Narnia stories. And quite often, she confessed, she would come home and simply sit and cry. At all the loss in this child's life. All the hopeless horribleness. At what would make two women who were entrusted with his care want to make him go away. Then, the next day, she would get up and go right back to it. To play through the last out.

She is very much a non-believer in the matters of Biblical faith. But she has been around the church for a great deal of her life. I told her about the latest Presbyterian controversy, some seminary students being angry about their ordination exam covering a passage from Judges about the hopeless horribleness that can happen in life. That it triggered some previous trauma responses in them, and they want an apology for the exam being insensitive to their trauma. She was incredulous. "Is it in your book? The Bible?" I told her it is. She thought for a while. "They want to be ministers but they made this about themselves and their trauma. It got hard, or uncomfortable, and the wannabe ministers said don't make us deal with this?" I said that was one way to look at it. She thought long and hard. "What if the man who did those horrible things was in prison? Would they go minister to him, the traumatizer? The thief, the killer? The child abuser? Isn't that where the church is supposed to be, too?"

I honestly don't know. Playing through the last out may not be the church's way. Then again . . .

Words are magic and writers are wizards.

MILEPOST 62

It is just a road. Appears over there and goes beyond over in the other direction. Each mile is marked by a milepost. This is the story of milepost 62. It was driven into the ground some eighty-eight years ago, and still it stands. A silent witness to the passing of time, weather, seasons, some livestock, and of course vehicles. Vehicles with people inside of them. And with people come stories. Which is where a storyteller comes in . . .

A small sports car pulls off the road at milepost 62. GPS is a dream of some science fiction writers and Popular Mechanics 'in the future' enthusiasts. A young man slumps back against the driver's seat and scratches his head, checks his watch. Discharged from the Navy, he put his savings into this roadster convertible. After all, you only live once. She wrote to him once a week during his deployment. He wrote back maybe once a month. She was attending the university in the big city, out on the town with her friends when they met. He saw her and asked her to dance. She had big dreams and he just wanted to know what it would be like to kiss her. In the week before he shipped out, they spent as much time together as they could. He is back and she now lives in a small town. He hasn't heard from her for a month. He pulls out a map and traces a route with his finger, checking the return address on her last letter one more time. Hopefully she likes surprises because he is back early. Hopefully there is still hope. He crushes the map onto the seat next to him, guns the engine, and takes off.

The minivan arrives at the side of the road with a lurch, dark smoke, and a distress call. "Mommy, I gotta go peeeee!!!" A harried woman hurries out of the driver's side, rushes around to the side door and tugs it open. The car seats in the back hold different aged progeny. The five-year-old girl with red hair has already unfastened herself and slides down with a pout of exasperation. "Now what? You don't expect me to just do it?!" The mother sighs and grabs the plastic potty chair off the pile of laundry and toys in the back and sets it beside the milepost. "Daddy would never make me go out here like this." Her four-year-old brother contributes, "He'd tell you to hold it and give you candy if you did." Mom sighs again and points to the potty chair. "Well, Daddy is not here right now, so either go now or sit in wet clothes all the way home." The red-haired girl finally obliges with a last, defiant, "Daddy wouldn't take this road anyway." Mom takes a long longing look back in the direction she just came. Hopefully there is still hope. Empties the plastic chair, and in a cloud of burning oil, they resume the journey.

The shiny new coupe rolls to a stop just beyond the milepost. It is night. The woman behind the wheel sits rigidly, knuckles turning white on the steering wheel. She blinks slowly. Once. Twice. With a jerk on the handle, she is out of the car, bent over gasping. Of course, the lying bastard bought her a new car. He felt guilty. She stumbles to the front of the car, leans hard against it and stares up at the stars. With the rising bile of betrayal and fear, she screams at the top of her lungs the penitent's most honest petition: "Goddamnit! Goddamnit! Why? Why me?! TELLLL MEEEE, PLEASE . . . please." She crumples to a heap on the dirt and stones, unmindful of them as her tears flow unimpeded in great wrenching sobs. Finally, she rouses herself. What happens to hope? Who steals it away, she wonders, before getting back in and slowly driving away into the night.

The coupe is several years older, a bit worse for wear. The two teenagers in the car are listening to music when they pull over in front of milepost 62. "Hey, this looks familiar," says the girl with the red hair. "I think Mom used to bring us this way," says the boy. "Well, Dad was no big help," says the girl. "I think he's trying," says her brother. "Hopefully there's hope for them yet." The girl laughs. "You're such an optimist, you little dweeb!" They sit for a moment in the glory of youth. "Oh, turn it up," says the girl. "This is my song . . . " He pumps it up and without looking, pulls back onto the road . . .

The police cruiser, lights flashing, pulls up. The officer checks the milepost and notes it for his report. Keys his mike, "I'm at the scene. Milepost 62. Fire and rescue are out here but it looks like there's two DOA. Kids." Sighs. "About the ages of my two." A fireman comes from the burning wreckage and hands him two wallets. He pulls out the id, notes the ages and address. Brother and sister. Damn. Keys the mike. "I'm going to make the notification now." He turns off his flashing lights, pulls around the accident and heads back the way he came.

The old pickup wheezes to a stop. The old couple look tired, worn, and weary. The man says, "I stopped here on my way to find you again." "That's a long time ago," the woman says and then falls silent, her eyes fixed on the milepost. "Is there hope?" she whispers. He gives her hand a squeeze, climbs out and limps over to her door. He opens it and helps her out of the truck. "Maybe that's up to us," he offers as he leads her past the milepost and the two battered, decaying crosses and into the field of wildflowers beyond. After about thirty yards they stop and help each other to the ground. They lie back and, together, they watch the sky . . .

Words are magic and writers are wizards.

THE BROTHERS CARAMEL-SLAW

When Joshua Slaw married Frieda Caramel the struggle for equal rights for women in the 1960s was gaining deserved momentum and they proudly joined their surnames together as a show of solidarity and a surfeit of simple love. Eventually they bought a nice home along Route 220 between Greensboro, NC and Martinsville, VA. They raised their two boys, Simon, and Jacque, amidst the rolling green hills dotted with truck and tobacco farms, textile mills and furniture factories that claimed the small towns nestled in the privacy and, at times, privations of a world that changed, through no fault of their own, where it made and grew such things. Decisionmakers at the top of large companies and national governments chased cheaper labor and easier profits, no prisoners taken, and Joshua, Frieda, Simon, and Jacque were caught in the backwash, as were so many folks.

Now, Simon turned out to be a tough son of a gun, a Supreme Realist and Businessman. Jacque, on the other hand, aspired to live in the Way of Faith and Nurture. Well, Joshua and Frieda were of the age, in the time of the Great Virus, that they were sacrificed on the altar of those paragons of politics, fear and greed. When their will was read, it was discovered that both sons inherited the house along Route 220. Their parents expressed the belief that the brothers Caramel-Slaw could share it or find those that could benefit from its safety and comfort. Now, it also turns out, that both men were in love with a local woman of inestimable beauty, one Miss Sybil Fremont. Miss Sybil's father owned the largest car dealership in four counties and was president of the biggest church. Oh, and he was quite the drinker and philanderer, which is as good of a place as any to make my apologies to Fedor Dostoyevsky.

Their love for the same woman drove quite a wedge between the brothers Caramel-Slaw, so much so that they could no longer stand to be in the same room with one another. So, they divided the house in half and went their separate ways. They had two separate front doors, two separate kitchens, two separate front porches with awnings, and a wall built right through the middle to keep the other out, or in, depending on which side you were on. Simon worked his way up to being head salesman at Miss Sybil Fremont father's car dealership and Jacque became head pastor at the church where Miss Sybil Fremont's father was president. Both men wooed and courted Miss Sybil, but in the time of the Great Virus people were not buying cars nor going to church. Each of them sat in their half of the house pining for Miss Sybil, plotting and planning ways to persuade Miss Sybil Fremont's father to influence her decision.

Late one night, there was a knock at Simon's door. When he opened the door, Simon saw Miss Sybil standing there, holding the hand of a frightened young woman who appeared to be of Cherokee descent. "Simon," she said with a toss of her hair. "This is one of my father's many daughters. She has no home, and her life is in danger. Can you take her in?" Simon was skeptical. "One of many? Why doesn't he take care of her?" Sybil stepped inside. "My father is away getting financing for his new meat packing plant. She needs food and shelter." Simon scratched his head. "Will your father reward me? I don't have any spare masks. And besides, I can't get sick. Your father has promised to make me CEO of the new plant and our future will be brighter, Miss Sybil. There must be somebody else." And Miss Sybil and the girl from the Cherokee tribe departed into the night.

Another night, late, there was a knock at Jacque's door. When he opened the door, wearing his mask of course, Jacque saw Miss Sybil standing there holding the hand of a strong, somber Mexican young man. "Jacque," she said with a coy smile. "This is one of my father's many sons. He has no home, and his family is being held in detention. But my father needs him to work in his new meat packing plant so that the food supply chain is continued, and the economy doesn't crash." Jacque scratched his head. "One of many? That doesn't sound good, Miss Sybil. What would people think if they knew?" Miss Sybil stepped inside. "Jacque, my father needs to keep his business going. People are depending on it." Jacque shifted his feet. "Will your father build a new wing for the church? He could stay in there. I've got to go make some zoom calls to my members so they will welcome us, Miss Sybil." And Miss Sybil and the man from Mexico departed into the night.

Still later, at night of course, the brothers Caramel-Slaw were in their divided home and a great rush of roaring engines and screaming sirens enveloped the house. The brothers Caramel-Slaw threw open their separate doors. Prison buses and transport ambulances from nursing homes circled the building. Miss Sybil Fremont's father watched from his limo, wearing a mask that said Make Humanity Humble Again. When the sun rose, the house was gone. All that remained was a door, set in the wall the brothers Caramel-Slaw had built. With an ancient lock. If you want the key, you'll have to find the lovely Miss Sybil Fremont . . .

Words are magic, and writers are wizards.

THE MIDDLE OF NOWHERE

I was awakened by a dream.

She is standing under a fire-spray of fall leaves. Beside a two-lane road that bends west in the distance. She teeters on six-inch platform shoes and her auburn hair reaches halfway down her back. I shoo the dogs into the back as she climbs into my pickup. "You humans fascinate me," she says in a drawl that is pure Alabama. I turn down the radio where Little Big Town are singing "The Daughters." "Excuse me?" I sputter. "Hiya." She thrusts perfectly manicured French nails toward me. "I'm Terralessa." I shake her hand. "Jack. Jack Goo."

I lost my religion and found faith.

"Where ya headed, Jack?" She flings her hair back with a flourish. "Just driving," I mutter. "It don't make no nevermind, darlin'," she peers at me from beneath too long lashes. "You go where you gotta go." I downshift in silence, too fast, gears grind. In the back, Pepper, an Australian sheep mix, lets out a howl. "Shut up!" I holler. Terralessa throws me a frown, turns around, makes a soft clucking sound to the dog. "Don't you listen to him, Sweetie. Let it rip!" She looks around the extended cab F150. "Real nice. Real nice. You thirsty?" Before I can answer she hauls up a huge handbag and plumbs its depths. She comes up with a can of Coke, the real thing. Delicately pops the top, careful with her nails. Extends it toward me. "Here. Take this. Drink." I cast a baleful eye. She bats her lashes, pushes the can toward me. "C'mon. Take. Drink. All of it."

I decided not to choose between fire and ice.

"So, what did you mean?" I ask after a mile or two. Her perfume is some strange, intoxicating heather in a high mountain meadow. "Wait, turn it up. I love this part," her voice commands like a crisp fall breeze. I look at the radio. This is strange. It's still playing the same song. I turn it up. She sings along. "I've heard about God the son and God the Father. I'm just looking for a God for the daughters, I'm just looking for a God for the daughters." As she rummages around in that enormous bag, lips pursed, she asks, "Mean about what, Darlin'?" "Us humans . . . " I begin, but she interrupts. "Ah, found it!" Holds up a half-eaten Hershey bar. "Here. Take. Eat. All of it."

I closed one door to open my heart.

"I don't want your candy." She sighs. "Well, I brought it for you. I can't, well, give it to the dogs, now can I? That wouldn't do a body right, now would it? Go on, it's yours." She breaks off a piece, wiggles it between my lips. The sweetest of sensations. "You people fascinate me. That what you're askin'?" I nod, tasting the smoothness on my tongue. "It's a line from a movie, Sweetheart. All that learnin' but you got no sense." She arches her carefully plucked eyebrows. Watches me, a small Mona Lisa smile on her lips. "Jack Goo. I know you." Giggles at this rhyme.

The afternoon sun is causing problems on the smeary windshield, making me squint to see. "Terralessa. That's an unusual name." I slow down as the road curves toward the mountains. She gives a playful shrug. "I'm an unusual kinda girl." She pops the door and is gone. I stand on the brakes. The dogs howl. The tires smoke. I throw it in reverse. Back up. Jump out.

Nothing. No one is there. The wind ruffles the leaves. The dogs fall silent. I look around. I'm in the middle of nowhere. Slowly, I return to the truck. There is no song playing now. But on the console sits a half-eaten Hershey bar. In the cup holder is a half empty can of Coke. The real thing. And I will remember. Her. Always.

Words are magic, and writers are wizards.

COTTONHEART

Cottonheart started every day the same: two biscuits with apple butter. Except the Lord's Day. Then she added fatback and grits just to keep it special. Cottonheart was all about finding the special. Those passing by her shack at the edge of the fields saw only what they wanted to see. What they didn't know was that for Cottonheart, on the inside, and always on the inside, was where she made a home. Mama named her Cottonheart, she said, because she knew her girl had a heart that could not be easily broken, soft but courageous. Cottonheart prayed every night to the Good Lord for a man who would come along and make her feel that way, that when they were together, wherever that happened to be, it was home. Being with him would be home. Until then, she had everything she needed.

Six days a week she worked hard, sunrise to sunset, following her nimble fingers as they pulled cloth through the big machines, stitching together clothes she could never afford. Dreams can be expensive while hope can arrive on a breeze. She tried to get through town before dark each night because there was danger all about, and she had to walk alone. More than once as she wound her way through the Settlement section of town she had to skirt around mobs of people, gathered around a burning cross, its flames sending the heat of hate towards heaven. All she wanted was to reach her home, rinse out her dress for tomorrow, eat a simple meal, then pass the time reading her Bible. She liked the stories of Ruth, along with the one about baby Moses in the bullrushes, and the one about Jesus and the woman at the well.

Cottonheart loved her church home. On Sundays, she walked the few miles to the church, back under the dogwoods, for a daylong marathon of preachin' and prayin,' eatin' and singin,' may the Good Lord's name be praised and lifted up, our One True Hope! Drenched in the pure sweat of being slain in the Spirit, the good folks gathered outside for dinner in the midafternoon. Cold drinks, fried chicken, ribs, potato salad, sweet potato pie—a true feast of the Kingdom. And among them all, a shared grief, a burden none could lift alone, other than the beseeching of their voices in song to be delivered from a fate thrust upon them, mixed with the hope of angels that could make the very stars weep and the trees catch their tears, forever nourishing the roots of a land that only grudgingly offered them lodging, rather than a true home.

Cottonheart saved what little money she could so that one day she could get a record player. People were talking about Chuck Berry and his new music, and she knew that would surely brighten her home. She grew distracted by this plan, trying to figure how much more she needed to save one night as she was walking home. The car was upon her before she had a chance to run. Three white boys pulled her inside . . . and when they were finished with her, they dumped her out down near the river. She dragged herself home, and even went to work the next morning. Without being able to eat her two biscuits. She felt broken inside. Then one day not long after, she realized that she was pregnant.

Cottonheart sat alone in her home after work for days and days, not sure what to do. Finally, she summoned Miss Gracie, the midwife from the Settlement. Miss Gracie told Cottonheart what to do and what to expect. The foreman at the factory started to give her more and more work, always threatening to fire her for having the nerve to get pregnant. He called her slow and awkward, just like "the rest of you people" except he didn't put it in so many words. It only takes one. Cottonheart was terrified she would lose her job, and then her home. Finally, the time came for the baby to be delivered. Cottonheart strained and struggled as Miss Gracie guided the birthing. She presented a squalling little boy and asked her about a name. "Jesus," said Cottonheart, "his name is Jesus Moses Cottonheart."

Cottonheart loved her son dearly. But his heart was not strong. And one night in his sleep, Jesus Moses Cottonheart slipped away at the age of one month. A shattered Cottonheart, gathered up all the money she had saved for the record player and Chuck Berry records in order to buy a small coffin in which to bury her son. The Settlement folks all gathered at the church under the dogwoods to say farewell to little Jesus Moses Cottonheart. For some reason, grief is often rewarded with more grief. And it can serve to be too much.

The next morning, Cottonheart started the day with two biscuits with apple butter. Then she carefully locked the door to her beloved home. She walked to the banks of the river and kept walking. Into the darkness and the bullrushes . . . wondering if there would ever be a pharaoh's daughter to give her a home.

Words are magic and writers are wizards.

BRACHIATE OR BREAK

I WAS BRACHIATING WHEN I broke my first bone. Five years old, midweek of the annual family vacation at Camp Lambec on the shores of Lake Erie, first grade awaiting as soon as we got home, I was eagerly demonstrating my new skill. Okay, okay, maybe a little bit of showing off. Monkey bars were a challenge to me. Up the ladder, brachiate across, get your feet on the rungs of the ladder on the other side, dismount. Thunderous applause. Simple and elegant. In my imagination. Reality was an altogether different animal.

I was fine getting up the ladder, reaching out and grabbing the first bar or rung, letting my feet drop and swinging hard by my arms to get across the distance. No problem. Kick your feet for momentum, reach for the next rung, grab it. Rinse and repeat. Until I reached the other side. Dismounting meant swinging my feet to latch onto the top rung of the ladder, then swinging out on arm strength alone to grab the bar at the top and climb down. It was a complicated maneuver for this particular five-year-old. So, I came up with a shortcut. When I reached the last rung of the horizontal brachiating, I would simply let go. In my heart of hearts, I blame Dan and Sue, my siblings a year on either side, for not teaching me better. I needed to practice until I learned the proper technique. But it was so much easier just to let go and drop.

We had just left the dining hall after supper one evening. The grounds were big, beautiful, and safe. All seven Tuftmuffins could play to our hearts' content, safe in the knowledge that we were not the only preacher's kids there, so no big magnifying glass was on us. Again, let me point out that Dan and Sue were not around at that moment and need to be held accountable. I was walking with my father and begged him to stop and watch me do the monkey bars. Up I climbed and out onto the brachiating part. Hand over hand I proudly swung. All of a sudden I was at the end. Time to dismount. Dad was walking away, telling me to get a move on, it was time to get back to the cabin. Probably for a bath. All of a sudden, when I looked down, the ground seemed very far away. The ladder was right in front of me. But I didn't have the confidence. I hadn't done the necessary to accomplish a new ordinary. I let go and dropped. And landed on my right arm.

My father heard my howls and quickly came back to the play area. Old Doc McLaren was summoned. He fashioned a splint from two boards and cotton batting. My father carried me in his arms into the back seat of a friend's car for the ride into Erie to the emergency room. My mother stayed back at camp with the rest of the Tuftmuffins. The next morning, I returned to the camp with a new, white plaster cast encasing my arm. Dan and Sue were wracked with guilt, bringing me Hawaiian Punch and s'mores on demand. At least, that's the way it should have been. At the start of first grade, I learned to print my letters with my left hand. Which meant I learned to be a terrific switch hitter. Okay, that really happened later, but let me have my five-year-old moment.

Fast forward to early summer when I was right out of fourth grade. It was the Thursday evening before the last day of Vacation Bible School and its excruciating closing program in front of all the teachers and parents. In that strange foreign land known as the United Methodist Church. The Tuftmuffins who had any sense were in the backyard taking on the neighborhood in wiffle ball. Cutthroat wiffle ball. Sue and Dan were present and accounted for. Bases are loaded. It is my turn to bat. Our dugout was my mother's flower beds around the crab apple tree. Visions of glory and going down in the Hall of Fame of wiffle ball danced in my head as I copied the big leaguers, swinging the bat to get ready for my turn. My mother had erected a low, white wire fence around her flower beds in hopes, I suppose, that her Tuftmuffins would respect it. Needless to say, it didn't work.

"Jack, it's your turn. Get in there and hit it!" My summons to fame and glory. I'm tempted to say that one of my older brothers, Alan or Paul, was the one yelling at me, but alas, there were no cell phones, and the moment is lost to history. I casually hopped the fence and hit the ball out of the park. Except . . . except my foot caught on the top of the fence and I crashed to the ground with a strange buzzing in my left elbow. I never even got to bat! The heart of the summer lost to another broken bone. But this time, Dan and Sue did sign my cast. And I did miss the final program of VBS.

My parents and Sue are gone now. The rest of the Tuftmuffins are gray and potbellied. I managed to add a broken leg to my CV. My brachiating days are long gone. But I still catch myself, at times, wondering what's the harm in not learning the right steps to doing something properly. Then I remember the number of times I'm asked, "How do I become a writer?" And the almost universal disappointment in my answer, "Go sit your butt in the chair and write. Show it to someone who doesn't care if you think that it's good and write it again. Rinse, repeat." It's what Dan and Sue would appreciate.

Words are magic and writers are wizards.

BOOG: SEMPER FI

He comes in every Friday like clockwork, at 1205 sharp, for his lunch. And every Friday it is the same thing: cheesy grits and shrimp. Mind you now, the grits have to be stone-ground, and only stone ground. Just like on Mondays when he comes in at 0700 for oatmeal, and only steel cut oatmeal. A body does have its standards, ya hear? Boog is very particular about those sorts of things. Lights out at 2230, lights on at 0500, thank you very much. Hoo Rah! A large, shallow bowl of stone ground grits smothered with melted cheddar and shrimp cooked just right with oregano, paprika, onions and garlic. Just like momma's and momma's been gone twenty years now. After serving ten years in the US Marine Corps, seeing action in Desert Storm and Somalia, with a loud and proud eagle and furls tattoo on his forearm, salt and pepper hair close cropped, Boog is pushing fifty but his eyes stare into forever. And his heart never stops aching.

It's always been about coming home. Desert Storm: big victory. Somalia: nobody remembers. Desert Storm: yellow ribbons. Somalia: body bags. Desert Storm: git 'er done. Somalia: get us out. You're a Marine. You go, you train, you do the job, accomplish the mission, keep your head down. Come home. Semper Fi. It ain't easy. Nobody said it would be. But God Almighty, Boog sometimes wonders, what was it all for? Now he puts on a uniform each day, that of a county EMT, climbs into the emergency vehicle and sets out into the mission to aid the suffering and abet the pain. It's right there on his name plate: BOOG, Semper Fi. Others tease him about displaying the motto, but to Boog it's no laughing matter. Plain as day. Plain as the tattoo. To remind him. Maybe someday he'll find a good woman, maybe kids, who knows. But he will never forget. It's not about him. Semper Fi is for the others. Always the others.

There's no night quite as black and bleak as a night in the desert. And there's a lot of black, bleak nights and a lot of deserts for marines in both Iraq and Somalia. Boog was nine years into a career when he deployed to

Desert Storm. Then detoured in 1992 to the Mog in Operation Restore Hope. Boog doesn't talk much about what he witnessed there: starvation, the violence, the abject cruelty all around him and his buddies. The Gunnery Sergeant and his recon platoon were sent into the stark desert country outside Mogadishu to exercise their skills. Back in Washington the mission changed; the Marines were sent home and the Army Rangers and Delta Force deployed. Except no one remembered Boog and his men, no accounting, and they were marooned in the desert.

The ship pulled out, returning the rest of the Marines home, as the Army moved in. Boog and his men waited for word in the hot sand, short on food and water, unwilling to believe there could ever be a violation of the Corps basic principle: Semper Fi. Always faithful. No man left behind. No choppers came. Radio silence. Boog cowboyed up and led his unit on the long, slow slog of a journey through the desert to the airport where they attached to the Rangers. Boog grows very still, his voice barely a whisper, as he describes the events immortalized in the book and film, Blackhawk Down. "It's all real. It's all too damn real." Then he looks away, staring deep into the ache. "It took a year to get back," he says. "We stayed attached to the Army and had to go with them. Rwanda happened in April of '94 and we were itching to go stop that genocide. We coulda done it. We were more than willing. What the hell else are we for? Nobody could tell me why to any of it."

He grows agitated, the words spitting out like gunfire. "I was going to put in my twenty. Honest to God, I was. But when we finally got back to California a year later, I marched into my CO's office and resigned on the spot. I was done. Finished. Sometimes I even think about getting my tattoo removed." He pauses, rubs his eyes. "Sometimes." He pushes his cheesy grits around for a moment. "But it ain't about me, now is it? I always told my Marines to watch their sixes. Know what's going on in front of you and behind you."

On any given Sunday, at 0800, you can find Boog at the same hill. It's not really much of a hill, more of a grassy slope alongside the highway. He's there in full dress, never mind the dirt. Trimming the grass, planting a few flowers, a bucket of white paint nearby. To use on the crosses. Scattered around the top. And straightening the flags. Of those from his county who have fallen. From wounds visible and invisible. The little church sits back a little ways. Watching their sixes. Semper Fi, Boog.

(Boog is not his real name, but the historical events described are real.)

Words are magic and writers are wizards.

OPHELIA

The path leads off the road, through the trees and into a small clearing where there sits a small house of weather-grayed boards with a red tin roof and the window casings painted in the same faded ruby rose. In front of the sagging porch is a garden of polymer: giant sunflowers, daisy pinwheels, and pink flamingoes on one spindly leg. Off to one side a giant Buick with fins from the 1950s sits on four cinderblocks, hood raised up as though drafting the yaw of an ancient dragon. A long dormant orchard crowds up close to an old shed and barn, with stacks of beaten apple crates of wired together slats leaning into the wind coming off the mountains to the west. Of course, there is a swing on the porch, and a collection of kitchen chairs in various degrees of disrepair and comfort. Over the screen door is a hand-lettered sign: **Welcome to Ophelia's**.

Jedidiah approaches the house with no small trepidation. Ophelia steps out the front door at the tremor in the air of approaching footsteps. She is the epitome of the words of Shakespeare: "Oh, when she is angry, she is keen and shrewd! She was a vixen when she went to school. And though she be but little, she is fierce." Raven hair streaked with gray, pulled back and tied with a pale blue ribbon, reaches nearly to her waist. She has the lines of experience of a proud woman at the edges of her expressive eyes and at the corners of her determined mouth. Praise does not spring easily to those lips, but the heart within is open and caring. Around her neck, a small pouch hangs from a leather thong, and a tiny silver feather dangles at the tie.

The two stare at each other for a moment of eternity. Jed's baggy work pants flap in the breeze, scattering small clouds of dust from the quarry as he slowly sinks to one knee, twisting a fisherman's cap in his hands. "Get up, you old fool," Ophelia admonishes. "It's been ten years, how long was I supposed to wait?" Jed is stricken dumb, and the labor of his years shows as he pulls himself erect. "Well, come up on the porch and sit a spell," Ophelia offers as she takes a seat on the swing. Jed pauses to look at the weary orchard awaiting someone to tend to it, prune it with prudence. Ophelia watches with narrowed eyes, pondering the preponderance of the evidence. Is this a midsummer night's dream, or a tired rerun of love's folly?

A mockingbird chatters excessively, invoking luck and charm from a nearby blueberry thicket. "Was it worth it?" asks Ophelia as Jed settles onto a chair with uneven legs so that he has to struggle for equilibrium. "You are a handsome woman," he offers. "Always was, always will be," she responds. Jed tries again. "The orchard needs some attention. Maybe it ain't too late." He looks hopeful and bashful all at once. Ophelia points to the sign over the door. "This is mine." Jed studies the sign for a long pause. "It also says welcome, woman." She sighs. "I'm doin' fine without you, Jedidiah. Do you want some sweet tea?" He draws in a deep breath, as though inhaling two lungs full of courage. "I love you, Ophelia."

"So, is that a no on the sweet tea?" Ophelia's eyes remain steady. Jedidiah is crestfallen. "A man's gotta try, Ophelia." She closes her eyes, breathing deeply of all the hopeful searches over the years. Ophelia opens her eyes and draws the leather tong from around her neck. She slowly opens the pouch and spills its contents into her hand. One hundred tiny shiny pebbles sparkle in the late afternoon sun. "I gather these from the creek. Hold out your hand," she commands the supplicant. He carefully obliges. Her hand hovers over his as she pauses.

"Love is 100 choices a day. Love is 100 decisions a day." She studies his face. "Love is 100 x 100 words and thoughts every day." The pebbles spill from her hand into his. "When you can fill this pouch today, and tomorrow, and tomorrow's tomorrow, you can ask for this feather." She smiled. "Now, do you want the sweet tea, or don't you?" And the breeze died to a whisper and the mockingbird stopped its chatter as she rose and stepped through the doorway where there is a sign overhead that reads: **Welcome to Ophelia's**.

AT FIRST LIGHT

THE ANCIENT OAK HUNKERS atop the hill, a perch that surveys a rumpled carpet of green meadows and distant smudges of patient orchards. It is twisted and gnarled, a testament to endurance and perseverance. It's been battered by storms, shaped by drought, and sculpted by the wind. Rain beats down upon it without mercy, yet it is nourished by a taproot that seeks out the lifeblood. It's been bowed but never broken. As have the two who approach it, she with a hand-stitched quilt over one arm, he with a laden picnic basket on his. They come here, in just this same way once every year, spanning the decades of hopes and dreams, faults and failures. The old tree offers them shelter, companionship, and certitude. And the presence of a serene listener.

She spreads the well-worn quilt on the ground and reaches out with a hand which wears a well-worn wedding band, touches him on the arm. "We made it," she murmurs. "We can rest a while." The man pats her hand, sets the basket down and turns to face her. "Our spot. Some things never get old," he says, with a gleam in his eye. "Just like you, my dear." She pokes him in the ribs. "You old fool!" she scoffs, as her cheeks are tinged with pink, that only adds to her beauty in his eyes. They settle into their feast of non-prolixity, for this is their season of joy.

"Did you bring it?" he asks. She gives him a sidelong glance. "Oh Tommy, in all these years have I ever forgotten?" she gently chides. "Tommy, is it?" He winks at her, feeling the warmth of her presence flowing through him. "Irena, you only call me Tommy when you're trying to butter me up for somethin'! Like preparing me for when your mother was coming to visit." He casually leans away from her pretend slap at his cheek and they both laugh. "You're terrible!" Irena exclaims as she hands him a sandwich. Tommy leans against the old tree, silent witness to this ritual of restoration. He takes a huge bite of the egg salad on homemade bread, smacks his lips mischievously hoping for a reaction. He's rewarded with a "You're never going to grow up, old man!" and a sigh. "Nope, I'm always dancin' at first light, Reenie!" He pauses. "And I always will, Lord willin'."

There is a moment of contented silence between them as they savor the combination of egg, Duke's mayonnaise, pickle and just a hint of mustard (no onion) as the birds in the distant orchards serenade with their treble instruments. "It's so peaceful here," sighs Irena. "Wish I could stay here forever." There's a catch in Tommy's throat as he tries to change the subject. "We never brought the kids here, did we?" She smooths invisible wrinkles from her dress. "This is our place, Tommy." She gets up, steps to the old tree, leans against it. Folds her arms around herself, as though seeking sheltering protection beneath the wizened oak.

"Read to me?" It's a question, a plea, a hopeful longing. Tommy drinks the last of his sweet tea and pulls her down beside him to the comfort of the quilt. He takes a dog-eared volume from the basket. "See, I told you I don't forget!" Irena says with some satisfaction. He gives her cheek a tender kiss, opens the book and reads: "Seasons of mist and mellow fruitfulness/Close bosom-friend of the maturing sun/Conspiring with him how to load and bless/With fruit the vines that round the thatch-eaves run . . ."

. . . Tommy blinks back his tears, trying to clear the image of the tired man he sees reflected in the window. That day seems so far away now. He prays for the strength of the old tree as he turns back to the room as the nurses finish their ministrations to the tiny figure in the bed. "Tommy? Are you there?" He swallows hard. "I'm here Reenie. I'm here." He pulls himself together and comes to sit on the side of the bed. God, she looks so frail. And yet, she's still the most beautiful woman he's ever seen. Always will be, he tells himself as her fingers, one with the well-worn band seek out his. "Do you remember the old tree, Tommy?" she says as her hand tightens around his. "Of course. It's our place," he answers.

Her breathing slows and his heart jumps. "Yes," she whispers. "Don't forget. You need to go back there." Tommy struggles for words. "It wouldn't be the same. Not without you, Reenie." Her hand slips from his and she tries to playfully slap at his face. He doesn't move and it becomes a sweet caress. "Hey, Tommy, don't forget. You're always dancing at first light. So dance under our tree. Promise?" Tommy holds her hand fast against his cheek. "I promise." She smiles. "Good. Now read to me, you old fool. Read me some Keats."

And in the distance, the ancient oak hunkers atop the hill . . .

Words are magic, and writers are wizards.

AT THIS TABLE

The `68 Impala station wagon turned in at the bottom of the hill and drove slowly past the rowhouses of the old company town. The small clapboard homes are arrayed in neat rows so that if you stood on a porch at one end and looked down the block, they all lined up, post after post of greying whitewash. The monotony is interrupted only by a splash of the occasional green painted porch swing hanging on rusted chains, swaying in the strong breeze that swept in from the mountain to the west, emitting faint squeaks in anticipation of weary souls seeking their solace. Jerry steers the blue behemoth past the first row, climbing the narrow street to High End, a row of exactly the same houses with exactly the same folks living inside of them. With the surrounding mountains and narrow valley formed by the North Branch of some river, it could be a mining town, maybe logging, or some sort of a mill. Jerry felt fortunate that he paid the company the extra money for an end house, meaning only one shared wall and a view out the two small windows facing east.

He parked in his coveted spot and trudged up the stairs, shaking his head as usual at the pink and lavender paint job of the swing claiming its spot proudly at the end of the High End row, daring the neighbors to give it a second glance. Switching the old tin lunch pail to the other hand, he inserted the key and crossed the threshold to home. "Papa!" Twelve-year-old Penny looked up from the kitchen table where she'd been writing in her diary. "I'll get your dinner now." Jerry looked at her as though seeing her for the first time in a long while. When had she gotten so thin? He wondered. And her eyes, they weren't as bright and lively as he remembered. A sigh escaped before he could stop it. "Papa? What's wrong?" She shut the diary and came to him. "Nothing, child. I'm fine. What have you been up to today?" He touched her cheek with fingers coated in the grime of hard labor. She rewarded him with a smile that tugged at his spirits.

"How was school, Pen Pen?" She half-frowned, half giggled at him using the old nickname from her childhood. He noticed her jeans sagged at her waist and stopped above her ankles. When did she grow so much? And her shirt... he stopped, something about it didn't seem right. But he couldn't put his finger on it. Not yet. "Go wash up, Papa and I'll get supper on the table." Jerry tossed his lunch pail on the table. It slid across the shiny surface and knocked the diary to the floor. Penny was busy at the refrigerator as he bent to pick it up. "Dear Mama," read the notation at the top of the open page. He couldn't help but read the neat, curly writing. "Papa is so sad. We both miss you so much. Tonight, we remember..." It ended there where she'd been interrupted. He quietly closed it. The shirt... it was Ami's, her favorite, with a painted peacock in full display. Of course.

As he washed up, Jerry stared hard in the mirror at the man he was becoming. "Help me," he whispered to the image. "I can't. Not alone..." Penny's voice summoned him back. He sat down to the feast she prepared: hot dogs, mac and cheese, green beans, and sweet tea. It was only then that he noticed the third place, set for the one no longer with them. Penny reached for his hand, a blessing in and of itself. "Say Mama's blessing. Do you remember?" He swallowed hard and nodded. "At... at this..." He had to stop. Penny chimed in, "At this table, all are welcome. At this table..." she squeezed his hand, and it gave Jerry strength. "At this table, there are no strangers." He closed his eyes, memories flooding every seed of his soul.

"At this table, we are free. At this table, all believe." He opened his eyes to find his daughter staring at him, tears in her eyes. "At this table, all are fed." They said the thanksgiving together, their voices growing stronger, catching the breeze that stirred the air and wafted out the windows facing east, across the North Branch, and shaking the mountain to the west. "At this table, all are loved. At this table, we find grace. At this table, this holy place. At this table..." They stopped and Penny laid her head against her father's chest. "Mama," she said, "we remember."

And when they finished the blessing, he took a piece of hot dog bun, broke it off, and gave it to her. And Penny took a forkful of mac and cheese and gave it to him. And when they had finished, they took their glasses of sweet tea, clinked them together and drank until they were satisfied. Then they sang Mama's favorite song, as they danced around the table, laughing at the memories and the times yet to come. When they were done, they collapsed onto their chairs. "Ami loves us," said Jerry. "Mama loves us," uttered Penny. And he took her hand, looked into her eyes and said, "And, Pen Pen, if God made you, He's in love with me. We can clean this up together." And they did.

Words are magic, and writers are wizards.

IF'N I'M FORGOTTEN

"Does the wind ever stop here?" Those were the only words written on the last page of her diary. It's a miracle that anything survived the fire, especially a child's homemade book of blank pages awaiting the squiggles and hearts of her thoughts and deepest secrets. The folks in town debated what those words meant. Was she complaining about the constant wind? The ceaseless howling, tearing at leaves and grass, hair, and clothes? Always billowing up dust to drive it through any crack in the walls, around the windows and doors, coating everything? Or was it something more ethereal? Does the wind ever stop here, like she was waiting for it, hoping for the wind to come, pick her up like catching a ride on a train, and whisking her away to somewhere else? Or even perhaps something more ephemeral? Would the wind ever stop here, pay a visit, enjoy a cup of tea and some cookies, and answer her heartfelt questions and whisper secrets of its own just for her? The detective set out to solve this mystery.

Jake Trotter was his name. He came highly recommended. He arrived in town in his beat-up VW Beetle, with his faithful partner, Ellie, a golden retriever who had trouble minding her manners. But Jake put up with this lack of manners because Ellie had the gift for sniffing out the truth. It was truly uncanny how she could tell when a human was lying. She had been raised by a woman in a cabin up in the mountains with too many cats. Neither Jake nor Ellie could remember exactly who found who, but now they were a good team—as long as they didn't talk about cats. The two of them immediately went to the ruins of the burned home to nose around. They carefully examined the ashes, the charred beams, the remnants of the lives lived there. It was Ellie who sniffed out the charm bracelet, almost completely buried in what remained of the girl's bedroom. Ellie alerted near the remains of the nightstand, pawing at the fine ash until Jake came over and dug out the charm. He dusted it off, a jagged fragment of metal shaped like half a heart. He turned it over and found these words engraved: IF'N I'M FORGOTTEN.

Those words gnawed at Jake's heart. Who was this winsome little girl, who wondered about the wind's travels and made plans to be forgotten? No one in town could remember seeing her since the fire. In fact, no one could give Jake and Ellie a good description of the girl. "I think she had red hair," offered one of the teachers in the school. "No, it was brown, dark brown," insisted the principal. "She was just a child, with a gap in her front teeth," said the local minister. "Sorry, but she was a young woman, and she had perfect teeth," said the butcher. Ellie did her best to sniff out the truth, but people aren't lying, except to themselves, if they aren't noticing, not paying attention. "She was always so quiet," said a girl who insisted she was the best friend. "I told her people would like her if she smiled more," said the handsome quarterback for the high school. "What really concerns us," pontificated the mayor, "is the answer to the mystery, does the wind ever stop here? That's what we hired you to find out. If she is still around, she should show herself."

Jake did what he always did when faced with a tough case: he took Ellie for a long, long walk. Ellie would nip at his heels or try to chew on his hands, when she wasn't trying to get underfoot as he walked because, well, minding manners and such. As they walked, he noticed that the wind was growing stronger, picking up leaves and dancing them around the trees. Eventually it grew so strong that even the birds gave up on flying and settled into shelter. Dark clouds rode the wind and swept over the woods and town. Then, as Jake and Ellie watched in amazement, a funnel cloud formed and touched down to the earth. Where it touched a brilliant light appeared in the distance. Jake and Ellie started running to see if this was the wind stopping here.

They burst through the trees into a small clearing. There sat the girl, smiling as she held her hands out to the swirling cloud, forming a light all around her. From her wrist hung a bracelet, a gold chain from which hung a charm, the other half of the broken heart Jake and Ellie found in the ashes. Ellie barked and ran to the girl to cover her face with puppy kisses. And just like that, the wind was gone. Jake approached in the stillness and silence. The girl held out her wrist for him to examine. He took the broken heart charm in his hand and in the light made out the words: I HOPE YOU'RE NOT LONELY WITHOUT ME. And she left with Jake and Ellie that day, riding away in the old VW Beetle, off to solve the next case, not talking about cats . . . leaving the broken heart for the town to mend.

Words are magic and writers are wizards.

IF I BE WRONG

The ancient willows hang their weeping shoots over the old tombstones in an abandoned graveyard just off the tired dirt road, tucked back in a far corner of the county in southcentral Pennsylvania. Locals call it the Demon's Hide. Human beings, being what they are, have made concerted efforts over the years to find reasons to declare graveyards frightening places, and this one is no exception. Of course, that only applies to after dark. In the darkness, shadows and sounds, fears and fretting have us peering with the faint tickle of unease into the dark corners of what it means to be alive. And we don't like to admit to ourselves that we often find reasons that have no rhyme or reason. If something has a beginning then, by definition, it is finite and has an ending. Except the graveyard is too deadening, so we fill it with ghosts and demons, vampires, and vagaries.

The Demon's Hide is the home of Old Sam. He of the grungy coat, whiskered chin, pained expression, and world-weary attitude, walking with a slight limp among the stones of memorials and monuments to endings, overgrown with the fruits of discarded seeds and casual misplaced weeds. He stops in front of two simple stones. One reads Ebenezer. The other says Josiah. That is all. The area around the stones is neatly trimmed and fresh flowers adorn the twin graves. Old Sam fills his pipe, tamps it down, lights it and tells me the story.

Josiah was a Mennonite farmer in the Shenandoah Valley when the Civil War broke out. Being a confirmed pacifist, he hid when the Confederate soldiers came looking for conscripts. They burned down his barn and took his mules, so Josiah set out on foot for his parents' homestead up north, near Gettysburg. The second night, sleeping in the woods in the mountains, he was awakened by the sounds of horses galloping, dogs barking, and ungodly screams. Fearful of his safety, Josiah made his way to the stream. As he hid among the rocks he came upon Ebenezer, a runaway slave, fleeing for his life.

Ebenezer jumped up to run into the shadows of the trees. Startled, Josiah shouted for him to not be afraid. The bounty hunters shot blindly, striking Josiah in the leg. Intent on their prize, they rode on. Josiah lay in the stream, bleeding and in pain. After a long while, he felt someone lifting him up and taking him underneath the canopy of the forest. It was Ebenezer, who laid him down, built a small fire, then disappeared. After long hours, right before dawn, Ebenezer returned with bandages and medicines he had taken from a doctor's office in the town at the foot of the mountain.

For weeks, fearful of being discovered, Ebenezer crept into town through the dark, getting food and dressings for Josiah. He returned and nursed Josiah back to health. When he could travel, they decided to make their way north together. Trying to avoid surging armies from both sides, they traveled a circuitous route, sometimes ending up in North Carolina, other times stuck along the Dan River in Virginia. They decided to try to catch a train and head for Washington, DC. Ebenezer pretended to be Josiah's slave and Josiah carried a forged pass to get through the Confederate lines.

Somewhere around Richmond, the train was stopped and the two were caught. Refusing to carry a rifle and insisting that Ebenezer was his, the Confederate Army forced them to be stretcher bearers. Before they knew it, the two found themselves in the middle of the Battle of the Wilderness, carrying broken men out of danger. In the awful fury of the battle, they were surrounded by Union soldiers and taken captive. The soldiers declared Ebenezer free and left Josiah in the mud with the other prisoners. That night, Ebenezer came back for his new friend, untied him and they escaped into the wilds.

Dodging patrols and scrounging to stay alive they traveled north. Along the way they promised each other that they would never be apart again. Josiah said Ebenezer would be welcomed at his home. As they neared Washington, they devised a plan. Josiah found a broken rifle and they pretended that he was bringing Ebenezer with him. But as they neared the Union picket line, all the soldiers saw was a raggedy Confederate holding a gun on a Black man and fired. Josiah fell, mortally wounded. After he died, Ebenezer would not let the soldiers touch him. He made a wooden casket for his friend, found a wagon, and took him home to his family in Pennsylvania.

Old Sam finished his story. "Ebenezer made his life here and insisted that he be buried next to his friend, right here." He started to walk away, but turned, and said, "Don't spend your life trying to avoid dying. Everyone has the opportunity to take a look around at the times they find themselves born into and ask, 'If I be right, this is all about me. But if I be wrong. . .'"

Words are magic and writers are wizards.

HURDY GURDY MAN

THERE WAS A FIRST one. There always is. Nobody knows who or where or when. Nobody knows why. But then again, each and every one of us knows why. Maybe it was lightning behind a rainbow. Perhaps thunder rolling down a canyon then echoing back again. Maybe someone looked into the eyes of a newborn child and saw the reflection of forever. Sparks in a fire snapped and popped and soared into a blanket of stars while nightingales performed a doxology. Two humans drew near to each other and felt the pulse of the earth hesitate while some strangely irresistible force like the beating of the wings of a million butterflies brought their lips together. Maybe. Perhaps. And the result was the first one. The birth of music. The first song.

Beat, rhythm, scales, pitch . . . melody, harmony, simplicity, complexity. Communication, ritual, celebration, unity . . . dance. Of course, dance. Music and song are "sound that conveys emotion." And so much more. A siren call, abandoning oneself, listening with your soul, yearning for the stars, free to be, hovering on the horizons, call of the wild, down and dirty, whispers of angels, triumphs of the kings, rock and roll, feel the beat, beseech the gods . . . Tell me that you love me. We are the world. The water music. Morning has broken. Whistling in the dark. ABCDEFG. Happy birthday. Beethoven's ninth. The echo of the drums. Please don't forget me. Hit all the right notes. Sing it loud, sing it clear . . . Marry together touch and sound, sight and soul, heart and mind and we make music. Create it, express it, perform it, dance to it . . . lose ourselves in it, draw closer to those around us. And if we forget how, we may need a visit with the hurdy gurdy man.

In and around the hills and mountains of Appalachia there are certain places one does not go to unless one is invited. Close knit communities, where the blood of your ancestors is the most potent capital, who are protective and understanding of those with unique gifts. Some say there are clues to the location hidden in the music of the Kruger Brothers over Jonesboro way, but others say that's just mountain legend. Somewhere west of Asheville, NC, near the border with Tennessee, at the far end of Britches holler, in a small house framed by ancient trees, by invitation only, one can find him. Approach with honesty and humility. Come with nothing in your hands and a heart wide open. He's there, just on the other side of that crooked door. He is waiting. The hurdy gurdy man. The only living soul who knows the first song.

He sits in his old rocker, behind him plain wooden shelves piled high with ancient texts and stocked with Mason jars cradling white lightning. His hair's gone white now, thick glasses magnify his striking eyes. He will look you up and down, silent, and still, like a field mouse that knows he's been spotted by an owl. Because he wants to know if you can do it, be silent and still before the music. His voice is a bit gravely as he asks, "What'cha going to do with it if you hear it?" You don't need me to tell you there is only one answer to that one. After a bit, he says, "After you hear it, you're going to spend the rest of your life trying to catch the wind." Weigh that carefully. Because everything might change. It could change what you call your favorite music, your favorite singer or group. Even what you sing in church if you're so inclined toward such things.

The hurdy gurdy man pays no nevermind to distractions like time and distance. "Remember me to one who lives there," he murmurs, staring out the window at the distance. "For she once was a true love of mine." He blinks hard, as if summoning himself back from a faraway place. "Is the song a gift?" the visitor feels inclined to ask. He looks surprised, claps his hands together hard. "What isn't?" Claps his hands together again, softer, then again. He starts a beat, sits up straighter. "You bring a guitar?" he asks, with a twinkle. Oh, the joy for those who do bring something! "Is it a love song?" the visitor is eager to know. "What isn't?" comes the reply from the hurdy gurdy man, keeping the beat.

He begins to sing. The very first song. The first melody. That expression of what it means to be alive. Of what it means to be us. At the sad part, his eyes water and the flames in the fireplace bow low. When it soars, the whole place lifts off. When it ends nobody wants it to end. When it ends, nobody wants to leave.

But that's just it. The hurdy gurdy man insists that you take it with you. Just don't forget the words. Or the melody. You have been entrusted with the very first song.

Words are magic, and writers are wizards.

iPHONE JESUS

It began in the dead of night, as these things usually do. The soldier cleared the ridge, a dark silhouette against the desert night sky. Then he realized that he was exposed and ducked down below the dunes, rolling over and over, keeping his weapon high, arms outstretched. A machine gun opened up, chewing and spraying the dirt where he had just been standing. That was followed by the 'crump' of a mortar, which landed short. As he dug himself down into the warm earth, he could hear the mortar rounds being walked toward his position. Panting hard, he scrambled farther underneath the overhanging rock formation at the bottom of the slope. That's when he heard the clank and rattle of a tank being maneuvered around the top. A pause, pregnant with dread. Then a shell slammed into the rock and his world exploded in a dizzying whirl and deafening roar of flame and smoke.

When he came to, he found himself lying dazed and hurting on the hard floor of a dank cave. He tried to get up but discovered his left leg was shattered, his desert fatigues soaking through with his own blood. The soldier slowly dragged himself away from the opening to the cave, which showed jagged edges against the stars, silently watching high overhead. He was trapped, alone. The opening was higher than he could reach. He turned on the Phantom Warrior special flashlight to blue and shone it around. It kept enemy night vision goggles from spotting him. Nothing but rocks and more rocks in the eerie light. He was trapped, no way to escape. If he called out for help, the enemy would hear and come finish him off. Or capture him and take him God knows where to do God knows what.

He leaned his helmet back against the wall of the cave and tried to stay calm. His platoon was on the other side of the valley, waiting for the evac choppers. His buddies called him Skippy because he liked to skip all the rules which he felt did not apply to him. Regs were for those who didn't know any better, who didn't know how the world really worked. Which was why he slipped away from the patrol to explore this little ravine, to see what he might score. "And here I am," he muttered to the emptiness. The blood, his blood, was forming a small river across the cave floor. Something about it reminded him that he'd brought his iPhone with him, definitely not something permitted. There would be hell to pay from his sergeant when he got back . . . if he got back.

He dug behind his tactical vest and pulled it out, hesitated, then switched it on. He shielded it close as he turned it on. No service. His wounded leg that felt like it was on fire was now growing cold. He thumbed to TEXT, paused. "Jesus? Are you there?" he typed, hesitated, pushed SEND. He was shaking his head at his foolishness when the screen lit up. WHAT DO YOU NEED? Skippy stared in disbelief. He chewed his lip as he typed, "Where are you? What do you look like?" Seconds later: IS THAT WHAT YOU NEED TO KNOW? He sighed. "Yes, I'm scared and alone." Waited. BEEN THERE, DONE THAT. Skippy shook his head and decided to go for broke. "Send a selfie."

The pause was long, too long. Sweat poured down Skippy's face, but he grew ever colder. Finally, he typed, "Jesus, don't do me like this. I'm hurting, dude." After a moment: WHAT DO YOU NEED? Skippy typed, "Why can't I see you? I don't want to die." The screen lit: I DID MY TIME. YOUR TURN. Skippy slammed the phone down, heard the glass crack and instantly panicked. The lens had a spiderweb distortion, but he tried anyway, "Jesus, you still there?" His heart was starting to race. WHAT DO YOU NEED? Skippy grunted and said a few choice words before typing, "I just want to see you." Right away came the reply: SEND A SELFIE.

The big, strong soldier, encased in the garb of efficient killing for warfare, broke down and started to cry. Great sobs filled the cave. His heart stopped racing. He could barely feel it any longer. He could barely feel anything at all. With his last strength, he held the phone out at arm's length and snapped a picture of his tear-streaked face, caked in his own blood. He put it into the text box and hit SEND. The phone dropped into his lap. It is not known whether he saw the reply: THAT'S WHAT YOU NEED.

High up in the surrounding mountains an eleven-year-old girl in the clothing of the Pashtun studied the image on her cell phone. Ever so slowly she reached out one finger and traced the tears on the man's face. Then she gently pulled it to her and gave it a gentle kiss.

Words are magic and writers are wizards.

JUST AS I AM

BETTY CLOSED THE DOOR and approached the mirror with dread. Maybe if she didn't look herself in the eye it would change things. Maybe if she just washed her face, brushed her hair, put on a touch of make-up. and smiled, this would all go away. Maybe, just maybe, she hadn't felt what she thought she did. Maybe if she didn't look herself in the eye in the mirror, the sense of panic would pass, it was all a silly mistake. She could cancel her visit to The Breast Center and the discomfort sure to follow. It was all an honest mistake. After all, she was certainly healthy looking. She ran a few times a week, watched what she ate, loved her children—she'd do anything for them—and her husband, despite all his obvious faults and annoying habits. Her only vice was chocolate, and as everybody knows, that's not really a vice. More like a necessity for good and right living.

As she drove through streets strangely missing their usual traffic, she barely noticed the empty restaurants and shuttered businesses. Life was already changing too rapidly, maybe she could wait until later, put this off until things got back to normal. Maybe . . . she looked in the rearview mirror and scolded herself, "I'm tired of maybes." The classic oldies-that-your-kids-can't-stand music station on the radio blared "Cause" by Rodriguez, and the phrase " . . . but the sweetest kiss I ever got was the one I never tasted . . . " brought tears to her eyes, but she stopped them with a sigh, "Damn music." Next thing she knew, though, she was singing along to " . . . and I make sixteen solid half-hour friendships every evening . . . " She shook her head at her reflection, muttering, "Welcome to the new world."

She parked the car and headed into the imposing medical arts building. The doors of the elevator opened onto the third floor and after checking in she took a seat and looked around. Patients were doing their best to stay six feet apart like some sort of life-sized game of tic tac toe. She noticed a man watching her from across the way. He had a close-trimmed white beard and the corners of his blue eyes crinkled when he smiled. "You know, they only let the special ones in," he said. Betty looked away, then back. "Are you waiting for your wife?" He shook his head and touched his chest. "Nope, it's on me. That's how I know." He smiled. "I don't know how you ladies do it. That machine squishes down hard!" She gave him a questioning look. "Yep, nice sized mass. Right about here," he indicated his right breast.

"I'm sorry. What did they do?" asked Betty. "A little nip and tuck," he said with a twinkle in his eyes. "A biopsy. Don't worry yourself none, they take good care of you." She noticed the other women nearby rolling their eyes. He went on, "I'm here today for my results." Betty studied him a moment. "I hope everything is all right." He spread his hands out in front of him. "The way I figure it, it ain't about where you been. Or where you're going. It's about who you are. Right now. Being a 'just as I am' person." Betty caught herself biting a fingernail. "Aren't you worried?" He folded his hands and leaned toward her. "I don't want to be sick if that's what you're asking. I don't want to be spending all my energy chasing some ghost around inside my body. But nobody sitting here in this room wants that, either. Whether it be this or some invisible virus. We've all got better things to be doing!"

He looked at her closely. "You haven't told anybody, have you." It was a statement, not a question. He looked her in the eye. "You don't even want to look at yourself in the mirror. Don't be afraid of who you'll see in there." He sat back and smiled again, patted his belly. "Being a just as I am person doesn't mean being like me, my friend. It means seeing everybody else the way you want them to see you. Right now. Right here." The door opened and one of the techs in pink scrubs came out. "Reverend, you ready?" He stood up and took a step toward Betty. "It's always for all the marbles. Every day. Today is for all the marbles." He turned to follow the tech. "For every one of us."

After Betty finished her appointment, she rode the elevator back to the ground floor, the little ice pack soothing the irritation of the invasion. She noticed an older woman sitting alone on the bench outside the door to a neurologist's office. As Betty passed the frail woman looked up. "Excuse me," she said. Betty stopped in front of her. "I don't mean to bother you. It's just . . . " Betty gently urged her, "No bother, dear." The woman reached out a hopeful hand. "Could I trouble you and ask you for a hug? Please?"

As she drove home, Betty flipped on the radio. Andy Grammar sang 'Don't Give Up On Me' to her: " . . . even when nobody else believes, I'm not going down that easily . . . So don't give up on me . . . even when they say there's nothing left, even when I'm down to my last breath . . . I will fight for you . . . "

Words are magic, and writers are wizards.

JACKPOT

It was a dark and stormy night. The rain came down in sheets, obscuring the view down the narrow alleyway. The solitary streetlamp cast a feeble glare that gave up less than a third of the way through the gloomy space. Garbage bins stacked along one wall overflow with the refuse and effluence of the various bars and restaurants that fronted onto the main square. Back here lies the realm of rats and restless wanderers without reason to wait for hope to find them. Down this dark, damp, foul smelling alley walks the man they call Pirate Patch and his cat, Cameo. Pirate Patch is dressed in an outfit befitting his rank, an old chartreuse ruffled tuxedo French silk shirt, worn over pantaloon breeches from an old costume shop, motorcycle boots, and a pale blue gentleman's waistcoat leftover from a prom rental outfit. In his arm is a one-eyed calico with a damaged ear, Cameo.

They duck down the wooden stairs and through the weather-beaten door of a joint called Susan's Floor. At first glance it appears to be not all that out of the ordinary: plank tables and benches, low ceilings, dim lighting. He passes on through this great room and through a hallway to a door with a thick, velvet curtain hanging across the opening. Inside the dingy room, a poker game is in progress. Pirate Patch sits down in the waiting chair, sets Cameo in his lap, and looks around at the players. "I'm the shadow on the windowsill in late afternoon, I'm the forgotten bulb planted in the fall under the leaves, I'm the hidden ace in a royal flush . . . " he started his spiel. "Shut up and bet," yelled a woman with blue/silver hair, dressed in a pink taffeta gown and clutching an old Raggedy Anne doll. "I don't want to be late for the fundraiser." Across from her was a man with a monocle and a Daniel Boone coonskin cap. "Gambling is the purest form of prayer," he wagers.

"Dealer's choice," sang out a thirteen-year-old girl with freckles and red hair, wearing a plaid school uniform, an AR-15 slung across her back, as she shuffled the worn deck of cards. "Everybody remember what's in the jackpot?" She looked around the table at each player, holding their gaze as she flipped the cards to them. "Place your bets on the table, the most valuable thing that you have with you. One hand, no wild cards, aces high. The game is death fears." The players picked up their cards, looked at them, and put on their best poker faces. "The jackpot is one look," the girl reminded them with finality. Monocle man thought long and hard. "Death fear is non-existence," he said, carefully removing his hat and placing it in the pot. "It's knowing ahead of time that we won't know anything at the time. For the rest of time." And he laid his cards upon the table.

Taffeta-dress went next. "Death fear is not making the Big Guy happy. Eternal anger." She kissed her ragged doll and placed it in the pot. "We don't know anything before we are born, but then we are like dolls, being told how to dress and how to act. Who to love, who not to love. Death fear is that we won't be happy. For the rest of time." And she laid her cards upon the table. Now Pirate Patch studied his cards long and hard. He finally sighed and put Cameo into the pot. "Death fear. The scariest thing about being dead? Nothing." He leaned back and studied the ceiling. "Going through dying doesn't seem like a lot of fun, even scary, but then that's it. It is all over." And he took an old sandwich out of a pocket and started to munch on it. After he laid his cards upon the table.

Dealer-girl hesitated about even looking at her cards. "Death fear? I hardly know what life is about yet." She tried to lean back but the big rifle made it too uncomfortable. "They told me to carry this around with me all the time. That I'd be less afraid." She looked at the items in the pot in the middle of the table. "What means the most to me . . . huh, I mean most valuable?" She found a pin in her pocket and pricked the end of her finger. Then she leaned over the table and let a single drop of her blood settle onto the Daniel Boone coonskin cap. Another onto the doll. "All this talk about dying and then wanting to come back to life. To what?" She hesitated. A tear ran down her cheek and dropped onto Calico as she whispered, "To what?" And she laid her cards on the table.

"The winner!" cried the other three, and sure enough, the girl won the hand. They stood and escorted the girl down the darkened staircase, further down and further in, until they reached a great room. Across the center of the room was a huge cloth, finely spun, almost like gauze. "There it is, the jackpot," said Pirate Patch. "Beyond the veil, you get to look at death. And beyond. We all want to know . . . "

The girl stepped forward, drew back the veil, and stepped beyond. They waited. And they waited. And they waited . . .

Words are magic and writers are wizards.

BEAUTIFUL WAR

NICKLEBACK WAS IN HIS headphones singing "Far Away" when Johnny, manning the .50 caliber machine gun on top of the up-armored Humvee, looked up at the gloriously blue sky through his combat shades and smiled. It was good to be out in the countryside rocking and rolling, prepped and primed for mayhem. He was outside the wire, patrolling some of the territory that their unit controlled. Word came down that the insurgents were back in the town causing trouble and hopefully a show of mighty force would dissuade. He snuck his cell phone out and surreptitiously made a video of himself as a warrior on the warpath. It was a shaky video of his dusty helmet shielding his dusty smile, then dusty rocks on a dusty road being traversed by dusty armor laden vehicles loaded with young soldiers laden with fear and bravado. His vehicle brought up the rear.

He held the phone at arm's length and smiled for his parents back home. "This is beautiful, guys," he exclaimed just as the Bradley fighting vehicle leading the way ran over an IED and the world dissolved into flames and black smoke. The Humvee swerved hard, throwing Johnny hard against the edge of the turret. As he righted himself and swung the gun to cover the mountainside to his six, somehow the phone landed beside the gun, still going. He pulled the bolt, and the phone recorded his grunts of exertion as he squeezed the trigger. Adrenaline pumping, eyes wide, Johnny laid down covering fire for those rushing forward. Sweat stung his eyes as he concentrated. Then, in a blink, everything went black and quiet. Too quiet.

When Johnny opened his eyes, all was still. He raised his head and looked around. The convoy was gone. Instead of rocks and dust, the area was green and lush. The mountainside was covered with trees and vegetation and a breeze blew across his face. A river flowed nearby in the flat valley. A figure approached, silhouetted in the sun. It stopped and bent over him, extending a hand to help him rise. "I am Thunder Rising to Lofty Places," said the man. "In your time, I am known as Chief Joseph of the Nez Perce,

The People. You are welcome here." Johnny got to his feet, noting the man's strong features and dark hair hanging in braids. "Where am I?" he asked. Chief Joseph nodded toward the water. "This is the Snake River. It is where my people paused to rest as your army pursued us. Come and sit and talk for a while before you continue your journey."

Johnny and Chief Joseph sat down beside the river, under the vast Montana sky. "Why was the army chasing you?" asked Johnny. "Your country declared war on us because we wanted to stay in our homeland. Our homeland was back in what you call Oregon. We did not want war. We wanted to stay where our fathers are buried. Your people came looking to take gold out of the land, more and more of you. The seven million acres that your government 'gave' us was reduced to less than one tenth of that. When some of our young men struck back against the settlers, they were called terrorists and," he paused, a sad smile on his face, "the die was cast."

He sighed as he continued, "I tried to lead my people to Canada to seek asylum. Your army chased us. It is said that they even admired us, the way we fought and defended ourselves. We were vastly outnumbered, and your army had far superior weapons. I was called the great peacemaker." He dipped a hand in the water and drank the cooling liquid. "I would not have needed to be a peacemaker if there had not been war. A war declared on us for wanting to stay home." Johnny dipped his hands in also and drank. "That's a long time ago." Chief Joseph looked out over the valley. "It was yesterday." He faced Johnny, imploring, "The old men are dead. It is the young men who say yes or no. I am tired."

The breeze picked up, rippling the water. "Don't worship the warrior," he added. "Must it be that a basic premise of the people is that we must kill each other to get what we want? All in the name of bringing them what we insist they must have?" He stood up to go. "We just want to be home." And he left Johnny there beside the water.

Johnny's mother answered the knock at the door. FedEx handed her a padded envelope. Taking it to her chair she opened it and let out a loud cry of pain. It was Johnny's phone. She held it to her cheek, her tears washing his blood onto her fingertips. Finally, she dared to push the button. The screen flickered to life. A video started to play. A shaking image of her son came into view, one hand on the machine gun on the Humvee. As the dust rose around him, she heard his voice. "This is beautiful guys."

Words are magic and writers are wizards.

THE SECRET TO LIFE

Sitting over a plate of grilled stickies, hot coffee at the ready, a mulcting for getting started with his day, Jerry looked around at the other diners in the Eat n Park. Retired men gathered around a table, their eggs, pancakes, and decaf punctuated with loud laughter and the freedom of no wives present. Nearby some college students studiously ignored their books and chatted about Tinder vs. Grindr. Across the room a couple of families with small children did the dance of eating of expectations and expectations of eating. A tiny woman in an old-fashioned pill hat and worn thin overcoat sat at the counter and ordered oatmeal and a bran muffin. Jerry made a mental note to pick up her check on his way out. A server with a beautiful smile poured him more coffee and he watched her walking away. Which is how he missed noticing when the stranger slid onto the opposite bench of the booth, settling himself across from Jerry.

"Hi, neighbor," said the man. "Do you know the secret to life?" Jerry's head spun back to the table. "What are you, Mister Rogers?" The man threw his head back and laughed a deep laugh. "No, but I do need a minute to think about the people that made it possible for me to be here." Jerry grew annoyed. "Look, buddy, there's other tables. Why don't you and King Friday XIII take it somewhere else?" The man smiled. "Because you have been chosen. You have no control over that." Jerry sipped at his coffee. "Chosen for what? Publisher's Clearing House?" The man sat back, and his smile vanished. "You get to decide which is more important, more valuable: your life or your love." He slid a piece of paper across the table. "Take this. Use it when needed."

"Why should I? Maybe I don't want to be chosen." The man thought about Jerry's response a moment, shrugged, and spread his arms out wide. "The response time for fire and police here is seven minutes. It takes ten minutes to evacuate this building. In five minutes, this place will be devastated by a bomb hidden in the kitchen near the gas lines." He paused to look at his watch, fiddled with the time and pushed a button. "Ten minutes ago, your ex-wife and your children left home, traveling west on the road you see out that window. Your wife left her cell phone at home. If she's not stopped, in five minutes a drunk driver is going to smash into the car. The clock started. What is the secret to life?" With that he nodded, got up and left.

Jerry stared after the man. Finally, he glanced at the piece of paper. His eyes grew wide, and he looked around in a panic. He jumped to his feet, rushing past the retirees, the college students, the families, and the woman in the pill hat. He shoved past the server and crashed into the kitchen, all the while mentally ticking down the seconds. He shouted at the cooks, "Gas, gas? Where's the gas line?" Food flew and some man in a white apron tried to tackle him, but Jerry cast him aside and knocked pans and plates of food aside. He thew open the door to the pantry and frantically searched. Finally, he spied a large briefcase with a blinking red light attached to a timer ticking down past three minutes. Panting for breath he grabbed it and retraced his steps through the restaurant, ignoring the shouts and curses.

Outside, he dashed through the parking lot, his mind filled with images of his family heading down the road to tragedy. A car flashed past him at high speed, weaving across lanes and turning onto a ramp to the expressway going the wrong way. He glanced at the timer. Under two minutes. Tears of frustration filled his eyes and his chest ached from the exertion. Up ahead there rose a small hill, overlooking the expressway. Jerry held the briefcase close and struggled to force his legs to go up the slope. Less than a minute to go, the flashing light seemed to mock him. Sirens sounded in the distance, too late to be of help. As he reached the top, he turned to face the traffic down below, so no one could miss seeing him. He held the briefcase high above his head...

Back in the restaurant the server picked herself up from the floor and went to Jerry's booth. As she picked up the piece of paper, a loud explosion rocked the establishment, rattled the windows, followed by a quiet silence among the diners. She looked outside and saw that traffic on the expressway had come to a complete stop. The manager came over to check on her. "What was that all about? What was that crazy guy trying to do?" The woman tried to speak, but nothing came out. She handed him the piece of paper. He read it, shrugged, folded it over and tossed it back on the table for the bus boys to take care of.

A breeze blew it open so that any passing that way who cared to, could read the words, written in ancient Aramaic: *Eloi, Eloi, lama sabachthani?*

Words are magic and writers are wizards.

BILLY'S TRAIN

Eight-year-old Billy lay quietly in the hospital bed. Without irony, his favorite song, Just Breathe by Pearl Jam, played on the iPad under his pillow. The Idiopathic Pulmonary Fibrosis made it an honest to God struggle to breathe, each and every solitary breath. And it explained the whispers and gurgles of the equipment used to help his failing lungs stand a fighting chance. The absolute, unequivocal miracle was that he had survived a take no prisoners, no holds barred disease for this long. But that's the kind of kid Billy's mom and dad were raising. In fact, they had just stepped out to go have a late lunch while Billy tried to take a nap. Billy figured that he was too old for naps, but you do what you gotta do in these kinds of situations. That's according to Grandma Vernie, his favorite person in the whole world. Just please don't tell his mom that. She wouldn't understand what goes on between special friends.

Grandma Vernie wasn't his real grandma, mind you. When the IPF started and mom and dad went around with their worry faces and tried too hard to smile, Grandma Vernie, the widow from next door, just kept on treating him like an ordinary, dyed in the wool, kid. "Gotta cough, Billie? Cover your mouth. Nobody wants to kiss a barn door!" Billie had no idea what that meant, but the way Grandma Vernie said it meant it had to be something grown up. And maybe a little naughty. And if he got a little too wound up when the two were playing a board game and he started getting too intense because he hated to lose and groused about it, she'd say, "Well kiss my foot and call me an angel! Your head's gonna bust right out of your britches you're so goldarned important! Nobody misses you if you're the only winner in the world, child." And somehow that was enough to do the trick.

A couple of afternoons ago, Grandma Vernie had showed up, leaning heavy on her cane. "My arthur-itis be actin' up, child. Mind you, I'm not complainin'. Fat lot of good that does folks, ya hear me?" And, of course,

Billie heard her. She knew enough not to fuss at him about being sick and he appreciated that fact. She handed him a box wrapped up as a fancy gift. "I brought you Pap's old mistifier. It vaporizes the water so you can breathe it easier, child." She filled it with water, plugged it in on the table next to Billie's bed. "Where's Pap?" asked Billy. "Oh child, he done caught the train to be with Jesus. Don't pay that no nevermind, now ya' hear me? I'll be catching that train soon enough myself." She stopped short, looking at the boy in the bed, tears threatening to break the dam of grief in her eyes, as he asked, "Is the train coming for me, Grandma Vernie? Remember you said, friends gotta be square or the bread don't rise." Her whole body trembled as she whispered, "Oh child, if the train be acomin' for you, it better be arunnin' over me first." True friends can speak of these things.

So, Billy lay there this afternoon, watching Pap's mystifier 'spootin' up puffs of vapor like steam from a railroad engine. As he watched, the train came around a bend in the distance, the whistle starting low, then getting louder. He could see it stopping at a farm outside of town. Then some people got on. Doors slid open, big boxes filled with mysterious gifts were loaded onto huge freight cars. Then the train pulled out and to his amazement a big, black as midnight, puppy with a smile on his face, leaned out the window of the engine and waved. Billy laughed at how silly he looked in an old blue and white striped engineer's hat. Behind the engineer puppy stood an old man, dressed in a fancy white suit. He doffed his fancy hat and waved a cane at Billy as they drew near. It looked suspiciously a lot like Grandma Vernie's cane, noted Billy with wonder.

The next thing Billy knew, the train stopped and the black as midnight puppy and the man in the pure white suit were motioning to him to come aboard. He hesitated. "Come on," said the puppy. "We're going to go through a big tunnel. There's a beautiful lake on the other side with lots of sunshine." The man in the white suit added, "And clean air. Lots and lots of fresh, clean air. I tell you, it's the truth. You gotta be square or the bread don't rise!" he added with a big laugh that went through Billy like Christmas morning. And he got onboard the train.

When his mom and dad returned that afternoon, they were greeted at the nurse's desk by the doctor and the chaplain. It was hard news. Very hard news that no one wants to hear. And they were truly mystified when the nurse brought them a cap. An old railroad engineer's cap with blue and white stripes. And they cried. They cried very hard. Because how could they know?

But to this day, if you make your way to 30th Street Station in Philadelphia and make your way to the benches in the main concourse, you will see her there. An old woman, leaning on a cane for support, holding a box wrapped like a fancy gift, watching the train schedules. True friends can speak of these things . . . or the bread don't . . .

Words are magic, and writers are wizards.

BE THE SONG

Charles and Nancy lived in a blue-collar section of Baltimore. Charles drove a bus for the city and Nancy was a music teacher in the public schools, back before the world decided that being plugged into the internet automatically added twenty points to one's IQ and bestowed experience in several professions all at once. They gratefully raised two daughters in an era when many a son of the workers was drafted and sent to Vietnam because wars never fight themselves. The girls were taught to love music and keep to regular schedules. Nancy always exhorted her daughters, as she did all of her students, as they struggled to master positioning, chord transitions, technique, not to mention hitting the right notes, to "enter the music, surrender to it. Be the song!"

One day her youngest, Lillie, stopped mid Tchaikovsky, to ask, "Momma, what do you mean by 'be the song?' I am fingers and bones, blood and breakfast, dirt, and hot dogs. I am not a song." Nancy corrected Lillie's hand position and patiently explained, "Did you ever get a song stuck in your head? It's magic. It is as though the song is alive inside of you!" She saw Lillie pull a face, ignored it and went on, pointing to the sheet of music. "See all those squiggles and marks? Mister Tchaikovsky saw swans swimming gracefully as though they were dancing. He tells us a story about a prince and a swan queen who fall deeply in love. But an evil baron puts a curse on the swan queen, and she can only become a human and be with her lover between midnight and daybreak, never forever. Mister Tchaikovsky uses these squiggles and marks to tell the musicians the story and they play it to give the dancers the story to act out. If you want to play well, play with the beauty it deserves, be the song. Be the swans, be the prince, be the queen, be the evil baron. Anytime the music for Swan Lake is in your imagination, leaping and soaring, you will yourself be the song."

Lillie rolled her eyes and kept practicing. On her regular schedule, of course. The daughters grew up and left home. The other side of the coin is, of course, that Charles and Nancy grew older and eventually more feeble. Nancy's fingers became less nimble on the piano keys and, as her eyesight dimmed, household chores that used to be routine became physically overwhelming and sometimes downright dangerous. Charles faired a bit better, and he worried watching Nancy's decline. The old house on Guilford Avenue needed repairs and upkeep that became more and more challenging for him to maintain. But it was their home, the one they labored and sacrificed for all these years. When Lillie could make it home she would spend time with her mother in the front parlor, playing Mister Tchaikovsky's story of love and longing. "You're the swan queen, Momma. The song is part of you. Be the song, Momma." And Nancy would smile and sway, her head filled with magic and wonder always within reach.

Sadly, the time came when the daughters realized that Momma needed more help than they could manage. They searched the city for a nursing home that could make her comfortable, feeling cared for and welcome, two of the essential elements to being human. She was placed on the waiting list for one and made Charles promise, swear up and down and sideways, that when another spot opened up he, too, would move there and they could be together forever. Nancy finally moved into the home and set about trying to adjust to a much different world. Lillie would come and take her to the dayroom where a piano sat. Each day felt like a week to Nancy, each week more like a year. This strange new world seemed like a place where she could never be the song again. Time crawled but finally the home told the daughters that a place had opened up. Charles could move in now to be with Nancy.

But Charles changed his mind. His visits to the home had been too depressing for him, the cost of leaving his home too high. He decided, after sixty-seven years together, he would not move into the home with Nancy. Lillie made the long journey to tell her mother. Even as she told her mother the news, she could see the Swan Queen begin to wilt and withdraw. "Tell him it's midnight, and I only have a short time till dawn," she pleaded with her daughter before taking to her bed. Lillie tried everything, even bringing a portable keyboard to her mother's room to play for her. But the spell of rejection is a powerful one. For six weeks the Swan Queen hovered, as though dancing just above the waters, unable to swim, unable to fly. Finally, Lillie brought the keyboard one more time. Before she played, she took Nancy's fragile, withered hand. "Momma, it's okay. Go on now. Be the song." And as Mister Tchaikovsky's magic filled the room, that is exactly what happened . . . .she danced beyond never forever.

Words are magic and writers are wizards.

BREATHE WHILE DROWNING

HIS WIFE CALLED ME late in the evening. Her profound infirmities kept her from getting to the hospital, could I please go and spend some time with her husband during his last hours. "He's always telling me about you, Preacher Boy. He thinks so highly of you, he really enjoyed coming and talking to you all the time." So, late at night, I find myself walking through the hushed hallways of the hospital, reflecting on my time of knowing Pete. Plucked from a small town in West Virginia by the draft in World War Two, Pete went into the 506th of the US Army, immortalized in the Band of Brothers book and HBO series of the same name. Pete is small, wiry, a bulwark of determination, smelling of Marlboros and cheap gin. "Preacher Boy, I ain't offering no excuses, but when your life is filled with terrible pain, at some point you realize you have to breathe while drowning."

After basic training and the required pitifully few parachute jumps, it was off to England to prepare for the big one, the invasion of France. "As the time for the invasion drew near, we all knew in our bones that we were dead men," Pete said one day, sitting with me on the steps of the Post Office, puffing away on the ever-present cigarette. "That's the secret, Preacher Boy. Knowing ahead of time that you're a dead man. Don't matter what you do, just take care of each other, and keep moving. We were coming to kill or be killed, no sugar coating." He tapped me on the knee. "That's why before we boarded those planes, we boxed up our shadows and shipped them home. Let people remember us the way they wanted to." He looked off in the distance. "Nobody wants to know what blood and piss and cordite smell like or what the sound of boys out there in the hell of shell bursts and tracers, wounded and crying for their mommas all night until they die, sounds like."

"They dropped us all over damnation. A few of us found each other in the dark and stumbled across a captain who took charge. But then we found one of my buddies. Parachuted into a tree, broke his back, and got run through by a branch. He's up there screaming and hollering. There's

Germans all around. The captain asked for a volunteer to take care of him before we all got killed. I went up the tree with just my knife, Preacher Boy." His voice lowered to barely a whisper, more of a gasp. "I took care of it." The old collie dog that followed him everywhere let out a mournful whine. The demons threatening to drown him demanded their due and he shambled off to drink until he could breathe again.

Another time he told me of the horrors of the winter in the Ardennes during the Battle of the Bulge. "I ain't ever been so cold in all my born days." He quickly changed the subject and dug some black and white photos out of his pocket. "That's me in the Eagles' Nest, Hitler's resort up in the mountains." A young man with haunted eyes stared back at me from the cold lair. The horror drew him back, unrelentingly, to the frozen Ardennes . "The Germans used artillery on us in the forest, it was like it would never end, day and night. The shells would explode up in the treetops, trying to use the trees to kill us, if the cold didn't get us first. Poor bastard in the next hole took a direct hit one night. Preacher Boy, I stuck my hands in his open chest to try and get my hands warm." He stood up, gasping and wheezing. "Pray for me, won't you?" he pleaded.

Pete made it back, but he never came home. He married, worked in the mill until drinking got the better of him. A trail of petty crimes and misdeeds led to nowhere. Townspeople eventually shunned him, one by one. Churches did not want a drunk bringing his dog to worship. "Millions of good men made it home. God only knows how many of them are trying to breathe while drowning," he pondered before going off to buy birdseed. "I put out sunflower seeds for the redbirds, Preacher Boy. The cardinals don't know anything about what I done, who I am. They eat, and sing, and fly away, knowing old Pete will have seed for them whenever it snows."

I arrive at his hospital room and pull a chair close to sit beside him. Imposing machines wheeze and whirl as his lungs fight the fluids of emphysema. He is drowning. I take his hand as he struggles to breathe against the approaching tide. I whisper that his wife sends her love and caring. He stirs. "She'll see to the birds," I add. Time slips away, minute by minute. His breathing slows and I wipe the sweat from his brow. "Rest easy now, Pete. Rest well. Your shadow is welcoming you home." As he slips away I sense something at the window. I look up. A bright red cardinal looks in, as though waiting. Then with a nod, he flies away.

Words are magic and writers are wizards.

BROTHER JOE BOB CARL'S GAS AND GOSPEL

I AM DRIVING THROUGH the mountains of western North Carolina, following the Cullasaja River from Franklin to Highlands along US64. The Cullasaja flows from the Tuckasegee to the Little Tennessee through the Cullasaja Gorge in Macon County in the Nantahala National Forest. And if you think the names are tongue twisters, the road itself might make you a bit queasy. Lots of sheer rock walls on one side of endless blind curves following rusty guardrails along steep drop offs into the river gorge. At one point you can make a tiny detour to drive under Bridal Veil Falls, if you're so inclined, though if you're not childlike be prepared to be disappointed. Turning off at Turtle Pond Road, I climb Little Scaly Mountain, following the gravel one and a half lane trail through thickly wooded forest, wending back and forth across the Georgia state line until all that matters is that I'm on The Mountain. For some reason I may never discern, I am drawn to an unmarked dirt lane that wends and winds and climbs some more before its dead end at Brother Joe Bob Carl's Gas and Gospel Stop.

It's a ramshackle affair with an antique service station visible gas pump sitting proudly all shined up and standing at rigid attention before a wooden building that crouches against the fierce winds, just like the stunted white oak trees that surround it and looking every bit of the centuries of weathering that the humbled trees also exhibit. All are surrounded by a carpet of lichens that seem to part and bow before the footsteps of Brother Joe Bob Carl as he steps out of the battered door and casts a wary eye towards a weary traveler. How do I know that it's him? The hand lettered sign leaning against the pump tells me so. It is the first of many signs . . . and wonders of that day.

"Gas or gospel?" he asks with the look of a mischievous elf. "Some of both," is all I can think of to say. The antique service station visible gas pump whirls and gurgles while he whistles a tune that seems so very familiar somehow . . . but I still can't quite place it to this day. "Let me ask ya sumthin'," says Brother Joe Bob Carl. "Does a singer own the song? Does a reader own the story?" He takes off his camo cap and scratches at the salt and pepper hair underneath. "Do a piano's keys own the melody? Or more to your point," though I wasn't aware I'd been making one, he continues, "Does a writer own the alphabet?" I'm astonished, and it shows. He meets my confused shrug with a laugh. "I'm just riddlin' you. Don't pay me no nevermind." He goes back to his tune and tops off the tank. "Nice truck," he murmurs, before motioning to me to follow.

We go through the door, squeeze between racks of every last known knickknack, urgent Amazon purchases, and body improvement aids from the last twelve decades and enter a dingy office. He continues on to the rear, kneels and opens a small door, and crawls through. Still whistling that tune. I get on my hands and knees and crawl into the darkness. It is cold and damp and uncomfortable, but I stay tuned to his . . . okay, you got me, his tune. Finally, I emerge into the light to find Brother Joe Bob Carl perched on a small ledge, feet dangling over the edge, a couple thousand feet above the Cullasaja River. I gingerly sit beside him, my terror of heights notwithstanding, and peer down between my feet. In one glance I magically see the specter of the might and fury of the Cullasaja Falls thundering over impossible rocks, as well as the wonder and dancing of Dry Falls, the majesty and awe of the tree covered slopes and peaks.

"What do you see?" asks Brother Joe Bob Carl. At least I think he said that. I look into his eyes, then down below, then back to his eyes. "Power," I offer. He nods. I looked again, then back to his eyes. For some reason, although I never see his lips move, that tune fills my head. "Beauty," is all I can say. He closes his eyes. The afternoon stretches on. A movement catches the corner of my eye and I watch a hawk floating on the breezes and updrafts. I grow uncomfortable when it seems like the hawk is the one doing the watching. Of me. I close my eyes in fear. When I open them, I'm startled to see Brother Joe Bob Carl gazing at me, his hand over his heart. And I know. "Longing," I say. "I see longing. My own."

He smiles and reaches into the pouch at his side. He removes a piece of cloth, neatly folded. A book with gold imprint. And two sticks of wood. Brother Joe Bob Carl carefully arranges them before me on that high ledge. "When you are ready," he says, "you will know where to go, what to do." Then he took off his cap, scratched his head some more, and crawled back the way we'd come. I sat there for the longest time before knowing. I left them there. And followed the echo of his tune.

Words are magic, and writers are wizards.

THE PRISONER

Some people say, to this day, that it never happened. Some people say, to this day, that it never could happen. Still others say, to this day, that it never, ever should happen. Some people insist, to this day, that it actually did occur. And then there are those of us who fervently believe with every fiber of our being that of course, it could happen. And, by God if it could happen, who's to say it didn't, wouldn't, or shouldn't? Isn't faith acting like we believe a lot of things that did, could, would, or should happen? Or is it; is that what is faith? "Aye, there's the rub," to quote Willie, whose fondness for strong Iron City ale and bawdy jokes earned him the nickname, 'Shakes Beer', otherwise known as inmate #798334 in the Western Pennsylvania State Penitentiary, later transformed into the West Penn State Correctional Institute or, as it's known to everyone who's been inside, The Wall.

If you dip your left foot into the waters of the Monongahela River and your right foot into the waters of the Allegheny River and walk north, you're walking on the Ohio River, a feat in and of itself. And yes, the Ohio runs north by northwest through Allegheny and Beaver Counties before it makes a lazy turn where Pennsylvania, West Virginia and Ohio hold hands, just to show there are no hard feelings as it leaves the homeland of its headwaters. A few miles above the point (yes, I'm going full Pittsburgh on you) along the Good River, The Wall sits encamped. It is the product of that most human of all inventions, civilized society. A forty-foot-high fieldstone wall encloses some twenty acres, built in the years following the Civil War to house up to 1100 of those who committed serious crimes so they could become penitent, or corrected. The Wall hovers above the tows and barges and party line cruises on the river below, and looms over the souls encased within its confines.

Jonesy entered the penitentiary as a young man, just a few years removed from adolescence, that time of wanting all of the freedoms, none of the responsibilities. Jonesy had gone for a ride with a friend who held up a gas station. Two years into his stretch Jonesy, whose father worked in the J & L mill on Second Avenue and his mother at Kaufmanns downtown, was put in 'the hole', or solitary confinement, or Restricted Housing Unit; take your pick. Seems that at one point, while going through the North Block, Jonesy came upon a guard beating a young inmate named Willie, who had said the wrong thing. Jonesy stepped in and pushed the guard who fell, hit his head, and was injured. Jonesy was locked away. The key was thrown away. No appeals. No contact. Three ten-minute showers a week. Locked up 23/7/365. Five times a week an hour of exercise, alone. Strip searched. Lights on 24/7/365. Eating alone. For weeks. Then months. Then years. Then decades.

It changes a man. Of course, it does. What saved Jonesy from this expression of civilized society was being allowed to write letters. To one person and one person only. So, he chose Willie Shakes Beer. After his parents died, Jonesy sent letters to Willie for other prisoners who needed encouragement. To those feeling despair, to those needing hope or strength. He even wrote to the guards. Oh, he made his legal appeals, had his benefactors and detractors. To no avail. As the years went by the steel mills disappeared, Kaufmanns disappeared, but the Ohio flowed, and The Wall remained. And Jonesy eventually needed glasses, then bifocals. His hair turned gray, then white. Nobody could explain why he needed to remain in The Hole, but regulations stipulated it. The color of his skin helped many to overlook it. Letters from Jonesy became coveted currency within The Wall. People memorized them, shared his words, cherished them.

When word came down that the prison was to close in 2005, Jonesy decided to write one last letter to each and every inmate before he was shipped across the state to another hole. He wrote to Willie, "Whether it's to be or not to be, I hope that they take me at night so that I can see the stars one more time. I hope it is raining so that I can feel like I'm in the river one more time. I'm out of fight. I don't know if it's better to suffer the slings and arrows of this misfortune or fall asleep and find out it's all been a dream . . . to just shuffle off . . . " Willie busied himself with the authorities, begging and pleading for leniency. Compassion. Humility. And that most fragile: hope.

The night Jonesy was to be moved everything was arranged. He was brought out to the middle of the yard. Then, mysteriously, the guards left him alone. He looked up. The floodlights went off. Stars. Welcoming him. The silence was deafening. The stillness complete. He looked around. In every window, along every tier, each walkway, lining every stair, from the office windows of the administrators, the chapel, gymnasium, clinic—all were lined with people. Prisoners holding his letters. His words. His thoughts. His imagination. A door opened and a child stepped out, coming across the yard, hand outstretched. As she approached, an Ohio

River Valley fog rolled in without warning. Thick, billowing, it blanketed The Wall. Shouts went up. Alarms sounded. People yelled. As quickly as it came, the fog lifted. The lights came on.

The Yard was empty. Some claim they heard a splash down at the river, but Jonesy was never seen again.

Words are magic, and writers are wizards.

THE UNICORN STORY

THE GRANDPA DROVE CAREFULLY, his precious cargo ensconced safely beside him in the person of his 9-year-old granddaughter, Haley. He steered the old battleship Pontiac along the Parkway West, from the Pittsburgh Airport toward the city. "You don't give up on a car if it ain't giving up on you," was his theory of the 8-cylinder behemoth. "Whataya thinking about, Grandpa?" the girl asked, as they descended the steep, sweeping curves toward the Fort Pitt Tunnel. He glanced over at her trusting eyes. "In winter with warm tears I'll melt the snow/And keep eternal springtime upon thy face," he murmured. She gave him a quizzical look. "What's that mean?" He allowed a small smile. "Just Willie's way of painting a picture, my dear. Just ole' Willie's way." Haley giggled. "Grandpa, your heart is so big it sticks outside of you!"

The man dug into his pocket, pulled out a peppermint and gave it to her. As she savored its sweetness, the old battleship broke through to the other side of the tunnel and all the wonder of the three rivers uniting at the Point, tall buildings etched against the clouds in the Golden Triangle, trains, tugs, tows, sports stadiums, cable cars climbing Mount Washington, all framed by the hulking girders of the giant bridge brought forth a rush of excitement. "Oh Grandpa! Look. It's America!" Haley exclaimed. He looked at her again, the lump in his throat tightening at the sight of the ugly bruise on her neck. Her mother, his daughter, sent her for a visit. 'Until Charles calms down. He didn't mean to get so angry. Really, Daddy, he's a good man. Just for a while. Please.' The man shook his head, as if he could clear the pain from his heart.

After a bit, he pulled into the parking lot of an Eat N Park restaurant. While they waited for their order he handed Haley a small box, wrapped in red paper and a silver bow. With eyes wide, she opened it, and withdrew a bracelet. It was made of yarn and thread, from which there dangled a small charm, a pink and blue unicorn. "Do you like it?" he asked, a bit hesitantly. When she tilted her face up towards his, he could see the unmistakable reddened fingermarks on the soft skin below her ear. "It has special power," he continued, dread and bile gagging him. "Unicorns always look for the truth. Unicorns have hearts full of courage." He leaned across the table, inches from her smile. "And unicorns can remove poison from water. And to those who aren't truthful, the unicorn pierces their heart with its horn." He gently stroked her cheek. Haley giggled. "Grandpa, your heart is so big it sticks outside of you!"

Their food arrived. Haley got her favorite, pancakes, and bacon. Extra bacon. Her daddy wouldn't let her get the extra bacon, but grandpa didn't seem to mind at all. "I want you to wear that," he said, with more intensity than he intended. "All the time. You hear me?" She frowned. "Are you mad at me, Grandpa? Do you want me to go away, too?" He clutched at his heart, as though pierced through. "No, child. No." His lips trembled; his courage faltered. He sought the truth, a way to draw out the poison. There seemed no way open to him. "Grandpa only wants to hold you safe. I want you to remember the unicorn. No matter what." She looked at him with absolute and complete trust. "But I don't need a unicorn, Grandpa. I have you."

The man's vision blurred through his tears. "Oh, child. Grandpa won't always be here. But unicorns live forever." He slipped the bracelet onto her small wrist and held her hand for a moment. "Remember. Only you can decide who you are, Haley. Now, say it with me." And so it was that the patrons at the Eat N Park that winter evening heard the old man and the little girl reciting together: "Unicorns look for truth. Unicorns are full of courage. Unicorns take away poison. Unicorns pierce the heart." Three times he made her recite it. Always ending with, "Only you can decide who you are." And all those around fell silent. Wondering at the site of the holy haze that seemed to envelop the two in their booth. Maybe it was just the lighting gone awry. Maybe it was smoke from the kitchen. Maybe . . . But none who witnessed it ever forgot it.

And so it was, that the next morning, when the Pittsburgh Police found the old Pontiac apparently abandoned in the parking lot of the Eat N Park, it's engine running, no sign of any foul play, no sign of the old man and the child, many wondered. To this day, if you stand at the Point on a cold winter's night, after the river traffic dies down. And look out at the mist rising. Some say they see pink. Some see blue. But they all swear that when the wind comes down the Ohio, you can hear a child's voice whisper, "Grandpa, your heart is so big it sticks outside of you."

And etched into the stone lining the bank you will find these words: "In winter with warm tears I'll melt the snow/And keep eternal springtime upon thy face."

Words are magic, and writers are wizards.

THE GREEN DOT

THE STRANGER ARRIVED UNANNOUNCED, as strangers so often do. He stood in the public square and began proclaiming, "In three days there will come the death of imagination." People walked on past him, scoffing, "Imagination could never die. That's preposterous." At noon of the first day after he had been proclaiming his message for hours, a woman approached. She had a puzzled look on her face. "We don't need imagination anyway. We have a special book that tells us all we need to know. It has all the stories we need, explains all where everything comes from, and why we are here." The stranger looked at her with great patience and asked, "What if something new comes along, or what if there is new knowledge?" She replied, "Oh, we make everything new fit the old." The stranger shook his head. "Then I cannot imagine giving you the green dot."

The stranger moved along, still proclaiming, "The end of imagination is near. If you do not have the green dot when imagination ends, you cannot enter the Kingdom of Light." A group of theologians and pastors were just leaving their weekly luncheon and heard him say this. "My good fellow," said one of them, "this is quite the epistemological syllogism, wouldn't you agree my fine colleagues? We pursue the thoughts of the Great Guy in the Sky, historically and righteously, so without imagination what would be the eschatological purpose of things, let alone a green dot?" The rest all nodded in sage consent. "How does one even possess a green dot?" asked a pastor, fresh from seminary. "Unless you receive a green dot, you can never enter the Kingdom of Light," said the stranger. "Well, there you have it!" announced a senior pastor who had all the theologians' books on his shelves. "It's discriminatory and biased." And they moved on.

And it was night, and it was the second day. The stranger took up his place and made his announcement. "In two days, imagination will vanish. Receive the green dot so you may enter the Kingdom of Light." A television news crew arrived and assured the stranger they simply wanted to tell his story. "Are you making a political statement?" the ever so eager to prove herself journalist inquired. The stranger stood there in silence. "The cameras are rolling, sir. If you don't make some noise how will anyone hear you?" She pushed him. The silence of the stranger became deafening. The journalist tried again. "What's your story? If imagination disappears, won't that be the end of stories?" The stranger finally said, "Without a green dot, you can never see the Kingdom of Light."

At that moment, an Amazon delivery truck was passing by. The driver stopped to consider this spectacle. The reporter thrust the microphone in his face. "Sir, what do you make of this green dot conspiracy?" He shrugged. "I'm just trying to feed my family, make a living. What's a green dot going to do for me?" The journalist faced the camera. "And there you have it. People are saying if you don't have a green dot, you won't be allowed to make a living, worship as you please, talk to the Great Guy in the Sky even. Where will it all end? Now, back to you in the studio." The stranger helped her pack up her equipment and got her something to drink in the heat of the day. Before she left, she turned to him. "Do you think I could get a green dot?" It was only much later that she considered his answer. "I imagine that's up to you."

And it was night, and it was the third day. The stranger took up his place and made his announcement. "In one day, imagination will vanish. Seek the green dot and enter the Kingdom of Light." The entire town had had enough of this foolishness. Social media was lit, as they say. They were the butt of internet memes. And they gathered around the stranger to demand that he leave them alone. Just at that moment, a child named Johnny was walking in the square, tapping a stick on the ground before him. Johnny had been born blind. The stranger called the boy to come to him and Johnny came.

"Johnny, what is light?" the stranger asked. "I have never seen light," Johnny replied. "Is it music you can touch all the way to your feet?" he asked. "Is it the warmth of the sun that I can drink? Is it the vibration of my stick when I tap a rock? Is it the excitement of my puppy when we play? Is it the feeling in my heart when I know my mother is smiling?" The stranger smiled. "Johnny, what do you dream?" Johnny reached up and took the stranger's face and pulled it to within an inch of his own. Slowly his fingers traced the stranger's features. "I dream of you," whispered Johnny. Then he felt the wetness of the stranger's tears and pressed his lips to them. "I dream of light."

The stranger touched his finger to Johnny's forehead. "I'm giving you a green dot." But the people grew angry. "There's nothing there. That's no green dot." But they were too late. It was the end of the third day.

Words are magic and writers are wizards.

THE GOD CULT

The night sounds of the woods composed a chorale of insect songs, small animals rustling, tree frogs harmonizing, gently carried on a breeze off the lake. The campfire burned on the rocky beach, the cool mountain air quickly drying our soaked clothing. "What were you thinking?" asked Billy, shaking his head at the recollection of getting my foot unjammed from the rocks as the cloudburst caught me in the open in a dry creek bed. "I thought I could jump over it," I shrugged. "Thanks, by the way." "Couldn't let the new preacher drown like a rat, now could I?" Billy flashed his easy smile. "I don't know anything about managing the faithful," I confessed. "What's there to know?" replied Billy. "It's the God Cult. You don't need faith to run a church, you need to be a prop master."

"The God Cult?" I wondered whose absurd idea it was to bring me here. "Yeah," he said. "Cults have a superhero, somebody at the top. You're supposed to worship him, listen, do everything that makes him happy and prosperous, right?" I shrugged, "I suppose." He continued, "Is that all written down somewhere?" His eyes reflected the sparks from the fire. I reached into the Preacher Bag Jodie gave me as a joke earlier that day. I pulled out a Bible. "Prop number one," Billy declared. "You can hold it over your head, wave it around, thump on it, open it and point to magic words to back up the cult, and so on and so on. They'll love you for that." He pulled out a flaming stick from the fire and pointed it to the book. "Or" and he waved the stick toward the flames. "It's just an object." I ran my hand over the cover, took a deep breath, and heaved it into the fire.

He studied me with unwavering eyes. "What else you got in your preacher kit?" I rummaged around and pulled out a small wooden box. It opened to reveal a small plate, little glass bottle and a few small cups. "Ah," mused Billy, "the 3 in 1 Oil of the God Cult. " He stopped to chuckle at his own joke. "Memories and spirits and ghosts and invisible prayers, all live inside that little box. Made to look like breadcrumbs and fermented fruit.

For the God Cult you have to be able to look very serious and be a good actor. Can you pull that off, Preacher? Make the invisible visible? Corral the furthest reaches of the imagination into a vaudeville act? Tall tales told well to the perishables in the pews? Big, big job." I snapped the box shut and pitched it into the fire.

"Keep going," he urged. I reached in and extracted a small wooden stand. In the middle a cross was fixed, gleaming with polish. To one side was a tiny American flag and on the other the flag of the God Cult. "Well, isn't that just precious!" Billy scoffed. "Preacher, let me tell you. I was the sniper in a Marine Scout platoon. We went rockin' and rollin' through Iraq. I have 43 confirmed, if you catch my drift." He nodded toward the set and his voice went soft. "I was protecting my buddies, my kind. God and Country. Sacrifice and service." He took the set and held it up to examine it more closely. "Your Dear Leader's boy got himself killed. Now every clubhouse has one of those or it can't be in the God Cult. They're all props." And into the fire it all went.

We sat for the longest time in silence after that, watching and listening. I heard him heave a deep sigh. "What now?" I whispered. As he got to his feet, he said, "One of the strangest things about the cult is that they all are convinced God gets furious and then disappointed if He doesn't hear from them at least once a week about how great He is. That they have to tell Him every day how they would never make it without Him, or what? His feelings get hurt? He's that much of a narcissistic bore?" I reached into the preacher kit and took out the shiny worship songbook and into the flames it flew. "Looky there," Billy cried. "Now, that's a fire!"

The night settled in around us. The fire died down to a few glowing embers. "Now what?" I asked. Billy came and stood before me, his eyes inches from mine. "What do you have left?" I picked up the bag and shook it. "Nothing. It's empty." Something funny happened in his eyes. I've never been really sure just what, but it happened as he said, "Check again." Reluctantly I undid the tie and searched around inside in the darkness. Something cool and hard touched my hand. I pulled it out. In my hand was a small mirror. "It's enough," chuckled Billy as he turned to go. Then again, over his shoulder, "It is enough. Try to keep up."

Words are magic and writers are wizards.

THE HOLY DARK

Winston Freeman is furious. So furious that he cannot fall asleep. He sits in his study brooding. And drinking. Looking for numbness. Looking for clarity. The alcohol provides neither. He entertains notions of retribution. How good it would feel . . . to knock the snide right out of that son of a bitch . . . to scream "SHUT UP" to that prattling fool. How good it would feel, satisfying even . . . to stop in the middle of traffic and run up to the window of that pickup truck and shake a fist in that jerk's face . . . to rip the foolish flag off the house of the insufferable neighbor. What a triumph it would be . . . to call his ex-wife and brag about dating younger, hotter women who hang on his every word . . . to march into his boss's office and proclaim from on high how much of an idiotic imbecile he is. Winston is certain he would feel all powerful, on top of the world, a bro among bros. After all, he deserves to feel that way, he is owed some peace and satisfaction. Why can't he have just one moment?

Winston feels himself growing more and more agitated. By the time the clock reads 3am, he is emboldened, full of the fire of indignation . . . albeit, fueled by the force of self-righteousness. He studies his collection of pistols displayed on the wall. What if . . . ? Their dark power is a lure, a possible cure for this helpless sense of being impotent in his own life. Who would it harm if he carried one of them with him? As he gets out of his chair to take a closer look, he weaves a bit, unsteady and blinking repeatedly as the display swirls in his vision. The words of the sage, "Object attachment to a piece of metal, whether it be a firearm or a cross, gives the illusion of power to an empty or troubled heart," find no root in his imagination this night, of all nights. At any rate, he needs more whiskey, of that he is sure. "I've had a few, I'll take my bike," Winston reassures himself, cloaked in a vague taint of responsibility.

Tucking a Baretta .9mm in his waistband, he sets off down the dark lane on his mission. Winston wanders across the two lanes, unconcerned as the road is deserted. The cool breeze on his face is helping him to realize that he has no idea where he is going. Where does one buy courage in the dead of night? He concentrates on following the center line, absorbed in his quixotic quest when the headlights of a car come rushing up behind him. The driver sees him at the last instant, jerks to the right, slips off the surface, overcorrects and careens across the pavement, hits the low retaining wall, and rolls over and over in a metallic screech and shower of sparks, landing upside down in the drainage ditch, wheels still spinning in a helpless appeal to the laws of physics. Winston stares for a moment, stunned by the suddenness and ferocity of the crash. Then he shakes himself, drops the bike and hurries to the wreck.

Kneeling beside the driver's window, broken glass crunches under his knees as Winston bows low to see the interior. A young woman in obvious pain is suspended by the seatbelt, upside down. Her red curls dangle toward the roof as she turns to look at him, her face shockingly pale. "I'm in a wee spot of trouble," she manages with a grim smile. "Me granddad told me to not be trying to drive through the holy dark." Winston reaches across her, searching for the release button. "Can you move okay?" She groans, and attempted movement brings a sharp gasp. Winston looks at her lap and has to swallow hard. The impact has fractured her right femur and bone is poking through her jeans. A small bloodstain is rapidly growing larger as he watches. "Don't leave me, please," murmurs the girl. "You're hurt. I need to get help," Winston manages. "You be my help," she says, pleading in her voice.

"I'm afraid to move you. But you can't stay like that." Winston quickly takes stock. "I'll crawl in the other side and maybe I can keep your leg from getting worse when I undo the belt." He pushes back out and goes around the car. The fumes of gasoline spilling out bring an expletive to his lips as he remembers his phone is back in his study. The sides of the ditch make it impossible to open the doors, so he wriggles through the passenger window, his back on the interior roof. "What's your name?" he asks. "Miriam," comes a weak whisper. In the light of the dash, he can see the bloodstain growing with each beat of her heart, saturating the cloth and starting to drip free. Winston struggles out of his shirt and reaches up to try to put pressure on the wound. "Miriam, I'm right here. I'm staying right here, okay?" "I'm cold," she manages, "and the spirits of the holy dark be whispering to me. *Mo ghradh*, I'm not ready to go on alone . . ."

In the early morning, police responded to a call about a wrecked vehicle on old Route 219. When they arrived, they took note of the skid marks across the road tracing the path of the accident and called the fire department to handle the spilled gasoline. But when they looked inside the car, it was empty. Empty that is, except for a blood-soaked men's tee shirt. "Nobody could lose that much blood and live," one surmised. And none could figure out why it was tied to a Baretta pistol as though fashioning a crude tourniquet. Nor was there any explaining the tire tracks of a bicycle leading off into the distance, toward the holy dark . . .

Words are magic and writers are wizards.

THE HONORABLE

THE CLOUD-SHADOWED MOUNTAINS SPENT the day like they spent every other day; impassively watching as the sun worked its way across the wintry sky over fallow fields in the valley. The golden-brown stubble leftover from harvested crops served as the winter beard protecting earth's skin. A pile of giant rolled hay bales nestled in the corner of a field, each wearing a protective white shrink-wrapped plastic robe against the elements and hungry field mice. On the next hill, hay barns brimmed with the sweet smell of last summer's bounty, the mixture of sun and laughter and patience that if you know enough to look for it, is its own reward. Behind a stand of oaks and poplars sits a large white house with a two-story portico entrance and black shutters at every window, a long driveway winding down the hill haunted by antebellum spirits restless for expiation, atonement of any sort would do. Across the valley two large churches, one Presbyterian and the other Baptist, lurk like sentinels, guardians against foolish grace too easily redeemed.

Judge Chester Oaks presides over this domain. Well, to be truthful, Chester is the 'decently and in order' Presbyterian and his wife, Alicia is the wild, untamable Baptist, so the only parting of their ways is on Sunday mornings . . . and Alicia's Baptist-can't-make-it-till-Sunday-all-hands-on-deck-lest-the-devil-give-you-heck – Wednesday evening meeting. But the land has been in the Oaks family for generations, just a stone's throw from one Thomas Jefferson's summer home, Poplar Forest, to the east. And if you're fond of history, forty-five minutes to the southwest is the farm and national monument of one Booker T. Washington, mentor to one George Washington Carver, and if you don't know about these two gentlemen, shame on you. On the way there, you will pass the National D Day Memorial. And yes, I'm aware that Appomattox Court House is just a stone's throw up the valley. History. You can't take a piss in Virginia without soaking history, and some is more popular than . . . the other stuff. But we're here to learn about The

Honorable Chester A. Oaks. His love for Alicia, for the land, for his herd of black Angus, for the law, and what makes a person honorable.

Chester is a judge in the Superior District Court and as he nears retirement age he wonders if he has any true claim to the title of honorable. On the weekends, when he's going to either the Lynchburg Livestock Auction or the Farmers Livestock Auction up in back of Moneta, with the old trailer rattling along behind his truck, his farm manager, Harry, riding shotgun, talking weather and prices and markets and shots—modern cowboy conversation—sometimes Chester gets philosophical. Hard to tell what two men in a pickup who both have been cruising on the main highway of life for a good while with moderate success might talk about otherwise, but on this day Harry suddenly looked up and asked, "What's it like to send somebody to jail?" Now one thing honorable means is honest, so Chester replied, "It's something I never get used to. Am I sending somebody someplace where I wouldn't go myself?" Harry scratched at his whiskers. "But they're criminals. You ain't." And the Honorable Chester said, "But if I was standing in front of me, up there on the bench . . . or, if I looked down and it was me waiting for judgement and sentence, would it be any different?"

They almost bought a young bull that day, but when bidding went beyond Chester's willing to pay number, he walked away without a second thought. That night when they got home, Alicia met him in front of the portico, looking weary and a bit worn. Chester was alarmed and took her in his arms, asking what was wrong. "Doc was here. Mary Jean is in a bad way." She looked at him in a way that needed no words. "Did he put her down?" asked Chester. Alicia shook her head. "He knew how you felt. Kept shaking his head, saying, 'If I told him once, I told him a hundred times, don't name your breeders.' You old fool," said Alicia with breathtaking tenderness. Chester kissed her on the forehead. Without a word he went down to the main barn, got the backhoe, and went out to the old orchard and dug a hole. Then Harry helped him get Mary Jean down there without seeing the rifle and, under the new moon, the honorable Chester said his goodbyes.

The next Wednesday, after Alicia left for the Baptist big-long-name meeting, Chester stopped at Harry's house and asked if he wanted to take a ride. "Something wrong with the herd?" Harry was worried. Chester assured him all was well. They drove across the county to the Blue Ridge Regional Jail Authority in Bedford. When they arrived, Chester grabbed a briefcase and kept a nervous Harry calm as they passed through security. By 7 they were in a classroom facing inmates of various ages. "I'm Chester," he began, "and I'm here to help you prepare for your GED exam and to give you some college classes, as well. And Harry here, he can teach you everything there is to know about raising black Angus. It's good, honest work, you're outside a lot, and the cattle don't talk back. Much" Harry stepped forward, shy and awkward. "I can take an engine apart and put it back together blindfolded." Then to Chester's surprise, he added, "I draw, too. If you want to learn some drawing stuff, I'd be glad to show you."

The next morning, the sun came up over the same mountains, and they spent the day as always. Watching. Silently. Maybe because they already know that it takes much more than a black robe to identify what is honorable . . .

Words are magic and writers are wizards.

THE SECRET

It is a war story. "My tears for your scars" pretty much sums it up, as it does for all war stories. And the same can be said of love stories, my scars for your tears. So, this story is both: a war story of love and a love story of war. And to put the icing on the cake, it is a Christmas story, the ultimate 'my tears for your scars' story, especially for the descendants of white Europeans and everything that they have touched around the globe even with its elements of the Far East, Near East and Mid East. God bless the editor who looked at Mark's manuscript for these crazy gospel things and said, "Nope, keep the beginning as is. That's all it needs." It is a story told by one Bacon Puggle, a sergeant in the United States Army, fighting their way across France in 1944. It seems Bacon was captured in late summer and sent to a prisoner of war camp deep inside Germany.

Bacon filed into the drab camp, nestled at the foot of the Bavarian Alps, a majestic setting for so dreary a place. Rows and rows of wooden barracks sat filled with endless rows of crude bunks for countless captured soldiers, all harboring their fears about how this would all end. The commandant was a coarse and obedient soldier, as well. Prisoners were counted three times a day, rain or shine, hot or cold, lined up in rows in front of the barracks. Fierce dogs and men with submachine guns roamed the area between the two electrified fences and searchlights swept through the darkness all night long. Bacon was assigned duty in the camp infirmary, where he met an attendant named Aleudar. The two men struck up a friendship in this unlikely setting. Bacon could not tell if Aleudar had been a doctor before the war, or simply had experience working in a hospital. Once when he asked the mysterious man about his home, he answered, "We have no home. They hate us, call us gypsies."

Bacon helped him sneak extra rations for those suffering, sneaking extra bread or a tiny fraction more gruel. One wounded soldier seemed to garner extra attention from Aleudar, a boy of seventeen, who had lost his father at Pearl Harbor and his older brother in Sicily. His mother was alone now in Pittsburgh and Aleudar told the boy stories and encouraged him to be strong and make it through, but the young man grew weaker. The winter of 1944-5 was particularly fierce and cold. Many in the camp were dying just as liberation and victory seemed to be a real possibility. The German commandant was ordered to move the prisoners before the Allies advanced into the country. The guards were given orders to liquidate all of the weakest prisoners. One day they came to clean out the infirmary.

Aleudar pulled Bacon aside and whispered urgently to him, telling him that he had hidden a special box inside the camp and for Bacon to dig up that box and take care of it. What he found in the box would belong to him now, in appreciation of his friendship and trust and would make him rich beyond his dreams. Then Aleudar went to the guards and somehow persuaded them to let him take the place of the wounded boy. For some reason Bacon did not understand, the guards agreed to Aleudar's sacrifice and the boy was spared. Aleudar was taken to the garbage pits and executed because evil demands its pound of flesh, in all respects.

Under the cover of darkness, Bacon snuck out of the barracks and went to the place Aleudar had told him about. He dug into the dirt and uncovered the most beautiful wooden box he had ever seen. Beautiful and intricate designs were carved into a kind of wood he had never seen before. He eagerly tried to pry it open to discover what would make him rich beyond his dreams. But the strange thing was, he could not open it. No matter how he tried, it would not open. Although there was no clasp, no lock, nothing he tried worked. It would not open. Figuring that maybe it was some kind of heirloom, Bacon took the box with him and hid it away.

The camp was liberated, the war ended and at long last, Bacon was on his way home to his wife. On the ship back across the Atlantic, he would take the box out at night and try again to open it, but nothing worked. On the long train ride, he mused about what riches awaited him once the box opened. It was beautiful and obviously valuable, but what was inside? Finally, the train reached his hometown on Christmas morning. With snow silently falling, he walked up the sidewalk to the front door. His wife threw open the door and they rushed into each other's arms. Church bells pealed as Bacon pulled out Aleudar's special box, the only gift he had to give. He held it out to her and when her hand touched the box, by some special magic, it opened. And inside, waiting to be revealed, lay . . . The Secret.

Words are magic and writers are wizards.

Adapted from THE HEALER, a novel by John Thomas Tuft, AuthorHouse 2019.

TAKE ME TO CHURCH

Dusty sat beside the campfire finishing his coffee from a tin mug. His sorrel horse, Devil's Angel, grazed nearby, fidgeting a bit as fireflies rose off the mountain grass in the musky dusk. Dusty was helping move the herd from the summer pastures back down below for the winter. The life of a cowboy has more than its share of solitude and sometimes more than its share of misery. After his father was killed at Shiloh, Dusty left home and headed west. The youngest in the outfit at 17, Boss posted him on the eastern side of the herd that night to watch for the mountain lion that had killed two calves earlier. Getting one dollar a day was good, honest money, but the work meant twenty-hour days, fatigue, loneliness, and danger. He needed to be up before dawn when coyotes would sneak up the draws and dry creek beds looking for trouble, so he checked the Winchester repeater that he kept close at hand at all times.

After his triple B's chow—beans, bacon, and biscuits—Dusty stretched out and watched the stars arching over the wide valley below. The cattle seemed settled for the night, and he tried not to think about the task tomorrow of getting them across the river. Other than a stampede, that was the biggest moment of danger in this job, he knew. He loved the high country with its cool breezes and hawks soaring overhead, reminding him of home in the Great Smokies. He drifted off thinking about Momma and his sisters back east. He was dreaming about being in the woods with his old hound dog when a brilliant flash of lighting and a boom of thunder jolted him awake.

Dusty's first thought was for Devil's Angel because a man out here with no horse was a goner. Her eyes were wide, and her nostrils flared, but she was still there beside the embers of the fire. He went to her, speaking in a soothing tone, keeping one eye on the sky. He needed to check the cattle right away. As he saddled the sorrel and slipped the rifle into its scabbard, the wind picked up. The sky split again with a bright flash and the full-throated wrath of the gods. As he swung up onto the horse, the clouds opened up and over the drum of the rain he heard restless cattle bawling and bleating. He urged Devil's Angel forward with a kick and slap of the reins, heart in his throat. Hopefully Boss and the other cowboys were already there with them.

As he rode down the slope into the high meadow, in the next flash Dusty saw cattle milling around agitated, and unsure. It would be hell on earth if they started running downhill toward the river. Over the din he heard Boss and the others whistling and yelling out to the herd, trying to keep them reassured and controlled. Suddenly a calf broke away, terrified and heading pell-mell toward the gulch to the east. Dusty kicked Devil's Angel and gave chase. Wind and rain lashed at his face as he struggled to keep the calf in sight. The horse was sure-footed and the two operated as one, dodging around trees, wheeling to try and head the frightened calf away from danger.

With a snort, Devil's Angel abruptly stopped and reared on her hind legs. Dusty hung on and in the lightning glow saw the calf trapped down in the rocky gulch with the mountain lion snarling in a crouch on an overhanging rock. He jumped off the horse and clamored down into the gulch, in his haste forgetting the rifle. As he reached the frightened calf, his boot slipped on the wet rocks and his foot became inextricable wedged tight. Dusty ignored the pain and worked to free the calf as the water began to rise now in the narrow confines. With frantic tugs he finally got the calf free and pushed her toward the bank as the water reached the top of his boots.

The calf exhausted herself trying to climb the steep, slippery slope but kept falling back into the still rising water. The mountain lion snarled and licked its lips in anticipation of a fine meal. Then, without prompting, Devil's Angel stepped forward and placed her body between the predator and her cowboy. Dusty scrabbled at the rocks imprisoning his foot as the water reached his waist. The calf bleated in despair as she fell back one last time. Dusty made a desperate grab for her, snagged her by the tail and struggled against the rushing water to pull her to himself as the water reached his chest.

As the sky turned gray with the new dawn, Boss and the other cowboys finally reached the gulch in their search for the lost. They stopped in silence at the scene before them. In the rushing water, a shaken and weary Dusty stood battered and bruised, trembling with the effort. Clutched close to his chest was the prodigal calf, bleating for her momma. And on the edge of the channel, Devil's Angel, hobbled and staggering, bleeding out from the wounds of a mountain lion attack, yet still watching over them . . . with sighs too deep for words.

. . . For we do not always know how to pray as we ought . . .

Words are magic and writers are wizards.

LIVING MEMORY

On the first night of the annual FAWG Festival this year Margaret McMeade flirted with Pastor Cletus in an outrageous display of attempting to sway one of the key judges in the Baked Goods contest. But, she explained, "everyone is so tired of that Nellie Goodson winning the blue ribbon in both cakes and pies. For the last ten years, mind you, she's smiled sweetly and walked off with the acclamation as the Baker Supreme." Pastor Cletus, who looked like an old gunslinger with the droopy white mustache, swept back silvery pompadour, and black ribbon bow tie, gave a not unkind smile and did his best Yoda impression. "Do or do not. Trying is an option not." Margaret fluttered her eyelashes one last time and laid one hand on Cletus' arm. "But she's not even a member of Creeper Creek Community Church, Pastor!"

For the uninitiated, The First Autumnal Waxing Gibbus Festival is an annual three-day celebration for the entire town of Creeper Creek during the waxing phase of the first full moon after the autumnal equinox. Rows of canned jars of pickled beets, pickled hogs' feet, okra, homemade sauerkraut, or whatever one's heart desired to pickle and preserve, including fruit preserves, sat proudly displayed in countless booths, with the ladies of the Creeper Creek Community Church Women's Auxiliary bustling about organizing, exclaiming and secretly, or not so secretly, coveting each other's best work. The tent pavilion in the center is the tabernacle of baked goods, the hotly contested battle for Baker Supreme designation for from scratch pies and cakes, and to a lesser extent breads and cookies. Just beyond the tabernacle stood the fine display of the Quilting Guild, a riot of colors and schemes and patterns that brought oohs and ahs—but no boasting. Heavens no, quilters do not boast. The work is the reward.

For two days and two nights, the field behind the small, frame edifice that represents the Creeper Creek Community Church, filled with crowds streaming in past the old sign out front that still uses the metal letters that invariably get lost or jumbled in ways of indeterminate inspiration. "Livers for Jesus" appeared one week when nearsighted Old Ray misread the bulletin notes. His overcorrection to "Liars for Jesus" did not help matters any, either, but the Spirit moves in mysterious ways all agreed. Living for Jesus includes livers and liars of all persuasion. The FAWG Festival was for everyone, and Brother Brown of the African Episcopal Methodist Congregation encouraged his flock to participate. Matter of fact, it was Brother Brown and Pastor Cletus who put their heads together one year and came up with the Living Memory grand finale for the festival. It is as much a result of common sense as it is an opportunity for radical transformation in a community. Even more so than Livers or Liars for Jesus, but I am getting ahead of myself. I'm Presbyterian. All shall be revealed decently and in order . . .

With booths lining the perimeter and the baking tabernacle in the center, portable outhouses off to one end of the field, the other end is used for a makeshift stage and benches in a crude semicircle. At the end of the third evening of the FAWG Festival, all gather in this mock-up of a Coliseum. Quilts are auctioned off and the awards and ribbons are duly awarded, the last and crowd favorite always being the Supreme Baker. And yes, much to Margaret's consternation, Nellie won an eleventh time. Then while the joint choirs of Creeper Creek Community and the African EM sang a medley of gospel and popular music, the banner of Living Memory was hung high overhead and the ushers solemnly carried in the assortment of card tables and set them up on the stage, around the stage, anywhere there is room. When the singing concludes, the fine folks of Creeper Creek get down to the business at hand.

At a signal, all those who wish to, proceed to a small table, place a name placard, and lay upon it the talismans of their memories. Pictures, letters, ticket stubs, locks of hair, drawings, slave ship manifests, autographs, jewelry, photographs, newspaper clippings of violence like lynchings and beatings, and those of marriages. Clippings of birth notices and death notices. Ribbons of fairs and ribbons of war. Mother of pearl cameos and mother's pearl earrings. Union cards, draft cards, birthday cards. Memories are carefully placed and noted. Then the Quilting Guild distributes a homemade dump bag they've created for this very purpose to all those entrusted with the sacrament of Living Memory. When everyone has a bag, Pastor Cletus says a prayer and Brother Brown starts a clapping beat.

At this signal, the people approach and examine the memories. When they make a choice, they sign a pledge card with the owner of those talismans. Then it all goes into the dump bag. For the next year they have agreed to live with that other person's memories. For a year, they are entrusted to keep the other's memories alive. Examine them, touch them, and if they don't know the story of a particular memory, it is their responsibility to ask the owner to tell them. That is why, on any given night in Creeper Creek, porches are abuzz. Barber shops kept open late. The local diner brought in extra folding chores. Worship services delayed by extended coffee hours. It is all because of the Living Memory project. Living with someone else's memories until the next FAWG Festival.

I hope to see you there next time . . . do or do not . . . This is the way.

Words are magic and writers are wizards.

START FROM ZERO

"Hello, hello, let me tell you what it's like to be a zero, zero . . . " the woman of indeterminate age sings the Imagine Dragon song as she waits outside a McDonalds, before her voice trails off into aimless humming. "Zero, the place of nothing. The liminal holder between positive and negative," she cheerfully adds as she feeds an overstuffed orange and brown Tabby cat French fries. Zelda and her cat, PeanutButterCup, can be found most days scrounging their way through life. Her fifteen-year-old minivan waits patiently at the curb, an old steed that wheezes and gasps but still eats up miles. Zelda and PeanutButterCup move around a lot, and for good reason. For Zelda, life lived at zero is an improvement. Existing in a neurotic world as a psychotic takes a lot of energy and innovation, not to mention the constant restlessness. Zelda keeps a tattered paperback copy of THE ROAD LESS TRAVELED on the dashboard of the van, the M. Scott Peck tome her lodestar, she believes, for navigating the vagaries that paranoid schizophrenia has bestowed upon her.

Zelda earned a master's degree in education, at one point. Worked in public schools as a counselor who got along great with the kids. She seemed to have special insight into their struggles and anxieties. Until. Until around the age of 32 when it started to feel to Zelda that her thoughts were getting away from her. And the unshakeable sense that someone was watching her. Someone who wanted to hurt her. She was sure of it. So sure, in fact, that she began sleeping with a butcher knife under her pillow. Her family and friends noted this troubling trend in Zelda's thoughts and behavior. Zelda insisted nothing was wrong, that she was just being extra careful. Hoping to keep hidden from view the storm raging inside of her. But one day, when the school principal found her hiding in a closet armed with a staple gun and a table knife because, as she very calmly stated, "the janitor organized some of the parents who want to kill me because I know too much," Zelda, instead of submitting to a psych eval, packed up her van with what she could, along with PeanutButterCup, and hit the road.

In a country that accepts school shootings as the price of doing business with all ideology, and worships its mythology as history, a landscape littered with souls struggling to reach zero comes as no great surprise. Zelda's thoughts and paranoia continued to haunt her in ever more fierce ways. For her, it was just the way her thinking worked. But to those around her, the strangeness made it more and more difficult to deal with her. She drifted from job to job, mostly low-skilled labor in kitchens. Housing became more and more difficult to keep so Zelda took to living in her van. Hadn't Mr. M. Scott Peck himself assured her that breaking free from conformity was the path to true relationships? And behind true came truth, right? And the truth sets you free. Zelda thought of herself as a free spirit, a nonconformist, and the problems that others had relating to her were on them. "Life is difficult" read the first line of M. Scott's book (she felt certain that she knew him so he wouldn't mind her calling him that) and by God, Zelda knew he was speaking directly to her.

Zelda was genuinely surprised and touched when PeanutButterCup started talking to her. She had begged enough money from a distant relative who was unaware of her situation and gotten a motel room for the night, after joining in shaking her head at the relative's question, "What is wrong with your family? Leaving you out in the cold like this." In reality, her family was tired of the midnight calls, the begging, the schemes, the lies, the drain on their own mental health. Pity from a distance has its advocates. As Zelda settled in for the night in clean sheets, she read a bit from Road Less Traveled then started to turn out the light. Someone was trying to get in through the sealed window. She could see the man sure as you can see yourself in the mirror. Zelda screamed, grabbed the cat, and fled into the bathroom. Huddled there in the dark, heart pounding, she heard PeanutButterCup whisper, "Start from zero."

For anyone, protecting ourselves from all of our fears can be exhausting. But when a brain makes it a full-time job to create fears, the results are overwhelming. Zelda's screams brought the police to the motel. They deposited her at an emergency room for a 72-hour hold. "49 female, homeless, delusional, active hallucinations, some homicidal ideation . . . " read the top of the chart in the young doctor's hands. "Can I see Dr. Peck?" she asks him. "He should know I'm here. He understands." The doctor shakes his head. "There's no one on staff by that name." His voice stays calm, conversational. "Who do you want to hurt, Zelda? And why?" "I had to leave home," Zelda begins, "because my mother tried to kill me. She says she didn't, but I know. What are the gun laws in this state? I should get her before she gets me, right?"

"I want to help, if you think that would be okay," says the doctor in an even tone. "Give you some medication that might help you feel better." "You think I'm crazy," protests Zelda. The young doctor shrugs. "It's New Year's Eve. Let's just start from zero." Zelda sits up, startled. Looks at PeanutButterCup, who nods wisely. "Yeah, let's . . . "

Words are magic and writers are wizards.

THIS GLORIOUS SADNESS

She stands all of 4'9" tall, looking like she just stepped off the pages of a Dickens novel with her mop of brown curls, freckles on her cheeks, below eyes that have seen far too much of the world's raw side. Her name is Rapture. Rapture is a slinger. Her innocent looks are what make her a good slinger. She lives on the top floor of a trap house run by her uncle Brando. Trapping refers to selling illegal street drugs such as heroin and meth and Special K (ketamine). A trap house is a place where users come to buy the drugs and then shoot up, smoke it, or whatever it takes. Uncle Brando is a Yat from New Orleans, a descendant from the poor Irish of that area who shortened the greeting "where you at?" to Yat, as opposed to Cajun or Creole. Rapture adored her uncle Brando but didn't like it when he urged her to try and buy the other kids' Adderall at school so it could be crushed, repackaged, and sold to college students looking for a study aid.

Rapture put on her torn jeans, rainbow Skechers, and EXO tee shirt each morning, wondering what other little girls were doing. She looked like them but her friends at school said that their parents would not allow them to visit in her home. And they did not want their children inviting her into theirs. Uncle Brando made sure she had food and clothes and always asked if she had homework, but also expected her to pull her own weight in helping with the business. So, he made her a slinger. He didn't dare keep his stash of drugs in the trap house. That's much too obvious . . . and dangerous. When customers showed up, some of Brando's crew took their money and then sent Rapture to the stash to retrieve what was needed—slinging the drugs back to the trap house. Who would ever suspect a cute little nine-year-old girl, picking her way among the old houses, curls bouncing, of having an eight ball or some Molly or Scooby snax of crystal meth in her pockets for Uncle Brando's customers desperate to tweak, shoot up or whatever?

Rapture is in her room late at night, listening to the sounds of fights downstairs, loud singing, or snoring, and every so often gunshots in the distance. She sits on the window seat and dreams about what life might be like for other little girls as she looks out on the city. She remembers that her mother used to make her a birthday cake each year, whatever flavor she wanted. Rapture always wanted "banilla cake and fudge icening." "You can't wish away a life," Momma used to scold as she put candles on it. "Birthday wishes are a glorious sadness." It seems like a dream now, the time before. It hurts to think about it. Because then she remembers the Pain. The awfulness. Being so scared that she just wanted to run and hide. Feeling so alone, numbly going with Uncle Brando into this dreary place. Two more birthdays have come and gone, but no cake. No celebration of being wanted on this earth. Rapture looks at her calendar. Three more days and she will be ten.

She sighs and studies the moon. "Can I wish my way back to life, Momma?" Rapture comes up with a plan. The next time Uncle Brando sends her to the stash, Rapture sneaks an extra packet of a drug into the pocket of her jeans, heart pounding, the plan clear in her mind. Later that day she sneaks off and goes into a different neighborhood. When she spots a couple that she thinks might be a pair who have come to Uncle Brando's trap house, she approaches them and offers them the packet for half price. They make her follow them to a dark, scary basement and ask who is putting her up to this. Rapture insists everything is on the up and up. She just needs the money. The look in their eyes of pure hunger and desperate need frightens Rapture, but she holds firm. Wishes are not free, after all. Finally, they relent, and she leaves with the ten dollars.

Rapture stopped in a store on the way home and did her shopping. The next day, the day before her birthday, she spent the day carefully and joyfully making herself a cake, banilla with fudge icening, of course. She took the cake mix, eggs and oil that she bought and mixed up the cake. She carefully poured it into pans and placed it in the oven. When the layers were done and cool, she opened the icing and slathered it on. Then she opened the box of candles and carefully placed ten of them on top. On her birthday evening, Rapture proudly took out the cake and lit the candles. She carefully picked it up and started down the stairs, wanting to share the birthday wishes with Uncle Brando and the others.

None of the drug users and drug crew, and Uncle Brando himself, could ever forget the look on Rapture's face as she brought the birthday cake into the room, candle flames dancing and shimmering. "Make a wish!" They all cried together. For a moment, everything was alright. As Rapture closed her eyes to make a wish, cars came screeching up outside the trap house. A long burst of gunfire shattered the night, window glass flying, furniture being chewed up. Seems a rival gang was upset that Brando's crew had sold drugs in their neighborhood territory. A single sale. By a little girl trying to wish her way back to life. The policeman found her there on the floor, among the others, still breathing, but just barely. As he knelt beside her, she opened her eyes. "I got my wish," said Rapture. "I'm going to Momma on the moon. She's waiting there in glorious sadness . . . "

Words are magic and writers are wizards.

THE PONY MAN

The old man, Mister Mercy, has been doing it since forever. Trudge out the back door, across the porch, down the grassy slope past the pump, into the barnyard—sometimes muddy, sometimes frozen—dogs nipping at his heels the whole way, slide open the doors with a loud screech that sends the barn cats scurrying, take the harnesses from the tack racks, and line up the ponies. Dawn has barely pierced the mist, but he's there, nevertheless, scooping oats and brushing their coats. Almost no one knows where the pony farm is located. Almost. Children know. Special children. Elizabeth knows.

Elizabeth first showed up when she was 5 years old. He was brushing Pinto when he felt her presence and turned around. "Can I help you, Darlin'?" he asked the girl with the blonde braids and runny nose, eyes red from crying. She nodded. "Do you know the song?" he asked, not unkindly. She started singing, softly, hesitating, "When it's midnight on the meadow, and the cats are in the shed/And the river tells a story out the window by my bed," she sang, growing stronger. "If you listen very closely, be as quiet as you can/In the yard you'll hear him, he is the pony man." Mister Mercy smiled.

"What did the river say, Darlin'?" he asked as he scooped her up and set her on Pinto. "She said, don't be scared," Elizabeth murmured, as she petted Pinto's pretty neck. "Would you like to go for a ride?" asked Mister Mercy. She nodded. He attached a lead line and led the way out of the barn. All of the other ponies followed along, some were white, some were brown. Through the paddock, out the gate, through the field, and into the woods they all went, the ponies staying close, never letting the girl be out of view. They neighed and snorted, blew gusts of vapor through their nostrils, chattering like a group of middle school friends on their way to the cafeteria. Eventually they came to a stream of cool, clear water. And they all sat and listened. To nothing. To everything. Okay, the ponies didn't sit, but they did play in the water.

Elizabeth showed up at the pony farm again when she was 11. The braids were gone, and she brought her backpack and phone this time. Her eyes were red from crying. He made her leave the baggage behind when he set her on Pinto. She sang the song. "What did the river say, Darlin'?" he asked, per usual. "Mister Mercy, sometimes everything is too big. She said, don't give up," Elizabeth sighed, as she petted Pinto's pretty neck. "Would you like to go for a ride?" asked the pony man. She nodded. He attached a lead line and led the way out of the barn. . .all of the ponies chattering as they stayed close to Pinto's precious cargo, not letting her out of sight. Maybe it was the bag of carrots and apples she'd taken from the backpack. They came to the stream of cool, clear water. The picnic was grand. And yes, the ponies ate. Every last bit.

Elizabeth returned when she was 15. Wearing jeans with manmade holes in the knees. And pink hair. Only to announce that she was too big for pony rides, and besides, who cared about ponies anyway. Mister Mercy kept doing his thing, feeding, and brushing the ponies. And the river kept telling stories.

One day years later, the pony man did what he has been doing since forever. Trudge out the back door, across the porch, down the grassy slope past the pump, into the barnyard—sometimes muddy, sometimes frozen—dogs nipping at his heels the whole way, slide open the doors with a loud screech that sends the barn cats scurrying, take the harnesses from the tack racks, and line up the ponies. Dawn has barely pierced the mist, but he's there, nevertheless, scooping oats and brushing their coats. Almost no one knows where the pony farm is located. Almost. Children know. Special children.

He was brushing Pinto when he felt her presence and turned around. "Can I help you, Darlin'?" he asked the woman with short blonde hair, eyes red from crying. She nodded. "Do you know the song?" he asked, not unkindly. She started singing, softly, hesitating, "When it's midnight on the meadow, and the cats are in the shed/And the river tells a story out the window by my bed," she sang, growing stronger. "If you listen very closely, be as quiet as you can/In the yard you'll hear him, he is the pony man." Mister Mercy looked deep into her eyes.

"What did the river say, Darlin'?" he asked as he scooped her up and set her on Pinto. Elizabeth remained silent as she petted Pinto's pretty neck. "Would you like to go for a ride?" asked Mister Mercy. She nodded. He attached a lead line and led the way out of the barn. All of the other ponies followed along, some were white, some were brown. Through the paddock, out the gate, through the field, and into the woods they all went, the ponies staying close, never letting the girl be out of view. They neighed and snorted, blew gusts of vapor through their nostrils, chattering like a group of middle school friends on their way to the cafeteria. Eventually they came to a stream of cool, clear water. And they all sat and listened. To nothing. To everything.

"Mister Mercy, I'm pregnant. And I don't know what to do." The stream rippled. The ponies grew still. The pony man handed her Pinto's lead line. And swung up on the pony's back. "What do you need, Darlin'?" he asked, not unkindly. "What do you need?"

Words are magic, and writers are wizards.

ARE YOU READY?

"Johnny, are you ready?" We are lined up in a row, all seven of us, oldest to youngest in the kitchen of the church-owned home. My mother asks the question of me as I slip into line. Susan, 14 months older, is to my right, Danny, 14 months younger, is to my left. My bowtie is in place, a hand me down like the rest of my outfit. The small church on the corner in the College Hill area of Beaver Falls, PA, hired my father right out of seminary, after ten years in the Navy, and now four children have become seven by some mysterious process in the mind of six-year-old me. Mom goes down the line with a comb in hand, smoothing cowlicks, checking buttons, adjusting said bowtie, picking lint off sweater vests, handing out dimes for the Sunday School collection plate. The knees of my Sunday pants have patches ironed on from the inside so the holes in both pant legs don't show as obviously as the ironed-on to the outside ones do on my everyday play jeans. I'll be in high school before I wear clothes without patches. I will be that little boy for the rest of my life . . .

"Tuffy, are you ready?" Steve Tucker of Wilmerding, PA, who sits beside me for three years of East Allegheny High School home room, he of the ability to tear down a car engine and rebuild it with a four barrel so it will go faster for the weekends of drag racing at Keystone Raceway, and whose older brother is a Corvette afficionado (if you know, you know!), who has an after school job before I do, who has a girlfriend before I do to whom he is still married these days, and who will hopefully never ask me what Steve said about her in those formative years . . . where was I? Oh yeah, Steve punches me on the arm as first period bell rings and we're out the door into the swirl of chatter, hormones and unbridled anxieties masquerading as bellbottom jeans, miniskirts, forever romances and pep rallies. I settle into my seat as the teacher hands out graded term papers one by one. He passes me by and continues placing papers on desks, greeted by groans and muttered curses. This can't be good. I still don't have mine. How badly did I screw it up? I knew I shouldn't have gone with sarcastic humor. Wait, he's done. No paper? The teacher stands in the center of the giant square of desks. "I want to read someone's paper. It was so different, so creative, and funny that I wanted to read it aloud." And I hear the words I wrote coming from his mouth. I'm the quiet, shy oddity of a preacher's kid and all of 16. Oh. My. God. Take. Me. Now. Before anyone knows it's me . . .

"Jack, are you ready?" My father is standing there, calling me out of my cloud of nerves, waiting to follow him into the church for him to perform the wedding service for his 21-year-old son getting married, ready or not. . .

"Rev. Tuft, are you ready?" I'm following a stranger through a door out into a church sanctuary where a gathered group of perishables will listen to me preach and then vote on whether they want to ever hear more. Do they know all I have are stories, little else . . . ?

"Daddy, are you ready?" My oldest daughter is a vision of beauty in her wedding gown, ready to be given away to some giant peach of a football player turned future son in law. This can't be right. Aren't they supposed to stick around forever?

"Jack Goo, are you ready?" Sue leads me out the door of her farmhouse and into the fields and meadows. "Bill and Bob ride again," she says into the wind as her flock of sheep ignore everything but eating. Breast cancer is relentlessly taking away her life. "Promise me that you'll be there at the end. Okay?" I reach for her shoulder. "Yeah, Putt. I'm here . . . "

"Mr. Tuft, are you ready?" The surgeon leans over me, concern in his eyes. "We're going to try and get you some relief. I know you're in a lot of pain and that you've been through a lot. We can only do so much. Prepare yourself, it will probably be with you the rest of your life . . . "

"John? John, I said, are you ready?" I blink a couple of times. The young woman nearby is pointing a video camera at me. She had interviewed me earlier, asking about my life, my writing, my pain, my struggles . . . my story. At some point as we talked I noticed her eyes welling up and tears spilling over, running down her face. I stop the interview to ask, "Are you okay?" She swipes at the diamonds on her cheeks, nods. "You touched me," she says simply. Now we are in front of the building where I arrived full of uncertainty, anger, disbelief, darkness, fear . . . coming off a thirty-year expedition through the tribulations of narcotics and depression. Through storms of doubt and despair. And pain. Always the pain. I look at the young woman. A nod. "I have friends in there. Good friends that got me through. Come meet them. Are you ready . . . ?"

Words are magic and writers are wizards.

THE WEARY WORLD

Hot or cold, rain or shine, Marcie walks her little dog, Max, up and down the block. The little Yorkie is frozen in time, so Marcie puts him in a small wheelbarrow for the journey. At some point Marcie got some old paint and stencils and turned the wheelbarrow pink with flowers strewn around the sides. Every day he rides like a conquering emperor in front of adoring throngs, Maximillius Canine-ian the Third, Emperor of the Land and his Loyal Legions, Overlord of all points from the brick house at the end of the block to the cross street, Long May He Rule! The wheelbarrow has been in Marcie's life since her third Christmas, part of a toy gardening set, and its child size means that Marcie has to bend low to grasp the handles. Fortunately, she is a tiny woman, thin and wiry and short, who always wears black. Always. With her dark hair piled up high in a beehive effect, painted on eyebrows and dark mascara, a spot of makeup giving her artificially rosy cheeks, she is a dark elf.

On the other side of the street from Marcie lived an elderly gentleman named Josiah. Josiah watches Marcie taking her walk every day and takes his walk in the opposite direction. Each day Josiah puts on a dress shirt, bow tie, vest with a pocket watch pocket, jaunty derby hat, and sets off with his polished cane for a daily constitutional. When he sees Marcie heading up the lane, he is out the door and down the street, takes a right, makes for the park with the small lake, does three laps around it and heads home before Marcie shows up with her dog in a wheelbarrow and stale bread for the ducks. It went on this way for the longest time, the two going their opposite paths, wearing their chosen armor and markings, weary world travelers on a speck in the universe.

One day Josiah was delayed by the fact that he had neglected to iron his shirt. That just would not do. He ironed the shirt and put it on, hoping that Marcie was far up the street by now. He selected a favorite cane and headed out the door, down the lane, and right, toward the park with the lake. As he completed the third lap around the lake he spotted Marcie sitting on a bench, staring off across the water. "Drat," he thought, "now she'll see me. I don't want to listen to that crazy bat. I hope she's not waiting for me!" He decided to ignore her but as he passed by she spoke, "You forgot your hat today." Sure enough, so he had. Startled by this chink in his armor, he slowly came over and sat down on the bench.

A long uneasy silence ensued. Finally, Josiah could hold it in no longer. "Why do you push that ridiculous stuffed Yorkie around in a little girl's wheelbarrow?" Marcie reached into the wheelbarrow, rooted underneath the bag of stale bread and drew out an unopened envelope. She held it limply in her lap. "Why can't you leave the house without being perfect?" came her response. Josiah bristled, "I'm not perfect." He gestured impatiently, "Are you going to open that?" She shook her head. "Why not?" Josiah demanded to know. "It might hurt. What if it is filled with pain?" Marcie lifted the envelope as though weighed with all the cares in the world. Let it fall back into her lap. "Max understands." Josiah laughed, "Max? What does Max know of pain? Max never got a letter in his life. Filled with pain, filled with joy. Never."

Marcie looks at him with one drawn on eyebrow arched. Josiah sighs. "I got a letter from my son once upon a time. He was a Marine in Vietnam. A bright, strong, handsome boy. He was at the end of his deployment country, telling me he would be home in two weeks. My wife and I were filled with joy. We prepared everything just the way he liked it. Put his things out so his dog would remember him. The day he was to arrive a telegram arrived. I didn't want to open it. But I needed to be strong for my wife. Ripping open the envelope was ripping open our hearts . . . " Josiah cannot go on, so he fusses with the buttons on his vest, adjusts the brim of his nonexistent forgotten hat. "And your wife?" asks a tiny voice beside him. Josiah shakes his head as he stands up. "She took the dog and left."

He collects himself and makes a small bow. "Unopened envelopes . . . that just cannot be allowed." Marcie stares at her lap. She reaches with a shaking hand to touch Max, the fuzzy fur worn from years of touching and tears. "I'm afraid," she says. There is silence. "I'm afraid of what it will not say," she continues, her hand falling from the stuffed dog. "All I want . . . all I want, is for it," she stops, gathers herself. "All I want for it to say is come home. Come home." She looks up, but Josiah's bare head is disappearing around the corner as he makes his way back along the way he came . . .

Words are magic and writers are wizards.

THAT WASN'T ME

THE HOUSE SITS ON the outskirts of the tiny hamlet of Montvale, Virginia, along Route 221 (US460 for purists), between Roanoke and the county seat of Bedford, home to the National D-Day Memorial for heroically tragic reasons, and as advertised, sits in a lush vale between two rounded ridges of the Blue Ridge Mountains. An entrance to the Blue Ridge Parkway is not far away and for some reason known only to God, the village is the site of not one, but two large gasoline tank farms. One agrees to not bring up the War Between the States of Northern Aggression at the diner on a hillock, Dale's Diner, held in high regard by locals and travelers alike for its good food and friendly staff. (C'mon people, you know me by now!) Across the road and just to the east is the tired house. Tired paint holds it together. The furniture on the front porch is thoroughly fatigued. A lonesome shutter hangs by one hinge, as though caught in the act of trying to escape the fate of the other shutters beside the blank windows. An old glider is wrapped in blankets and plastic to help it endure the coming winds of winter.

In the tired house, wrapped in her knitted shawl regardless of weather, Annie sits in her wheelchair staring out the window. It is what she does all day, every day. Her Harold helped to service those tank farms before he caught what seemed to be a nasty cough that turned into what took him back in aught three. She taught at Montvale Elementary School on Little Patriot Drive, just down the road a piece from where she spends her days now. Looking out the window. Seeing what there is to see. And beyond.

You must understand, mountain people are different. Timeless ridges wear on you over time. The sacred is there every day, for those who have eyes to see. Mystery is majestic and those who try to confine it are most often disappointed. So, when I tell you that Annie sees things others do not, you have to decide. For Annie is a godling scion. Some say these mountains are full of them. Annie sat there all day, listening to Johnny Cash singing

The Man Who Couldn't Cry, waiting for someone to bring her biscuits and gravy from Dale's, staring at the crowding ridges.

Her daddy met her momma when he jumped off one of the old orphan trains in the 1930s, thinking he was in Roanoke. The family always got a charge out of that story, an orphan from New York City being shipped to the Midwest for child labor, thinking tiny Montvale was Roanoke. He met Lorilee, Annie's momma, when he hid out in their barn. Lorilee used to say she felt the spirit move in her when she saw the wretched boy, part of why the family considered her to be a godling. That and her second sight gift. It was Lorilee's momma, after all, who back in 1889 foresaw the Thaxton train wreck that killed 18 souls about 15 miles to the east. From Verna to Lorilee to Annie the gift made its way through the generations. Annie's daughter, Lillianna, lives on up Lynchburg way and doesn't get down to Montvale excepting illness or a holiday. She has never let on about whether she has the gift or not, so maybe the godlings line has ceased. Time only knows.

Annie watches the traffic on the highway in short bursts but mostly keeps her eyes on the tree covered slopes in the distance, listening to the mountains. The wheelchair is the result of a stroke back in '16. Some days she is so intent on the hills that when she blinks and realizes that the sun is going down, it's like she has been transported somewhere else for the time, away from disease and weakness. "Some of my students have gone on to being dirt farmers, some are lawyers and politicians," she smiles. "There's no accounting for taste." Laughs as she sizes up a visitor. "You're mountain people, right? Some holler outside of Hurricane, West Virginia. Your mother's people, right?" Another nod. Annie pronounces, "Flatlanders think forever is just over the horizon. Mountain people know they are looking right at it, living on it."

The roof creaks as the wind picks up, sweeping through the vale. "I could sure use them biscuits," Annie sighs. Her visitor makes a run to Dale's and brings steaming mounds of simplicity and redeye gravy into the tired house. Annie smacks her lips in delight. "Did you ever see such a sight?" A shadow crosses her face as she touches his hand. "You've known great pain." Her visitor shrugs. "Go ahead and ask me what you want to ask," she encourages. There is silence as she looks steadily into his eyes. "It wasn't your fault, you know. Sometimes things just happen. But you don't need to carry what isn't yours to carry. There's enough pain in this world to go around, and then some. But it is not your fault." She fills up the fork with a big bite of the sacrament drenched in gravy, sighs as she chews.

Waves the fork in his direction. "There's love in your life. Someone who cherishes you. And you cherish her." Another bite goes in, accompanied by sounds of pleasure and contentment. She swallows, sips at the coffee, and gives him a sly wink. "But that wasn't me . . ."

Words are magic and writers are wizards.

LITTLE LION MAN

His siblings gave him the derogatory nickname of Rumpelstiltskin. Short of stature, an unbecoming face, a hideous mole under his left eye, still able to wear young children's clothing sizes, and not lucky in life by any stretch of the imagination, drove Rodrigo to be a loner. Boys of all ages from 8 to 80 make a sport of comparing themselves to other males of the species as a way of attesting manhood by acclamation rather than maturation. If "humans are gonna feel alone when we go into the wrong room," and if "what would I die for" becomes a Jeopardy category in a world where people feel more and more empty and unmoored, then courage becomes a precious commodity indeed in a world built by big people for big people—of all measure. The vast majority of us are fixer-upper human beings, except that there is no next tenant. We are stuck with ourselves. Perhaps that is a clue as to why so many remember how Rodrigo, aka Rumpelstiltskin, became the little lion man.

One day his grandmother, Leona, gave him a special gift, a gold scarf she had made herself. "I spun the gold threads from straw," she teased. "For my little lion man. This scarf is your mane, and when you wear it you will become like a lion." Then she gave him a big poster, the face of a mighty lion. Underneath his regal countenance were the words, "Prepare for the thing that won't happen." Rodrigo was puzzled. "What does that mean? A scarf doesn't make me a lion. And prepare for what won't happen? That doesn't make any sense, Grandma." She gave him a smile followed by a slow, knowing wink as only grandmas can do. "If it won't ever happen, then there's nothing to be afraid of, my little lion man. Prepare for it by not letting your fears tell you what to do." Rodrigo still did not understand but he loved his grandma and trusted that she knew what she was talking about. Because, well, that's why grandmas were invented, after all.

Every day Rodrigo wore the gold scarf around his neck. Others teased him. "Look at Rumpelstiltskin, thinks he's better than us with that fancy scarf. Hey, Shorty, that scarf doesn't hide how ugly you are. Maybe you should wear it over your face!" That always brought on a round of laughter from the others. And every night he would lie in his bed staring at the lion on the poster, wondering what was it that would never happen to him. From the look of things in the mirror he would never be tall. And maybe he would always be ugly. Prepare for being tall and handsome? Rodrigo laughed at that thought. When he did, he remembered Grandma Leona telling him that he had a beautiful smile. Was that what she meant? He didn't know, and every day that is how it went: wear the scarf, get teased, feel humiliated, stare at the lion, wonder how to prepare for what won't happen, and ask questions till he fell asleep. Over and over and over again. Never did he seem taller or more handsome.

Then one day Rodrigo came upon a bunch of kids teasing someone on the playground, a thin and nearsighted boy they called Freddie Four Eyes. When one of them threw a rock that drew blood, Rodrigo moved in. As loudly as he could, he roared, "STOP. LEAVE HIM ALONE!!!" He ran through the group, straight to Freddie's side. He handed him one end of the gold scarf, nodded and together they ran as hard as they could at the nearest tormentor, the scarf stretched out between them. When they knocked the boy to the ground, the others scattered. Rodrigo then used the scarf to bind up the cut on Freddie's head and stop the bleeding. Of course, both were given detention that day—Freddie sitting there, head held high with the bloody scarf still wrapped around his head and Rodrigo, whose feet didn't reach the floor—a band of brothers, a pride of warriors.

Rodrigo caught the late school bus home, riding with the other dispossessed of the day, including Mary with the buck teeth and early development, including the requisite acne, in detention for making an obscene gesture to a teacher. As Rodrigo followed her down the steps of the bus at their stop, Mary was on her cellphone. As they crossed in front of the bus, she tripped, and her phone slid out of her hand and under the bus. What happened next is a blur of milliseconds. Mary crawled toward the bus to get her phone. Rodrigo reached to his throat for his scarf to wave at the driver, but it wasn't there. As he tried to roar "STOP! STOP!" to the bus driver, he heard the driver high overhead gun the engine and find first gear. As it lurched into gear, Rodrigo threw himself at Mary with the strength and ferocity of a full-grown lion, knocking her clear . . .

On the hill outside of town is a quiet spot. Folks said there were one hundred and thirteen cars in the procession for the little lion man, stretching all the way back to town and beyond. If you go looking, find the stone with the carving of the face of a roaring lion. No name is on it. None is needed. But you will know it's the right one when you read the words: PREPARE FOR THE THING THAT WON'T HAPPEN. A call to courage to all of us humans of the fixer-upper variety . . .

Words are magic and writers are wizards.

ONE DAY LESS

SHE LIES AWAKE AND weeps. The house groans and creaks as it endures the birthing pangs of the long night, hoping for the sun crowning on the eastern horizon. If true prayers are sighs too deep for words, guttural moans that defy the confines of language, what is she to make of well-wishers' endless drivel of chattering wish lists and protestations passing for prayers? Or hollow *Deus benedicat* scattered casually in order to salve disturbed conscience, with sacred trinkets hanging on hallowed walls like a child with the key to his house hung about his neck so he can let himself in, fearful of the very freedom he covets? Marilyn stares into the shadows, desperate to discern the very force that invented existence. Ghosts, holy and otherwise, appear to have the need to be recognized to validate their existence, leaving Marilyn to wonder what chance she has to challenge the unseen powers at work in her life. Maybe it would be best if the next day never came. One day less . . .

It seemed only yesterday she surveyed the world with the detached arrogance of an adolescent, listening to Bob Dylan singing "You're A Big Girl Now" on endless repeat. But now it was Shakespeare's words that chased her thoughts around: "Say that thou did forsake me for some fault, And I will comment upon that offence . . . " The eternal question of human frailty; what is wrong with me? What makes me unlovable? Why is life so hard? Or more pointedly, why do you reject me? Marilyn rubbed her eyes vigorously before letting one hand fall onto the lump of fur beside her on the bed, Rusty, the labradoodle who was frightened by most noises known to mankind. Her other hand brushed against the bedside table where amber liquid in a glass sat beside a bottle of sleeping pills, the lid casually tossed to one side. The pill bottle was empty. She drained the last of the whiskey from the glass and set it back down with a thump. Now it was empty, too. She was empty. The clock was ticking . . .

Born in the foothills of the Sangre de Cristo Mountains in New Mexico, Marilyn always felt like the oddball of the family. While the rest of the family busied themselves with school and church, she roamed the vastness of the area around Santa Fe. She read a lot and wondered about things. Things like what did the Apache people think of their land being called the Blood of Christ? Why wasn't it enough to believe in a Creator, Mother Earth, and the Four Directions? The stars above were forever, but they could not hold back an evil force that tried to wipe away the Apache food source, the buffalo, hunted into near extinction, leaving them to survive on bones and dust. Marilyn's parents told her she was too sensitive, too curious, too softhearted. She came east to go to college, discovered dance and theater, fell gloriously in love with the sense of freedom, shared exploration and discovery, friendship, and romance. Falling in love with utter abandon . . .

And landing with terrible pain. No matter how hard Marilyn worked at them, relationships never seemed to work out. Mother and Daddy passed away and still she had not found her roots, her place, her person. She considered having a child to raise, either by birth or adoption. She could give the child all the love she had stored up inside of her. She could take her back to Santa Fe and show her the mountains, reveal all of her secret places from childhood, introduce her to the land and lore of the Apache people. They would have a small house, lots of pets, lots of friends, shared adventures. She went to the doctor for a checkup as she began the search for how to fulfill this desire. The news was not hopeful. The news was fateful. Disease had taken root inside her and she faced troubling decisions. The clock was ticking . . .

In fairytales a handsome prince would come to the rescue, slay all the dragons, kiss away all the hurts. In a biblical tale a healer would appear and restore Marilyn to wholeness. In a tale from the Apache people, she might learn the deep meaning of the medicine of her ancestors and a song sung to guide her in the desert of her troubles. But, alas, this is none of those kinds of tales. This is a tale of a hurting and lonely soul. A tired of caring so much soul. A tale of someone who deserves one less day of pain.

Marilyn puts her head back on the pillow. She thinks of the mountains of New Mexico and how they were here long before her, long before anyone, and will still be there, unmoving into the future. She lets her thoughts dwell, one by one, on the people over the years who touched her life. One by one they appear to give her a smile, a look of recognition and gratitude. She's feeling very sleepy as she reaches to touch the Apache medicine wheel that hangs above her bed. A quick start as Rusty pushes his wet nose against the side of her neck. Her hand drifts to his soft fur. She smiles.

Rusty stirs, raising his head, thinking he heard something moving on the other side of the door. But it was nothing . . .

Words are magic and writers are wizards.

NEENEE'S TEA

It is a little before dawn when she makes her way down the hallway, after splashing some water on her face, pulling the old housecoat with the flower print close around her. The slippers on her tired feet have molded themselves to the corns and callouses, swollen ankles and wobbly toes. Life's imperfections are what make it worth the trouble, currency to present to whomever dares to man the tollbooth on the highway to happiness and a life well lived. She steps into her domain, the soul of her home, the expression of her desire to serve with humility and grace . . . and unmistakable pride, a modestly appointed kitchen. In a society seemingly determined to turn every life-sustaining chore into one more scheme in a consumer economy, she follows her heart and its well-worn path of care. Which requires tea. Lots of tea.

    Her wealth is measured in quarters and dimes, nickels and pennies, and the thought of spending the cost of a meal for her family on a single drink of coffee from a gleaming franchise boasting of its arrogance is as extravagant to her as the thought of ordering a new dress for herself from the Sears catalog for no other reason than that she wanted it. She fills the kettle and sets it on the stove. This is her time; this is her sanctuary and the first cup of tea to greet the day is her sacrament. If there does happen to be an extra dollar, and no one needs new shoes, she tries to determine who around her is in need. For she considers herself to be blessed, and not beholden to the world's demands for screaming what she wants into the vortex. The kettle whistles and she takes down her special tin of Earl Grey and carefully selects a bag and places in the chipped mug. Pours the boiling water over it, carries it to the table and sits down to let the steam steep her own thoughts.

    NeeNee knows that soon her husband will stir, but this is yet her time. He will spend time in devotion, reading a well-worn Bible and muttering well-worn prayers, trying to exorcise the demons within that have driven his anger all of his life that the Almighty is so demanding. He wields it like a sword, demanding purity of himself and others, never daring to admit that he is terrified of his own mortality like it is a fire breathing dragon coming to rob him of all pleasure. He is a good man, she knows, but it has been hard. Fifty years, seven children, lots and lots of tea. Oceans of it, marking the passage of time like the tide, trying to dissolve hurts and fears, wash away worries and unmet wants. And celebrating, quietly. And rest. Most of all a time of rest. A cup of tea is her oasis in a desert of constant demands.

NeeNee's tea is her prayer. A slice of lemon serves to quicken the spirit, and elevate the ethos of her supplications, seeking light and calm, a strength stirred from within. The hands cradling the cup bear the stigmata of sacrifice, a silent witness of swollen knuckles and inelegant scars. The small bottle of 'nerve' pills sitting beside the tin of tea bespeak her utter fear of confrontation and the remnants and echoes of her own mother's very demanding and critical voice. But everyone has their ghosts, she reassures herself. She uses the hem of her housecoat to clean her glasses. Paradise is a cup of tea and a good Agatha Christie story, perhaps a pleasure to savor later in the day. Her eyes tire so readily now, and her greatest fear is of no longer being able to read her books with this cherished elixir.

NeeNee's tea is the balm of Gilead for a wounded soul, parched by unrelenting reminders of fate's carelessness and the perils of grief. She brought seven lives into this world, now one has slipped away. They are supposed to leave home, but they are not supposed to leave her alone. Is this a test or a task? She rises to reheat the water and freshen her tea. Perhaps it is neither. She pulls the housecoat tighter, fighting the morning chill. She takes down a jar of apricot jam and slides some bread into the toaster. A good cup of tea can only be improved upon with some toast. And for this moment . . . and perhaps only for this moment . . . that is enough. It can wait. It can always wait. Can't it? Until that next cup of tea . . .

Words are magic and writers are wizards.

MY BIG, FAT BODY

Sherman shoveled the rich, earthy-smelling potting soil and peat into the wheelbarrow before pushing it across the lawn and unloading it into the patch of garden. He picked up a small trowel and got down on his knees to work it into the ground. If the rain held off, he might finish putting in Martha's marigolds and flox-pink, white and lavender ones-before starting on his tomato plants. "You know," he continues a thought that must have started in his mind before his mouth knew it, "in this part of the world, we have the luxury of deciding, of choosing each and every thing that we take in. Not everyone has that option. And yet, we act like we don't have any choice, that we can't make our own decisions." He looks up, wipes the sweat out of his eyes. "We all think we have a big, fat body."

He gets a twinkle in his eye. "Now I ain't no doctor and I'm not talking about our weight. I don't care if you weigh 110 pounds or 350, don't make me no nevermind. You ever hear of the Holy Trinity? Most folks think it's Father, Son, and Holy Ghost. But, nope, it is blood, air, and water. That's what our big, fat bodies need to keep functioning. Stop those and it's all over. Period. You're done." His eyebrows go up as he taps on his skull with one finger. "Up here," he says, "up here, we all have a big, fat body." There is a soft chuckle. "Listen to me preaching at you!" Sherman groans and grunts as he gets up from his knees. "But mess with one of those and what do you get? Pain, I tell you." He brushes the earth from his overalls. "These old knees have seen better days." A big sigh, with the twinkle still there. "But what's a body to do?" He laughs so hard at this it brings on a fit of coughing.

When he can catch his breath, he continues, "All this talk of healthy living, healthy eating, while we have less and less physical labor needed to keep up our supply of the Holy Trinity? Hell, gyms full of exercise equipment and people walking around with little gizmos on their wrists counting their steps? Why? Trying to convince themselves they don't got big, fat bodies." He spits in the dirt. "Want to know what prayer is? I'll tell you." He points to the white cumulus overhead. "Nobody up there needs or wants to hear from us. Religion is a bunch of people sitting around, looking at themselves, saying, 'yeah, we like these big, fat bodies. How do we keep this going?'" Sherman pulls a face. "I don't mean no disrespect, but who needs that?"

He takes a tray of new plants and kneels again to start planting them. "Praying is helping each other out. Life is physical. So is praying. Prayer is a choice we make with our big, fat bodies. It's taking our blood, air, and water and beyond using it to keep our own big, fat bodies going, making sure that somebody else can keep theirs going. Plain and simple. If you ask me, and mind you, nobody did, but Jesus' life was a prayer. He took his big, fat body and turned it into a prayer. Take away the razzmatazz, the flash and dash, the theology, eschatology, even phrenology, and it boils down to a physical experience. Healing, feeding, comforting—it's all physical. He used his big, fat body to take care." Sherman looks up, a faraway look in his eyes. "It's a Presence. Blood, air, and water give us a presence."

He carefully makes sure that all the colors will mix just right when the flowers bloom. "I don't understand why some people hate their bodies like they do. I hope Martha gets to see these." He busies himself a while, getting them just so. "She's in there," he indicates the house with a nod of his head. "Has oxygen tubing that reaches all through the house. But not out here." He swipes at his eyes and tries to cover by swatting at a passing bee. "Feelings are physical too, you know. Don't pray your thoughts and feelings at me, come and be with me. Get your big, fat body into someone's presence." Then he works in silence while his pain accompanies his labors of love.

The sun rises higher in the sky. The trees, now fully clothed following the winter, casually move with the breeze. A robin builds a nest in the crook of the downspout as a pair of mourning doves watch from the wires, as though hoping for pointers. A bell tolls in the distance which makes an old dog look up from his nap, yawn and go back to doing nothing. Sherman gets up, touches me on the arm, before heading into the house to share a meal with Martha. And me? I am on my knees, sifting the earth through my fingers, hoping. Hoping that my big, fat body will become a presence. A prayer . . .

Words are magic and writers are wizards.

LAMENTATIONS

BILL WALKS DOWN THE hallway, his pace slow but determined. He wears his light blue scrubs, his work clothes, as he heads for the first case of another long day. Being a doctor was his childhood dream, practicing back in the same place his mother and father practiced might feel a little strange at times, but worth it. Dad developed tremors in his hands at age 62 and had to retire from being a surgeon earlier than expected. But his indefatigable spirit kept him going as he consulted on cases and gave wet behind the ears first year residents pointers on surviving the grueling training to become doctors. Mom, a family doctor to generations had a stroke at age 75 and now lived in an assisted living facility. His parents taught him to love the people, love the patient, respect the work. Good science and a good heart would take him far in his profession, they insisted. Now they needed him in ways that tugged at his good will and sometimes tried his patience.

Missy is a charge nurse for the birthing suites. She grew up on Lemon Blend and hot dogs with popcorn. The oldest of five, she was the one left in charge while her mother worked cleaning hotel rooms. Their double wide on the other side of the tracks was always tidy, and she kept her siblings fed and clean and in some semblance of order, but the first chance she got, she was gone. Fred delivered bread to the gas station convenience store where she worked and he always made her laugh, made her feel special. They ran off and got married. Six months later he left her high and dry. She could give up or she could pick herself up and start taking nursing classes. Two of her siblings got lost in opioids and constantly begged for money. It was tough to cut them off, but she had to make something of herself. When she graduated from nursing school no one from her family was there. Missy brushed it off and settled into her career. The fact that she could not bear children herself somehow made taking care of those giving birth make a special kind of sense to her.

Danny is completing more training after finishing nursing school. His grandmother, who raised him through his teens, was a nurse back in the day when you received a special nurse's cap as a sign of entrance into the profession. And when a doctor stepped onto the floor, every nurse had to stand up as a sign of respect and remain standing until God in a white lab coat left the floor. She raised him because when he told his parents that he was gay, his father literally turned his back and never spoke another word to him. His mother begged him to leave for the sake of "peace in the family." Danny wishes Grandma could see him now, training to be a nurse anesthetist, smiling comfortingly to the patient as he wraps the blood pressure cuff around her arm and adjusts the heart monitor. He wants to be as reassuring as possible, so he smiles for the anxious father hovering nearby. He looks up as the doctor enters, waits for his nod, and then opens the IV to drip Pitocin into the vein.

Darla is the hospital chaplain who feels her faith leaking away like a tire with a nail in it. What the hell is the point of all this? She's holding a small book of prayers of comfort, but it might as well be a book of Sudoku: put the numbers in the right columns in the correct order and shuffle spiritual focus until it all makes sense, but it never makes sense to her anymore. The woman on the bed, hooked up to monitors and being administered drugs to induce the most natural thing in all of creation, to deliver the body inside of her to the uncaring world. The baby will look perfect, every last feature in place, fuzzy hair, tiny hands and feet with delicate fingers and toes. But unlike Darla's three-year-old rambunctious boy at home, this child will never draw breath. Not one. This is a stillbirth.

Clare lies on the bed, trying not to think, trying not to feel. She wants to be strong for Manny, her husband. They have been trying for so long to start a family. It was a joyous announcement. They did it, incarnated love. All the hopes and dreams, all the plans for a life together. Excited grandparents, eager to splurge with their reverse inheritance. The joy of movement and growth within her. Bound to her by blood. Now each contraction is a bitter reminder of what will not be. The terrible pain of lost hope. The desperation of abandoned dreams. The dry ashes of death delivered the same manner as life itself. At long last, he is delivered. Their precious boy. With form but without life. Except for the life which surrounds him in this moment. Swaddled in all our lamentations.

Clare holds him, tenderly kisses his brow. "My child. Our son. His name will be Theodore. For he is God's gift." And all those gathered there whispered, "Amen."

Words are magic and writers are wizards.

LAST CHANCE

In the darkness, the bare trees slip past like sentinel ghosts, watching for travelers along the road that begins beyond their sight and ends beyond their dreams. Headlights of passing cars briefly reveal their crooked arms and empty nests, awaiting the return of feathered tenants and the awakening of beetles, flies, crickets, and other creatures. Such is the fate of roadside forests, waiting for the briefest of moments of recognition and tentative waves, the sleepy blinks of nodding children safely tucked into the backseats of solitary SVUs or horse drawn carriages. Sometimes a little girl will look with wide-eyed wonder, or a little boy will nod and raise a finger in silent salute to the arborous apparitions aligned in silent attention along arbitrary Appian Ways winding through the darkened countryside.

Such it was that four travelers traversed this very road one winter evening. A nondescript vehicle with four strangers making a journey together, but wandering apart, for such is the lot of strangers, is it not. Two men and two women, all wearing different colored caps—Red, Yellow, Purple, and White. White was driving the vehicle, Purple was in the front passenger seat, and Red and Yellow shared the back, but each had a window seat. As the miles droned on, they cast about for topics of conversation. Finally, the trip became magical when White asked, for no particular reason, "What would you do if it was your last chance to do it?"

"That's a nonsense question," said Purple, tired of nothing but bare trees to look at, zipping by too quickly in the dark to mean anything. "Why is it my last chance? We always get more chances." Yellow spoke up from the back seat, a little fearful of the looming trees out the window. "That's not true. Or else it wouldn't be called a last chance." Red stared out the window, wandering if trees ever counted how many of them were tall or not, coniferous, or not, sunset fire maple or not. White persisted. "C'mon. It's a fair question. These trees are so close they make the road seem narrow. I need something to get my mind off driving."

Purple sighed. "Okay. I give up. What would you do if it was your last chance to do it?" White looked thoughtful. Red asked, "Do you think trees know we're here?" Yellow shushed Red. "I want to hear the answer." "I think I would take a vacation. Yeah, I'd just take off one day and go where I wanted to go, do what I wanted to do." Purple sighed again. "Where would you go? How much would it cost? And how did you get the chance to take this vacation?" Yellow exclaimed, "Oh, I like that idea. A last chance vacation. Much better than working all the time."

Purple glanced out the window, not wanting to answer yet. "That's a lot of firewood out there. Or lumber. You know, houses were better when they were all wood; floors, walls, ceilings, slap on some paint and you had yourself a nice place to live." Yellow spoke up. "Well, I'd move to California. If it was my last chance, I'd go to live near my daughter and her children." Red looked at Yellow, then beyond. That side of the road was lined with trees as well. "This used to be all one forest," said Red.

White flicked on the high beams to get a better view of the curves ahead. "Who's next?" Purple sighed. Again. "I'd start a business. Yep, I'd start my own business. Maybe a hotel, or a big park with rides and restaurants. Bring people out here to enjoy themselves." Purple surveyed the others. "If it was my last chance, that's what I'd do." White asked, "What about a church? Or a chapel? Maybe out here in the woods." Yellow exclaimed, "Oh, perfect. That would be nice. You should do that." Red noticed a road sign. Still one hundred miles to go. Hopefully, it would not be too late.

The travelers fell silent. The trees watched and wondered. In silence and stillness. "If it was my last chance," whispered Red, already certain. Purple turned. "What? Did you say something?" Red nodded. "Tell us," Insisted White. "Yeah," said Yellow. "You're one of us. What do you want for a last chance?"

Red pleaded to the trees for strength. "I would fall in love. All over again for the first time." Purple nodded. With a sigh. White turned off the high beams and smiled. Yellow's eyes misted. Red said one more thing. "For the rest of my journey. I will fall in love for the rest of my journey."

A breeze danced through the trees as the headlights swept over them and moved on. Into the night's journey. And beyond.

Words are magic, and writers are wizards.

THANKSGIVING FOR MONKEYS

Brady walked down the path, watching her feet make the steps instead of watching where she was going. Which is how she managed to walk smack into a tree and raise a goose egg on her forehead. She did not care because she had Uncle Paul with her, a bedraggled and well-loved stuffed monkey with gangly arms and a goofy smile below button eyes. Well, she did care a little because it hurt but Uncle Paul gave it a quick kiss and they continued on their way to the railroad tracks. Momma always said not to play near the tracks, but the pull was just too strong: putting a hand on the steel rails and waiting for that faint tremble, then peering up the tracks for that first glimpse of the engine headlight coming out of the tunnel a mile away and steaming toward where she and Uncle Paul waited. Because the engineer always waved to them. A friendly, cheery wave and a smile as the beast swooped past in a roar.

While she waited for the glorious spectacle, she sat down underneath the cool November sun and opened the canvas shoulder bag that held her treasures. Brady pulled out a small sack and dug inside it, lifting out a wad of monkey bread. "Uncle Paul, would you like some?" Now who among us can resist the sweet savory cinnamon goodness of biscuit dough dipped in melted butter, rolled in sugar and cinnamon, and stacked in a Bundt cake pan . . . with love, no less? I know, right! And Uncle Paul was no exception. Brady's momma made the special treat every fall when the harvest was in and the family hog was slaughtered for meat, smoked for the winter months. As the two munched on this goodness and held time in their hands, Brady wondered if the light of the old steam locomotive could shine the way beyond her wildest dreams. Because that is what children and the Uncle Pauls of this world wonder about. Or have you forgotten?

Lost in her reverie, Brady almost missed the long, mournful moan of the engine clearing the tunnel, sounding the whistle to alert all nearby. She jumped up and, in her haste, did not pay attention to what she was doing as she stuffed Uncle Paul into the shoulder bag and ran toward the tracks, much closer than she should stand. As the train bore down, she tripped and sprawled in a heap, the contents of the bag spilling across the tracks. Before she could recover, the train was upon her and thundered by just feet from where she tried to regain her footing. She missed the face of the engineer, his smile and cheery wave. The ground beneath her shook as though a mighty iron dragon had awakened from its spell and breathed hot wind down on her, there beside the tracks.

Finally, the train was gone, and Brady scrambled to gather her treasures. But, to her horror and dismay, Uncle Paul was nowhere to be found. She looked along both sides of the railroad rails, calling his name, searching in the weeds and bushes. But no stuffed monkey poked his head up, with the button eyes over a goofy smile. Heartbroken, Brady collected what was left of her shattered world, and made the long, crestfallen journey home. Once there she poured out her heart to Momma, conveniently leaving out the part about being too near the tracks. Instead, she told her Momma that Uncle Paul had grabbed the monkey bread from her and danced away, teasing her with it, and in his foolishness, stepped too near to the train. And now he was gone.

Momma brushed the tears from her cheeks, and knowing little girls as she did, hugged her close. Because little girls should not see the fear in their Momma's eyes at the things that their children do in the name of imagination. At long last Brady fell asleep. Momma called her brother in Omaha, and said, "Paul, Brady lost that monkey that you sent her while playing down near the railroad tracks. Her heart is broken. I told her she's not allowed to play there, but she doesn't listen." Her brother tried to reassure her that Brady, like her mother, would grow up to be a fine woman, full of love and fire. Unconvinced, Momma hung up, wondering what magic can cure the broken heart of a little girl.

Thanksgiving Day arrived. While Momma was busy cooking, Brady snuck out and walked to the railway tracks even though she was not supposed to go on such adventures. She sat, full of sadness, holding a packet of monkey bread, but not eating it. The train whistle sounded in the distance. But instead of thundering on by, it slowed. There was the engineer, waving to her, and remarkably, calling her name! She stood up and walked closer. He held something up and with a smile, tossed it to her. There at her feet, staring up with button eyes over a goofy smile, lay Uncle Paul, none the worse for wear. Before she could offer thanksgiving for this wondrous monkey miracle, the train was gone ...

Words are magic and writers are wizards.

THANKSGIVING MAGNIFICAT

The party really started jumping when Gertie took out her dentures and plopped them into her tumbler of water. Millie, with a trim 90-year-old body stuffed into her skinny jeans and tight pink sweater, laughed, and raised her glass of wine toward Wild Bill, perched at the end of the table on his super deluxe motorized three-wheel scooter. Wild Bill's shock of white hair bobbed up and down as he carefully constructed a perfect bite of turkey, mashed potatoes pressed into the peas to hold them on the fork, stuffing, gravy, and a bit of cranberry salad. The small salad of greens to the side could be safely ignored. The klatch of blue haired ladies in wool suits and drawn on eyebrows decided to roll the dice, and each took a piece of each of the four types of pie offered for dessert. Even mincemeat . . . which might be due to the extra dreg of rum added to the recipe by an understanding cook back in the giant kitchen. Guilty pleasures are quite often the best pleasures . . .

Over in one corner, the Bad Boys of Hallway C huddle around a stash of chocolates and beer, even though you aren't supposed to bring either to the dining hall. The BB of C all have missing limbs and/or failing eyesight due to the complications of diabetes. However, their motto is "you're never going to live if you're too scared to die." In fact, Billy J has it as a tattoo on his flabby belly and every time his tee shirt rides up, it's there for everyone to read. He's convinced that is part of his appeal to the blue hair crowd, but he can't be sure seeing as how they always ignore him. Billie Jean is a young 62, placed here by her family because she can't remember who she is. It's her first Thanksgiving in The Joint, as all the old hands call it. It's really not a prison, but neither is it a passion. Billie Jean is fascinated by the birds kept in a large glass cage in the lobby and is reluctant to leave them to join in the feast. Freedom is just another word for nothing left to lose . . .

Sandra sits quietly in the corner staring out at the traffic as the sun sets behind purple and gold. "What are we waiting for?" she asks quietly.

"Is this an airport, or is this a train station? There's so many here, we should invite them in for Thanksgiving. The travelers need to get home, don't you agree?" She directs this to Jim, her husband who sits on the edge of the chair. He is visiting her for the day, straining to remember the young, vibrant woman who said yes all those years ago. "We have so much food here, if the kids come they'll . . . " and here she smiles and sings the last as a sea chanty, "eat till their bellies are full, ho!" Jim manages to have a tight smile. His Sandra is still in there . . . somewhere. He spots Billie Jean entering the room and motions her over to sit with them. Billie Jean sits, hands folded in her lap. Sandra looks at her, one eyebrow raised. Billie Jean slowly opens her hands to reveal one of the birds nestled there. The secrets of the soul are shared in peace . . .

Earl helps himself to more of the sweet potato casserole. He is one of the seven men who sit with Margie at a double table. He's sweet on her but then again, they all are sweet on her. In her mid-80s, a firm grip on reality and a sly sense of humor, her rollator parked neatly behind her chair, she gives each gentleman an opportunity to sway her with clean jokes or stories of past loves. Earl feels fortunate to be included in the communion of saints at Margie's table. In his career as a systems analyst for the CIA, Earl has seen a lot of things, kept a lot of secrets. But his secret pain is the hardest to bear. At Thanksgiving, the nights are long, the days short, the loneliness a futile tool for battling despair. Earl ticks off the years in his head since Mattie died, leaving him alone. Back in a day when two men could not, should not, fall in love, two men fell in love. The beauty of youth quickly fades but the need for loving touch never dies. Margie knows his secret and sometimes at night they sit together and hold hands, just being there for each other. Choosing love is choosing grace and choosing grace is the only real power . . . .

Barry, wearing his Vietnam Vet cap, slides onto the piano bench. His wife, Rose Marie, takes her place at the microphone in her wheelchair. Since her stroke, the left side of her body just hangs there, attached but not participating much in the joys of life. The congregation of perishables gathered for this feast at times feel like the birds trapped in that glass cage. But they can still sing. Barry belts out "Fortunate Son" just to prove he's still a rebel, with Rose Marie trying to mouth the words as best she can. They finish with a flourish, then settle into more audience friendly songs. Thanksgiving is proclaimed for the lost and lonely, the forgotten and the forsaken. Thanksgiving is proclaimed for the families and the soldiers, the confused country and the tired world. Thanksgiving is proclaimed for all we meet along the way. Finally, Barry ends the evening with a solo. The old Tom Kimmel song, SHIPS. "We rest here while we can, but we hear the ocean calling in our dreams . . . Part of us would linger along the shore, for ships are safe in harbor, But that's not what ships are for . . . "

Blessings and peace to you and yours . . . thanks for giving of yourselves.

Words are magic and writers are wizards.

A RED WAGON THANKSGIVING

Little Danny was on a Thanksgiving mission. The weekend before the holiday he went to the garage and got out the Radio Flyer red wagon that his grandpa had given to his father when he was a little boy. Two Christmases ago, when Little Danny was seven, he found the wagon underneath the tree, all shined up, repainted, Daddy's pride and joy passed on now to him. No robot monster or exploding goo or iPad game put the same gleam in his father's eye as did seeing Danny get excited about the wagon. Other kids in the neighborhood did not quite see the appeal of such an ancient relic, but to Danny there was magic in the shiny steel and hard rubber wheels. And a very real connection to the men he most admired in his life.

The Saturday before Thanksgiving Danny told his parents that he was going to ask people for things that would help someone less fortunate have a better Thanksgiving. He wanted to pull the wagon around the neighborhood and collect donations from friends and neighbors for those who did not have the means to celebrate Thanksgiving in the way he was used to celebrating it. He set off with a pack of two frosted strawberry Pop Tarts in hand and a bottle of PowerAde in the wagon. Six hours later, as the afternoon sun dove toward early retirement, Danny had still not come back home. (Need I remind you, if you're a reader of JTT magic stories, you knew it was going to be a ride. In the placenta of our imagination, where our experiences and memories interact with inspiration and magnified silence, sometimes we have to get our hands dirty, dare I say bloody.)

Danny's parents raised the alarm and the entire neighborhood along with the authorities turned out to search for Danny and the red wagon. As Danny's parents began to talk to them, the story of Danny's journey that day emerged. Mrs. Wilson said, "All I had were some chipped and cracked pieces of my mother's China, so I gave it to Danny. I had no use for them." The thirteen-year-old Thompson twins reported, breathlessly, that "You know, he's always hanging around, annoying us walking around with that stupid wagon, so we gave him our old Beanie Babies. Really, duh, what were we going to do with them? We aren't into LARPing as children or anything!" Retired Mr. Grimley chewed on the ends of his mustache as he rubbed his eyes, "What was he doing out on his own? I gave him an old transistor radio, told him to learn a trade and sent him on his way."

One by one the people told Danny's parents about giving him that which they intended to discard. Still, Danny had not come home. Police issued an Amber alert and all the cell phones buzzed with the news. As the Hunter's moon rose in the sky, Pastor Kimberly opened the church to the searchers because, well, it's a building and you have to do something, right? Danny's Sunday School teacher offered that "Jesus will watch over him" at which point Danny's father rolled his eyes and went back out into the night, desperately trying to think how his son would be thinking. He wandered down to the river and began to walk its banks, dreading what he might find but desperate to know. Finally, up ahead, he spotted the flare of a barrel fire underneath the overpass of the road into town.

Heart in his throat, Danny's dad began running toward the sparks of the fire. As he drew near he saw the red wagon parked near the barrel. He began calling, "Danny! Danny, my son, where are you?" Out of the shadows emerged some discarded human beings, watching him carefully. One of them stepped forward and greeted the frantic man. "I'm Randy, 4th Battalion, 31st Infantry. Are you here for the feast?" Another stepped up. "Simon, Corpsman, Master Chief, I take care of these men and women. Are you here for the feast?" One by one they all stepped forward, introduced themselves by rank and branch, and asked the question, "Are you here for the feast?" Danny's dad, bewildered, asked, "What feast?" They all smiled. "He's brought us a feast" and stepped back to form rank around some old ponchos spread on the ground.

Arranged on the 'table' were place settings of old China, each marked by the favor of an old Beanie Baby. On each plate awaited a package of frosted strawberry Pop Tarts and each baby leaned against a bottle of PowerAde. "I don't understand," said the father. "Where's my son? What have you done with him?" Simon stepped forward, tried to speak, but had to pause to compose himself. "He's up top. Volunteered to stand watch so we wouldn't be bothered." With that they sat down to the feast, the old radio putting out scratchy Christmas music. Danny's dad grabbed the handle of the wagon and dragged it behind him around the abutment and up the bank to the road.

There was Danny, sound asleep, resting against the rail of the bridge. Above his head a small plaque was attached. As Danny's dad knelt beside him to lift his brave soldier of the heart into the wagon, the writing on the plaque caught his eye. "For those who came back but never found home. Rest in peace." And underneath were the names of the 22 veterans who had taken their own lives that day . . . the names of those sitting down to a thanksgiving feast . . . brought by a very special red wagon . . .

Words are magic and writers are wizards.

A CHRISTMAS RESURRECTION

THE LIGHTING IN THE diner is a harsh pale white, while the full moon beyond the windows glows with mystery, a silvery *segulah*. Through the speakers in the ceiling come the tinny sounds of Israel Kamakawiwo'ole singing "Somewhere Over the Rainbow." Two truckers in winter vests and wallets chained to their jeans sit in the corner booth sipping black joe around mouthfuls of blueberry pancakes. Molly the waitress, pencil behind one ear, stokes their imaginations with a flip of her hair as she turns and saunters back across to the counter and the man perched on a stool. He's in his mid-60s, thinning gray hair neatly combed, his Pittsburgh Steelers jacket falling open, revealing his red San Diego Zoo sweatshirt with two giant pandas fixed in predetermined adorableness. "What can I get you, Hon?" He stares pensively into the glimmers reflecting in his coffee, and asks, "Do you have malted waffles?" She smiles. "Anything else ain't a real waffle." He nods. She taps him on the shoulder with the pencil. "Eggs?" "Over easy." She leaves him to his musings.

Simon and Garfunkel's "Bridge Over Troubled Water" comes on as a teenaged girl slips onto the stool two over. Her short hair is a hazy shade of Lime Kool Aid, garnet colored lipstick writ large below sad eyes outlined in black. The effect is jarring and enhanced by the dissonance that in one hand is an oversized cell phone while the other holds a Cabbage Patch Kids doll with yellow yarn hair, blue eyes, and a pink polka dot dress, smelling of baby powder. She tucks the doll under one arm, thumbs in a text message and throws the phone on the counter. It spins slowly toward the man. He barely moves, but he can't help but see the words on the screen. He takes a slow sip of hot liquid, sets it down, lets his breath out slowly and looks again. It's still there: "I want to be ded."

"No, you don't," he says quietly. "You talking to me, Gramps?" Her disdain is clear. "Yes. I am." She looks him up and down, sneers. "What are you, some kind of perv?" He is undeterred. "You don't want to be dead." She snatches the phone up and tucks it into her shoulder bag, trading it for a pack of cigarettes. "What the hell do you know? Leave me alone, Creep." Molly appears and sets the syrup in front of him, refills his cup, and says over her shoulder, "Can't smoke in here, kid." The girl mimics her in a sing song childish tone, "Can't-smoke-in-here! Kid!" Then, biting, "What are you? My mother?" "If I was your mother you'd be eatin' those damn things!" Molly responds, flips her the finger, and walks away. The smokes disappear and the girl fusses with the doll for a moment. "There's stuff that's worse than bein' dead, old man," she says without looking. "I know," he responds.

"What are you doing here on Christmas Eve? Don't you got family waiting for you?" she challenges. He turns on the stool. "Are you hungry?" he asks. "No . . . Maybe . . . A little," she is defiant. He slides a menu toward her. "Get something." She makes a show of studying the offerings. He continues, in a soft voice, "I just got out. Had a bad habit that I kept choosing over them. Finally did three years for stealing to support my habit. I'm not sure I still have family. They've moved on. New kids. New home. New Christmas traditions." She stops fussing, looks at him. "Don't they want to see you?" He smiles. "Coming back from the dead isn't all it's cracked up to be." She looks puzzled. "But it's Christmas . . . "

He looks her in the eye. "Yet here you are." She looks away as "Calling All Angels" by Train filters in mixing with the chatter of the truckers. She brushes at her eyes before turning back. She looks so young. "I don't have a home." She is defiant as both their hearts break at her next words: "My mom's boyfriend . . . he . . . forces himself . . . when my mom's at work." She chews at the dark lipstick, some of it sticks to her teeth. "Does she know?" he asks, his chest pounding. "She's a child," the girl sounds mournful. "How do I tell her that?"

"Waffles, malted. Two eggs, over easy." Molly sets his plate in front of him, unaware that she's entered a holy space, as she hears the man say, "You need a home." The girl looks at him, one finger entwined in the yellow yarn hair. "Everybody does," she whispers. He slides the steaming plate across the counter. "Take this. Eat. All of it." One of the truckers' hands Molly his bill. "This place is halfway to somewhere and halfway to nowhere!" he exclaims. While the trucker pays his bill, the man in the Steeler jacket and Giant Panda sweatshirt calls to him, "Where you headed?" "South. Headin' south," comes the answer. The man watches for a moment as the girl digs into the food. He reaches into his pockets and takes out a small card and a ticket.

He sets them beside the Cabbage Patch Kids doll. She looks up. "What's that?" He rubs his tired eyes. "That's a train ticket to Pittsburgh." He points to the small card. "That's my daughter's address. She's a good person, thanks to her mother. Go there today. Please. Start a new life." The girl's mouth drops open. "What do I tell her? What about you?" He starts out the door after the trucker. "Tell her anyone can be born again." She jumps off the stool and runs to him. Pushes the doll into his hands. "It's a new Christmas tradition." And he's gone, into the moonlight, trailing the scent of baby powder.

Words are magic, and writers are wizards.

A BILL AND BOB CHRISTMAS

THE ORIGINS OF THE legend of Bill and Bob are buried deep in the minds of the children who lived through it. From deep in the bowels of a simple carriage house apartment on the North Side of Pittsburgh in the very early 1950s while their father attended seminary at Xenia, the story was born in the active imaginations of the children. Fair warning, if you don't learn through stories, this may not be the place for you. Paul, Janice, Susan, Daniel, this is for you, and children of all ages:

The blizzard came in out of the northwest without any warning. Bill and Bob hunkered down in the comfortable log ranch house, venturing out only when necessary to bring in more wood for the fire or pull down more hay for the horses in the barn. The wind tore through their heavy coats and tried to snatch the cowboy hats off their heads as they fought their way to the barn, kerosene lanterns swinging wildly, around six that evening. Trigger and Black Star each received an extra ration of oats, the two stallions that got them around the 1500 acres of pastureland, woods, and streams. The two siblings worked well together at the Circle T, protecting the cattle herd and flock of sheep against rustlers and assorted outlaws. The Colt 45s slung on their hips never came out of the holsters unless they needed to be used. Only then and with deadly purpose.

"I could sure go for some of Mrs. Cook's biscuits and gravy right about now," said Bob, who always minded his stomach. Mrs. Cook's cozy diner was conveniently located right near the gateway to the ranch, and the kindly warm woman who ran it reminded them of their mother. The taciturn and bossy Bill, grunted and pointed to the evergreen waiting next to the barn door. "Let's get that inside and decorated," he said. "The townsfolk are coming out for the Christmas BBQ and we're not near ready." They were dragging the tree toward the house when they heard it. A cow bawling in pain down near Cutter's Creek. Bill whistled for their trusty dog, Tin Tin, who tore out of the barn, barking to beat the band, as he disappeared in the swirls of snow toward the animal in distress.

Bob leaned the tree against the log wall and went back to the barn to help Bill saddle up their steeds. They urged the horses out into the bitter winds and followed the sound of Tin Tin in the distance. The horses snorted, sending up clouds of vapor through the glow of the lanterns as they plodded through the deep snow, Bill and Bob hunched over in the saddles trying to stay warm. They tugged their bandanas up over their lower faces to cut down on the chill. After an arduous journey they reached the hillside above Cutter's Creek. One of their best breeders was down, tongue lolling, as she struggled to give birth to her calf. Bill and Bob knelt down beside her, Bob at her head speaking in soothing tones, while Bill got in back and pulled on the reluctant youngster.

After one last mighty heave, Bill got the calf out. Bob offered his bandana to help rub down the newborn, who struggled to stand in the fierce winds and snow. "We got to save her," cried Bob. Without a word, Bill picked it up and placed it over the neck of his horse. As Bob started to remount he thought he heard Tin Tin barking down near the frozen creek. "You go on, Bill. I'm gonna check this out," he insisted. As Bill set out back to the warm house, Bob led Black Star down the slope to the creek. Through the blowing snow, he spied a new lamb out on the ice, her momma on the banks bleating her heart out. Without a second thought, Bob dropped the reins, and began to crawl on his belly over the frozen creek. Inch by inch he crawled, the sounds of the ice cracking no louder than the pounding of his heart.

Finally, he reached the frightened lamb who was now so weak she could no longer stand. Bob carefully picked her up, unsnapped his cowboy coat and tucked the lamb inside against his own body heat. Then he turned and ran for the creek bank, the ice breaking up as his feet flew as fast as he could run. With one last giant jump Bob landed safely, climbed on Black Star, whistled for Tin Tin and headed for home. He checked on his passenger, nestled close inside his jacket. "Welcome to the world. It's Christmas Eve." Then he noticed that the snow had magically stopped, and he could see the moon and stars overhead as he made his way back to the ranch house.

The next morning the household was awakened by knocking at the door. It was the townsfolk coming to celebrate Christmas at the Circle T. Mrs. Cook bustled in, warm cinnamon buns and fresh cookies in hand only to find Bill and Bob sound asleep under the half-decorated tree. Beside them were a newborn calf and a weary little lamb being licked by Tin Tin. As the ranchers stirred, Mrs. Cook turned back to the door and motioned for a young boy to come on in. "This orphan has nowhere to stay.

Why don't you two take him in?" And they knew better than to argue with Mrs. Cook. Especially on Christmas morning...

And that, Brother Dan, is how you got to be Little Joey in the adventures of Bill and Bob.

Words are magic and writers are wizards.

DON'T READ THIS STORY

It was a long, wearying journey. I arrived at my destination late at night, seeking lodging in a run-down inn, The Motel Calvinia. The Corrs were singing "Breathless" as I steered the pickup into the raggedy looking lot, the dogs were quietly sleeping the sleep of the virtuous—as all dogs do on Christmas Eve—and when Neil Diamond started singing "Lonely Looking Sky" my half blue tick hound, Jake, woke up, licked my hand, and went back to sleep. Journeys have beginnings and ends, as does life itself. As I collected the key and made my way to the room, the Hooters were swinging to "And We Danced," the closest thing to Christmas music I wanted that evening. The dogs needed no convincing that it was time for bed, other than having to push them aside to make room for myself. As I fell asleep, the tones of Loreena McKennitt singing "Dante's Prayer" filled my headphones, which may help explain what happened next.

I woke with a start, knowing it was the wee hours because, well, any hour after midnight is wee. I sensed someone else in the room and the rattle of chains gave it away. I peered into the corner and there on a chair sat the earliest incarnation of Yoda, my seminary mentor Dr. Gordon Jackson. Small, cute, white hair sticking out in tufts. He laughed and waved, setting the chains to rattle some more. "They make us wear these when we do this schtick! Pretty cool, huh?" Dumbly sleep drunk, I asked, "Am I late for class?" I also noticed that the dogs couldn't be bothered, still snoring away. "Every generation judges the one before it while insisting they themselves do not judge," he said in his soft voice. "Didn't Mike and the Mechanics have that in a song?" I asked, and we both laughed. He looked me over and stroked his white Fu Manchu. "So, you're a writer these days? Remember when I preached at your ordination? By the way, that means nothing over on this side, just so you know. I turned to your father, who I taught in seminary, and said, well, all he's got are stories. Let's see how that works out." Unbidden, tears came to my eyes. "Is he okay?" Yoda/Dr. Jackson shrugged. "That's not a soup question, now is it?" and got up and passed through the door before I could say another word, giving the chains one last playful rattle.

I fought to stay awake but before long, warm among the dogs, I slept again. "Jack. Hey Jack. Jack Goo, c'mon it's almost Christmas." I stirred. Blinked. Blinked again. "Sue? Susan? Wait a minute, you've been dead for twelve years! No chains?" She shot me a questioning look. "Chains, why the hell would I have chains?" "Never mind," I said. "What are you doing here?" Her eyebrows went up. "Those are my dogs you keep using in your stories. I wanted to see how they're doing." I gulped. "Well, Britches and Petey and Jake have all died but I like keeping them around in stories." She stood up and stretched. "I guess we could go find Mom and Dad and have memory time about Christmas. Remember when I told them I was gay and they me kicked out of the house? Good times, right?" I didn't know what to say. She gave me her signature mischievous smile. "I'd use the f word but then you might need a trigger warning! Take care of my dogs, brother." She turned to go, turned back. "I'm sorry about your pain, Jack." I reached for her. "I'm sorry about yours, Putt." As she faded from view I heard her say, "You get one more tonight."

I sank into the chair where she'd been sitting and stared at the bed. One more tonight? I hit the play button and Gordon Lightfoot's "Don Quixote" filled the room. My eyes got heavier as I fought to stay awake. When my eyes snapped open, Eva Cassidy was singing "Songbird." On the bed was a vision of beauty, a young woman of perhaps 13. She was lost in a dance, leaping and twirling, laughter tripping from bright eyes. I watched, mesmerized, not recognizing her from my past. When the music stopped, she collapsed onto the bed and the dogs slobbered all over her, vying for attention. "Who are you?" I asked. She laughed easily. "Don't you recognize me? I'm Poopsie." I couldn't breathe for a moment. "Poopsie?" More laughter. "Yes, silly man. It's Christmas Eve. You always share my story with your readers on Christmas Eve. I wasn't going to miss this one!" She perched on the edge of the bed. "I'm hungry, got anything to eat?" "Spirits can eat?" She shot me a puzzled look. "What's a spirit?" I handed her the ever-present bag of M&Ms.

I watched her devour a handful. "This is all imagination?" I asked. "What isn't?" came her reply. "Be it spirits, or afterlife, or faith, or any of it, for that matter?" she went on after another handful. She nodded to the pen and paper on the nightstand. "Don't read this story. When the real Christmas Eve comes this year, don't read this story. Live that one." She grabbed the bag of candy and made to leave. "Merry Christmas." A pause, then, "Next year I'm asking if I can use the chains!"

Words are magic and writers are wizards.

THE LAST CANDLE

REBECCA KNEW THAT THIS would be her last Christmas. Now, first of all, this is not a Christmas movie and, as you may already know, cancer acknowledges no holidays and only keeps one dreadful appointment. Also, if you need only good cheer and all sorts of trigger warnings to avoid being upset and a Norman Rockwell view of Christmas, perhaps this story is not for you ... That said, it being Rebecca's last Christmas she put a lot of thought into what gifts to give to her children. She put on her favorite album, THE ESSENTIAL SIMON AND GARFUNKEL, as she pondered this momentous decision. When the pain meds kicked in she sank into their relief and slept for a short while. When she awakened, she knew what she must do and set about preparing for her last Christmas.

As you may be wondering, yes, well-meaning friends and other assorted perishables full of faith-words, had made pilgrimages to Rebecca's home, leaking their anxieties around and upon her. In all earnestness, to be certain. But Rebecca did not share their certainties or their anxieties. When they asked, "Do you believe in life after death?" her response, "It doesn't matter," literally derailed more than one conversation. "What do you think happens when we die?" they asked. "I don't care," came her honest answer. "I knew nothing of this life before I was born, how should I know anything about after this life?" Indignant and worried faces pressed with, "BUT THE BIBLE yada yada yada ... " Rebecca, being of sound mind and more questions than answers, replied, "But the Bible is full of people just like you and me wondering about the same stuff we wonder about. Human beings are animals on two legs looking for food, shelter, and someone who cares about them. What makes my one life so important that thousands of years from now it will matter what I believe?"

"BBBBBUUUUUTTTTTTT . . . .!!!!!" Each supplicant friend inserted their own anxious blanks. But Jesus. But God. But parables. But healing. But the cross. But Easter. But eternal life. But heaven. BUT THE

BIBLE. But the minister won't do your funeral . . . Rebecca's personal favorite. "Why would I care about that?" she said. "I won't be here." "But don't you want to know where you WILL BE? Don't you want your kids to know where you've gone?" her friends pressed. "It doesn't matter," she said, keeping calm. "Nobody in their right mind wants forever. It just seems so selfish." She could see that it was pointless to try and explain how she felt, so she shooed them all away. Setting aside the deleterious effects of theology, she concentrated on wrapping the gifts that she chose to give to her children for her last Christmas with them.

On her last Christmas morning, she called her children one by one, into the bedroom and gave them their gift. First was the oldest, Nathan, who was 12 at the time. He sat down on the side of the bed, sullenness hiding his fear. Rebecca mussed his hair and handed him his gift. He unwrapped and opened the box. Inside was a picture that he'd made in nursery school, a creation of macaroni glued to construction paper. With a liberal dusting of glitter. "I wanted to give you the most beautiful thing that I could think of," murmured his mother. "But I made that for you when I was little," said Nathan. "I know," replied Rebecca. "And you gave it to me out of love. Anything of love is beautiful." And Nathan accepted the gift and kept it close.

Next to enter the bedroom was 10-year-old Becca, obviously named for her mother and made in her image. Being precocious, she sang a chorus of "All I Want for Christmas Is You" to her momma and they both giggled and cried in the same breath as they snuggled together. Becca carefully unwrapped the gift from her mother, an old compact with a mirror in the lid. Becca studied her reflection as her mother explained, "We all have secret places inside of us where we hurt, and we think that it makes us unworthy. But the mirror sees what it sees. You. And every time that you give to someone else you give them a piece of yourself, or else why bother? Give yourself away and the mirror will tell you that you are really you." And Becca accepted this gift and kept it close.

Last to come to Rebecca was 7-year-old Danny. Danny already needed glasses in order to see well and he liked to read and think. He stood beside the bed, chewing on his lower lip, for he was sore afraid. Rebecca summoned her strength and lifted him onto the bed beside her and gave him his gift. Danny unwrapped the box and took out a single, simple candle. "This is the last candle in all of the world," began his mother, very solemnly. "I'm trusting it to you, my sweet boy. For you must understand, that the special person who has the last candle is the one who decides when to light it." Danny thought for a moment. "When it's dark," he proclaimed. "But it's the last candle. You have to decide if you light it just for you or do you light it to help others see in the dark," whispered Rebecca since it was a very special secret. And Danny accepted the gift and kept it close.

Rebecca is gone now. But Christmas goes on and on. Come with me to her house. Come up to the window. Stand on your tiptoes to see inside. Look closely. The three gifts are still there. Waiting. The picture of beauty. Your love. The mirror of grace. Your grace. The last candle . . . Waiting. Waiting to be accepted and kept close . . .

Words are magic and writers are wizards.

POOPSIE

It was to be a glorious Christmas. Older siblings were returning to the family home for the holidays, bringing spouses; or home from college, bringing tales of new worlds. We would spend laughter-filled hours catching up, teasing, bragging, telling tall tales over homemade cookies and cups of holiday cheer among all the oh so familiar decorations. I was living at home as I attended the University of Pittsburgh and this gathering promised to be the highlight of my year. My sister Susan was being allowed back into the fold after having been banished when she came out to our parents, but . . . but she wanted to bring someone with her to enjoy the special atmosphere. I was beside myself. How could she? Didn't she know how special this time is? How much . . . how much I needed everything to be as normal and memorable as they used to be?

Christmas Eve dawned cold and crisp, new snow on the ground, everyone warm and home safe. Except for Susan. Finally, she arrived to complete the circle. She made her entrance through the back door to the kitchen and my heart sank. She carried a bundle of blankets in her arms and as we gathered 'round she beamed as she unwrapped the precious cargo. "Everybody, this is Poopsie." I stared at the tiny, scrawny, misshapen figure in her arms. Although she was 13, Poopsie weighed all of 30 pounds. Her painfully thin arms and legs were drawn up, her eyes stared sightlessly, drool ran from her mouth plastering thin, dull, tangled hair to her cheeks. Severely mentally and physically challenged. Cerebral Palsy. Requiring 24/7 care at the home where Susan worked as a kitchen manager. How could she do this to me, I seethed. How dare Susan bring this creature into 'our' enclave? What earthly reason did my parents have for allowing such a spoiler of nascent nostalgia?

Susan breezily ignored my pouting and set about providing Poopsie with the best Christmas ever. She made a nest of pillows and the softest blankets right beside her own bed. She carried Poopsie into the dining room, forcing us to make room at the crowded table for this strange creature. She patiently spoon-fed my mother's special Jello fruit salad into the gapped tooth mouth, softly encouraging her charge to enjoy the cool sweetness. And me? I resented this intruder, this usurper of attention and need. Susan and Poopsie were ruining my Christmas.

The afternoons would find Susan and Poopsie in the living room, the tree lights on, presents piling up in a display of barely restrained generosity. Susan described it all in a soft, soothing voice, as Poopsie made strange guttural moans and squeaks. Every day Susan would set Poopsie on the floor on her hands and knees. "She can learn to crawl. I know she can," Susan insisted to my grimaces. "And if she crawls, she can walk. Jack, don't you get it?" No, I didn't get it. "And if she walks, she can dance," she exclaimed with a smile, as she patiently moved each of Poopsie's limbs through the motions of crawling. Time after time, till both were exhausted. After they both napped, it was more Jello fruit salad. My mother cherished them both, welcomed both into the fold. Not me. No way. This was an outrage. I have no idea what gifts I received that Christmas.

Christmas Day dawned, birthed by the timeless light of hope. The family, and Susan and Poopsie, gathered for the traditional homemade sticky buns and Florida oranges. Okay, and cookies. Then my father read the Christmas story, we said a prayer of gratitude, and then we all gathered in the living room with our piles of gifts. Susan ignored hers as she cradled Poopsie, helping her uncover the plush stuffed duck my mother had wrapped with love. I took all of this in, coldhearted, sullen. Unyielding. That afternoon my brothers and I participated in the annual 'take out our adolescent need for pain in a rousing game of football against all comers' bowl. I needed it. Sorry to say.

I came home early. I crossed through the kitchen and stepped through the doorway to the dining room. Something caught the corner of my eye. I looked into the living room. There, in the fading afternoon light, sat my father. In his big easy chair, near the tree. Alone. Except for the bundle of blankets in his arms. The man who expelled Susan from the house for her sexual orientation, from the good graces of the family and church. Yet . . . and yet, no father ever looked with such love, sang with such softness, cradled in his arms with such tenderness, as he rocked Poopsie in that peaceful serenity. Christmas did not seem to be any disappointment to him in the least.

Susan returned Poopsie to the home and returned for New Year's Eve. That evening the phone rang. My mother silently handed it to Susan. Susan listened in disbelief. She hung up and stood there stunned. As she fell into my mother's arms, weeping, she managed to gasp, "Poopsie died this morning." And my heart broke as she proclaimed, "I bet she's laughing and dancing right now."

It was to be a glorious Christmas.

I wish a blessed Christmas to you and yours. And, for all the holidays, for whomever you include in your family. In this year and the next.

Words are magic and writers are wizards.

(Poopsie is a Yiddish term of endearment.)

IT'S A WONDERFUL LIFE

I STEERED THE FORD F250 4x4 through the streets of Bedford, Virginia. Snow started falling midafternoon and now as the light fades I steer past the courthouse, more lawyers' offices than you could shake a stick at, and enough churches for three towns including their heathens, idly noticing the way the snow outlines the tree branches and softens the lights. The dogs doze in the back seat of the Extended Cab model, Pepper and Petey, two dogs' dogs, who patrol the farm and keep the sheep entertained with their attempts at herding. The Lhasa apso on the seat beside me is a dust mop that yaps; Britches, queen of all she surveys and who never tires of reminding me of that fact. I turn onto Longwood Avenue to take care of the tiresome business of collecting rent at my sister's apartment building. Once upon a time it was used as a Civil War hospital because, well, it's Virginia, it is now slightly more than a half dozen cheap apartments and it is my Christmas Eve duty to collect some very late rent.

Randy in 2C drives a flatbed tow/transport truck. Always in grease coated jeans and an oily once-white tee shirt, he does repo work, talks about his glory days playing high school football, and is always doing some sketchy work, strictly for cash, of course. As he presses wrinkled bills into my hand, what he hopes doesn't get out is that a lot of his cash flow comes from being a drug snitch for the county sheriff's office, setting up buys, locating stolen property—anything to lessen his own sentence for some off the books transporting of stolen cars. A guy who goes by Silversing, in 1D, is definitely off his meds. His parents kicked him out, at their wits end, after he dropped out of Virginia Tech to explore the celestial harmonics of the Peaks of Otter, three sister mountains to the northwest up State Route 43. He greets me with a disbelieving, "No, man, it's Christmas. There's no rent on Christmas. That's Elf law 101."

Shay and Annie are in 1A, a mixed-race couple in their late teens expecting their first child. Her father is there, loudly complaining about the toilet not working and he knows Judge Peters personally, and nobody should have to live like this, oblivious to the fact that I had no say in how events conspired to bring them here. Sherry, a divorcee in 2A directly overhead, pounds on her floor with a shoe to quiet all the shouting below her. I climb the stairs once again to smooth the waters, quiet the beast. It becomes immediately clear that Sherry has been imbibing holiday cheer since morning. She covers her loneliness during this season, as in all seasons, with bluster about needing peace and quiet and why can't people just mind their own damn business and let her drink in peace. Her job as a hair stylist doesn't cover the cost of a Christmas tree so she has strung colorful lights around the front window and painted a smile on the glass with lipstick.

Mrs. Peters pokes her head out of 2D. "Jack, could you carry Mr. Peters down to the front so he can enjoy the snowfall. Maybe some carolers will come by. He so loves singing and it's too far to push him to the church in the snow." The Peters rented the last apartment, despite their need for a first-floor unit because of the stroke that confined him to a wheelchair, beside robbing him of the power of speech. I pull my work gloves on again and apologize for wearing my muddy work boots into her spotless apartment. Poor guy is stuck up here all the time unless somebody shoulders the load. As I lifted this sparrow of a man in my arms, I heard the dogs going crazy down in the truck. Carrying him down the steps with his wife close behind fussing over getting a knit cap on his head, I smell smoke. I hurry the rest of the way down and out the door, nearly dumping poor Mr. Peters in the snow.

The snow is coming down harder, blurring the scene as I skid around the side of the building. The smell of smoke is stronger, and the wind is playing tricks on my ears. It sounds like someone is singing. I let the dogs out of the truck and followed them to the rear. There I find a small campfire burning in the corner of the L shape to the building, out of the wind. Next to the fire are two men. One is missing an arm. One is missing a leg. One wears the gray of the Confederate Army. The other wears the Blue of the Union. Two old soldiers who could never go home. Warming their ghostly limbs against the snow and chill. One plays a harmonica. The other sings in baritone: "All is calm, all is bright . . . "

The dogs settled, and I noticed that the building has emptied out. The Peters, Shay and Annie, Annie's protective dad, Sherry, Silversing and Randy, pause to listen in this holy moment. Watching and waiting, hoping that the morning will bring peace . . .

Words are magic and writers are wizards.

PASS THE LIGHT

Associate Pastor Carol sits behind the pulpit, watching the passing of the light through the assembly of the perishables. The seekers and the wounded, the lonely and the upright. All are gathered here. She tries to be centered, tries to concentrate on what is happening. Tries to pray. "What a joke," she whispers, then quickly checks to see if anyone heard. The senior pastor, Richard, is lost in his own thoughts. "That message went nowhere. I lost the room with that stupid story. Chuckles and charity, people want chuckles and charity. There's an old-fashioned word. Nobody says charity anymore. If it's not on social media, it doesn't exist." He sighs and returns to watching the passing of the light so he can time their exit, in silence of course, just right-out into the night and what lies beyond.

Dorothy comes forward, feeling solemn and somewhat afraid. Fire has always scared her. She is wearing the ever-present long sleeves to hide the scarring. Henry was always getting upset when he was drinking, coming after her, threatening to hurt her any way that he could. That last night, he knocked her down, called her horrible names, poured gasoline around, then lit it on fire. The flames raced across the floor, and she threw up her arms to shield her face. At first it didn't hurt, but then the searing pain washed through her. She screamed and was still screaming when the firemen carried her out into the night air. She remembers lying there, staring up at the stars, little flickers of flame. Were they mocking or whispering to her to hang on? She keeps her focus on the Advent wreath in the front, four candles around the tall white one in the middle. Dorothy holds the one she carries into the flame of the big white one and it catches with a sputter. She turns to face the waiting faces, ready to pass the light.

In the quiet darkness, Mitch fidgets at the sight of the twinkling light being passed from candle to candle by his fellow perishables in the pews. Don't they realize how meaningless it all is, he wonders. The flare of a candle reminds him of the flash of a camera at the wedding reception for him and

Elsa. That was twenty years ago, years that started off well enough. But things changed, they drifted apart somehow, and Elsa seemed less and less interested in him and their relationship. She went back to school, got her degree, and made friends outside their circle. Now she travels a lot for her job. She texted to see if he was going to the Christmas Eve service. He sent back a petulant, 'who cares.' She was happier, it seemed, while he was miserable. Maybe he should find someone else—that would show her. The light comes closer to him, passed from candle to candle, while the organ chimes a solemn call. Mitch lights his candle and passes the light.

Mya claps her hands over her ears at the sound of the organ chimes. The sensory input of the moving light and the loud sound is hard for her to process. At eight years of age, all she understands about being "on the spectrum" is that life is too full of sights and sounds and touches that disturb. She is careful to stay six inches away from her mother's hip, six inches from her father's. She sees other kids holding hands with a parent, running to them for hugs. She doesn't understand the attraction to touch. She can see her mother mouthing her name, trying to get her to behave. But this is how she behaves. She stares straight ahead, idly wondering what it would feel like to hold her hand over the candle flame. Mya grabs the small white candle from her mother, takes a taste of the end, marveling at the smoothness of the wax. She grasps it firmly as the flames approach, one by one, person by person, the mystery behind her eyes reflecting the coming light. What does it taste like?

Able, a row behind her, bows his head, trying to will the memories away. White hair caps his seventy-one years, but in his mind he is that nineteen-year-old kid from Cleveland, slogging through the sticky air of the jungle in droopy fatigues, a pack of cigarettes tucked into a rolled-up sleeve. The twinkling flames of the candles turn into muzzle flashes flicking at him from cover, trying to kill him and his buddies. None of them want to be here. They grab cover and radio for the 155s in the rear to level the village they want to liberate. "Merry Christmas, Charlie," laughs the corporal to his left as the shells impact with a strangely satisfying whomp, whomp, whomp.

Then they are up and entering the burning wreckage of homes and lives. Able enters a semi-intact hooch. Everyone inside is dead except for a boy of about twelve. Both his arms are blown off. He stares into Able's eyes, showing fear and disgust. The corporal pokes his head in. "Finish the gook, private, we're not taking him with us." Able flinches in the pew as he hears again the sound of his rifle unloading into the boy. He realizes that his hands are shaking too badly to get his candle lit. The little girl in front of him, who tasted her candle, leans over the back of her pew and, careful to touch only the wax, steadies Able's candle so he can accept the flame.

Through his tears the flame fragments into a thousand fairies twinkling over the hushed space.

The darkened room is filled with hundreds of struggling flames. All is quiet now. It is still. Pass the light . . .

Words are magic and writers are wizards.